CW01650471

WHEN BRADFORD ROCKED

THE WHO'S WHO OF BRADFORD'S ROCK & ROLL YEARS: 1954-1966

By the same Author

BRADFORD'S ROCK 'N' ROLL
BRADFORD'S OWN
BRADFORD BORN AND BRED

WHEN BRADFORD ROCKED

THE WHO'S WHO OF BRADFORD'S ROCK & ROLL YEARS: 1954-1966

Derek A.J. Lister

BANK HOUSE BOOKS

First published in the United Kingdom in 2012 by
Bank House Books
PO Box 3
New Romney
TN29 9WJ UK
www.bankhousebooks.com

British Library Cataloguing in Publication Data
A catalogue record for this book is available from the British Library

ISBN 9781904408994

Typesetting and origination by Bank House Books

This book is dedicated to my late wife, Diana Mary Lister (1946–98)

Contents

Acknowledgements

I am deeply indebted to the following people for assisting me in various selfless ways during the preparation of this book.

My very special thanks to my partner **Sandra (Sandie) Parish** for her typing, and for giving me her utmost support (again) in improving my original scripts and putting them into the Queen's English. It was Sandie above all who convinced me that *The Who's Who of Bradford's Rock 'n' Roll Years 1954–1966* should be published to enlighten future generations, and after much deliberation it was Sandie who came up with the title.

There is a name that should be at the very top in my acknowledgements, and that is **Ray Moore**. It was Ray in his capacity as manager at the Gaumont ballroom who offered me the job of DJ in 1960 when my rock 'n' roll group dissolved. After the Gaumont closed in 1962 I spent the next few years at the Majestic. If all this had not taken place my previous rock 'n' roll book would not have been published; likewise with this one. Therefore it is all down to my old friend of over fifty years: I have to say thanks, Ray.

My special thanks to Bradford's own lady of pop music **Kiki Dee** for her kindness in writing the foreword for this book. Kiki, an international star, is a credit to the city of her birth, and is still for at the top of her profession..

Special thanks are due to former *Telegraph and Argus* journalist **Mike Priestley** for checking the text's grammar and consistency of style. Mike also came up with the title of the book: many thanks for your help.

My thanks to my friend and publisher **Reuben Davison** for his invaluable help not only with the text but also with the collation of the many photographs. When author and publisher are on the same wavelength, book writing is far more enjoyable. His guidance and wealth of knowledge about the publishing industry contribute to this book being published.

My appreciation to my publisher and editor **Simon Fletcher** for his constructive help and advice.

Special thanks to **Dave Randle** of Bank House Books for his support with paging, and the sorting of over 300 photographs.

My good friend **Bob Duckett**, one of 'Bradford's Own', deserves very special thanks for taking the responsibility of drawing up an index for this book, no mean feat given the many names and place-names to contend with. Thanks, Bob!

My thanks to my son in law **Richard Coatesworth** for his help with computer difficulties and grandson **Ben Coatesworth** for being my best mate, and granddaughter **Lucy** for being a princess.

My thanks to my good friend **Graham Herrington**, my book signing venues and exhibition manager for all forthcoming events with this and other books.

Dave Metcalfe deserves special thanks together with **Dougie Lamb**, both of whom initially made contact with former group members and pointed them in my direction to be included in the book.

Ronnie Thompson (Rocking Ronnie), through his very popular rock 'n' roll radio programme on BCB, has often gave advance publicity of the book, allowing rock 'n' roll groups to contact me.

Very special thanks to **Keith Artist**, my good friend, and rock 'n' roll colleague for over fifty years. His enthusiasm for this book (as for *Bradford's Rock and Roll*, 1991) knows no bounds. From the very beginning he has been a fund of knowledge – and a debt of thanks is owed to him. A debt of thanks is owed to him and also his lovely wife Anne for offering from the start of this book to help with any typing I needed.

Margaret Gray – BCB presenter on Tuesday afternoons. My thanks for the in-depth interview on her two hour programme. The publicity given for this book brought in many otherwise unknown contacts.

My thanks to **Dianne Kean** for information on her late husband Tommy, and photographs of their very popular Lakean ballroom in Shipley.

Thanks to **Sue and Ashley Barker** for the photographs of her late father Laurie Lawrence, and the Majestic ballroom.

I am very much indebted to **Cliff Dutton** of Crusaders fame for his many phone calls from his home in Germany with detailed information, and for many photographs of the era. My special thanks also for his kind permission to use parts of the diary that cover the early years of Allan Holdsworth's career.

Thanks to **Gary Cavanagh** and **Matt Webster** for their kind permission to use information and text from their bestselling book *Bradford's Noise of the Valleys* (Bank House Books, 2009).

My sincere thanks to the popular author **Michael Stott** for his kind permission to use text from his bestselling book *Within 15 Miles of Ossett* (2009).

Thanks to the lovely **Linda King née Wilkinson** for supplying the photographs of Wood's Music Shop and many others of the period 1960–1, and a special tribute for a wonderful feature about teenage life during our rock 'n' roll days.

Very special thanks to **Christine Pottage**, long-time partner of the late Spike O' Brian, for her help in furnishing me with details of Spike's career and photographs.

Many thanks to **Susan Trudgill**, aka Swinging Sue, and husband **George** for their kind help in supplying text and early photographs of her late father Dave Lee. Sue's website for her popular rock 'n' roll dance classes is www.swingingsue.co.uk.

Thank you to **Vivian Keeting** for providing me with the history of The Phantoms and their former members.

I am greatly indebted to one of Bradford's premier drummers (and vocalist) **Ken Hickey** for his kind help in contacting many former group members and personalities. Ken is the committee member representing Bradford and the North of England for www.ukdrumfair.com.

Thank you to **Michael Littleproud** for providing information about and photographs of the Ideal ballroom.

Thank you to **Pam Wiggins**, wife of the late Dave Wiggins (Telecasters), bass guitarist, for photographs and details of his contribution to the rock 'n' roll era.

Thanks to **Ian (Sandy) Anderson** for information about The Spartans and The Nomads. The Nomads are still playing today with some of the original members (see www.thenomads.co.uk).

Thank you to **Brian Tordoff** for his help with information about and photographs of The Strollers (Brian T. Strollers), who are still playing today with some of the original members.

Special thanks to **Barbara Pell, aka Diana Stevens**, originally with Terry Sexton and the Shakes, for passing on information about members of The Telecasters and others. See www.pandormagic.co.uk.

Thank you to **Pat Fillingham**, wife of the late Brian Fillingham (Telecasters), another of Bradford's talented drummers, for information about Brian's early days.

Special thanks to **Jaquay Royston**, wife of the late Clive Royston (Brian T. Strollers) for permission to use information and photographs from his superb memorabilia collection.

Thanks to **James Bordass** for his Elvis hairstyle and Teddy Boy photographs, and for information about Helen (Ellen) of the Tomboys.

Special thanks to **Emma Clayton**, leisure and lifestyle editor of the Bradford *Telegraph and Argus*, for her help through the newspaper in contacting some of the early group members.

Thanks to **Jeff Birtley** for his kind help with regard to The Flamingos, The Montanas and the Mark Russell Four, and for photographs.

My very special thanks to the late Mrs **Jane (Jean) Artist** (1918–2010), my number one fan for over fifty years, who made albums full of newspaper features about my rock 'n' roll career – and more! This fine lady has sadly missed seeing the book that she was so much looking forward to reading.

Thanks to **Richard (Have you any medals) Jennings** for information about the original Chillas and an early insight into Gary Lane and the Rockets.

My thanks to the very talented musician **Peter Stanley (Stan) Dobson**, not only for the information on his group The Tarantulas but also for his very descriptive and well-written text. Special thanks also for his gifted artwork for Geoff Chew's 'Twang Bang Boom and Zoom'.

Very special thanks to **Geoff Chew**, not only for his support and for introducing me to groups in the Otley and Ilkley area, but also for putting together his wonderful insight into the world of instruments and equipment.

Thanks to my old friend **Peter Clegg** for information and photographs of his days with The Phantoms, Charlotte and the Brontebeats and Three Good Reasons, right up to today.

Special thanks to **Roy Bould**, **Allan Davies** and the late **Malcolm Murray**, formerly of The Royalists. They were the first group members to contact me, laying one of the foundations of this book.

Linda Russell and Bruce: many thanks for information about and photographs of their successful career and that of other groups from the Keighley area.

My special thanks to **Dave Marshall** for his help with editorial and photographs of local groups, especially The Caravelles.

Special thanks to **Doreen Burns** for photographs and details of her time with the popular female trio the Three Ds.

Very many thanks to **Dave Pannett** for his help and photographs from his days with Lee Chevin and the Ravers.

Thanks to **Dave de Courcy** for his help in supplying photographs and details of his career with The Evergreens and other groups.

Very many thanks to octogenarian **Harry Foster** for taking the time and trouble to enlighten me about the time when he was a part of the Tomboys and Helen.

Ian (Sandy) Sanderson has my special thanks for helping with photographs of and details about The Nomads and other groups in the Keighley area.

Thank you to **Ian Brogden** and **David Wiltshire**, formerly of Gary Layne and the Rockets. They persevered in bringing the text about this popular group to a successful conclusion.

Thank you to **Josie Meehan**, formerly of Jo White and The Bluenites, for her help with information on this group and the family connection with other groups.

Thank you to **Jeff Birtley** for his help with and information about The Flamingos and Sandra and the Montanas.

Thank you to Mrs **Jennifer Speight, aka Toni Star**, formerly of Toni Star and the Meteors, for in-depth information about the group and personal photographs.

My thanks go to members of The Dingos and former vocalist **Keith Savyer** for his brilliant cartoon of the group the Brad Lads.

Thank you to **Mick Judge** of Mick Judge and the Jurymen for information about his group, including photographs, and information about other groups he was involved in.

Thanks to **Mike Stephenson**, formerly of The Telecasters and many other local groups, for information in the early days of writing this book. His photographs were also invaluable.

My thanks to **Mike Betts** for a very detailed insight into his group The Tradesmen in the early days of rock 'n' roll, showing all their trials and tribulations as they strove to reach the top of the pops. He contacted all the members of his former group and completed not only their history (in great detail) but also each member's biography.

Very many thanks to my old friend **Mick Kershaw** (Mick Novack) for his in-depth knowledge of his former days in our rock 'n' roll world, for which he has always been held in great esteem.

To my good friend **Terry Sexton** my thanks for helping with his groups The Telecasters and The Shakes, filling in many gaps.

Many thanks to my friend **John Pennington** (councillor) for permission to use photographs of the Mecca Locarno, later Pennington's Night Club.

To **Cliff Martin**, formerly of Cliff and Brenda with the Dominators, my thanks for helping to put together the story of this special group

Thank you, **Trevor Lever**, for your endeavours in contacting former members of 'The Tuxedos and obtaining information.

My thanks to **Janet Bentley née Kirby** for her kindness in sending me photographs of her and her friends in 1964 outside the popular Allasio Coffee bar and restaurant, New Victoria Street.

Thank you **Joan**, the wife of the late **Dave Lee** (one of Bradford's most successful stars) for her kindness for access to photographs of Dave.

Special thanks to all individuals, whether group members or not, who in some way have contributed to the text or photographs to make this book a record for future generations, so they can read about those wonderful years of so long ago!

JENNIFER ROBINSON **KYTE PHOTOGRAPHY**

Foreword

Ever since Derek Lister, alias Dal Stevens, included me in his book *Bradford's Own*, we have been firm friends. That being the case, I am thrilled he has asked me to write a foreword for his new book *When Bradford Rocked*. I recently received and read the manuscript and found that it is packed not only with stories and details about the musicians and performers starting out during this amazing time in popular music history but also tons of information about Bradford itself. I have been able to recall many of the fantastic department stores and shops that graced our good city when I was growing up, and I learned just how many clubs and venues there were for people's entertainment. How could I have forgotten the coffee shops, particularly the Alassio opposite the Alhambra Theatre, where I sat with my mates and made one cup of trendy coffee last for hours! There is even a section on the instruments that young musicians were using (for those with a technical mind).

I was glad also to read about old friends like Carl Gresham, who has done so many interesting things in the world of music and entertainment, including his work as a DJ live and on radio, plus John Verity, a fine singer and musician whom I have worked with over the years.

I send all good wishes to the many characters I have met who grace the pages of this expansive work and I will definitely be passing copies to my four great-nieces and nephews to give them a sense of their Bradford roots!

This is the story of rock 'n' roll and how it touched one city in the UK – but it also reaches out further and expresses the attitudes and feelings that were present in so many people's minds when rock 'n' roll hit the world like a hurricane.

Kiki Dee

Foreword

A map of the Bradford area.

OH NO ARNOLD!! WHEN I SAID WE SHOULD WEAR STAGESUITS ASSOCIATED WITH OUR LOCAL TEXTILE MILLS— I MEANT MANUFACTURED BY THEM, YOU DAFT IDIOT!
The BRADLADS
SiV 2010

Prologue
ROCK 'N' ROLL

In 1956 everything changed in Britain, as rock 'n' roll began to trickle in from America.

Many people do not realise that 'Rock Around the Clock' was much more than just a flash in the pan, as many later historians would have us believe. Bill Haley and the Comets had already had a major national hit with 'Crazy Man Crazy' in 1953 and they also recorded what are now acknowledged as the earliest rock 'n' roll records, such as 'Rocket 88' (1951) and 'Rock the Joint' (1952). Remember that this was *years* before a young man named Elvis Presley had even thought of venturing into a recording studio ...

1951 to 1954 was the period during which things started happening for Bill and his band, first the Saddlemen and then, as they became known from 1952, the Comets. These were the years in which they literally invented rock 'n' roll. Once Bill Haley and the Comets recorded 'Rock around the Clock' on 12 April 1954 the world would never be the same.

Rock 'n' roll shook things up in the 1950s and '60s. Many musical styles from around the world contributed to this new sound. Along with an African-American influence, rock 'n' roll also drew on the lyrical melodies of recent European immigrants and the country and western music of Texans.

The music first became popular in small clubs and on the radio, where DJs began to call it rock 'n' roll. Later, television programmes allowed teenagers to watch their favourite bands. Not everyone was excited about this music. Many parents didn't like the suggestive dancing, lyrics and loud, fast beat.

The golden age of rock 'n' roll is usually recognised as the 1950s and '60s, and this is the era on which this book concentrates.

Introduction

Most of *Bradford's Rock and Roll the Golden Years: 1959–65*, which I wrote in 1991, is about me, firstly with my own groups, Dal Stevens and the Blue Jays and Dal Stevens and the Four Dukes, and then with my life as a DJ for five years (1960–5) with Top Rank at the Gaumont and Majestic ballrooms in Bradford.

It was in 1965 when I decided that my rock 'n' roll world was changing and was being taken over by the beat boom, with Mod style and Beatle suits. Music tastes changed almost overnight, with the advent of blues, R&B, soul, harmony groups and pop art, progressing to psychedelically painted trucks, long hair, drugs, flower power, hippies and the music associated with them. Now the songs and music that explored the ups and downs of teenage romance sung by the Tabs, Bobbies and Frankies were on the decline. It was at this time I decided to 'pack my tent and slowly steal away' from my rock 'n' roll world. The book was almost finished, but as an afterthought I decided to try to add a few local groups and celebrities. I therefore devoted the epilogue to those of whom I could contact. Time was short, though, and I only managed to include a few, with brief details of their careers.

It has now become apparent that there is a need to record more detail about our very own local rock 'n' roll groups, who, through the period 1954–66 gave immeasurable pleasure to thousands of young people in Bradford and the surrounding districts. Bradford had a wealth of talent – vocalists, guitarists and drummers – who compared favourably with the top groups of the country. Our local groups exported their talent to other parts of the county, and in some cases nationally, but they were never recognised with a title like the Bradford or the Yorkshire Sound. They never quite achieved the fame that most of them richly deserved.

By the mid-1960s, 90 per cent of the city's indigenous music was silenced. Dozens of groups unplugged their home-made amplifiers and quietly went home. There wasn't anywhere for them to play, as bingo had already commandeered most of the dance halls. These days the defeat of the Bradford beat would be put down to market forces. It is a saga of missed opportunities, bad judgement, poor management and plain rotten luck. However what is missing from the recollection of the victims .fifty years later is any sense of grievance: just being part of that scene was enough!

The Legend of a Group

The following is an insight into the world of over fifty years ago that will give you, the reader, some idea of what our would-be stars had to contend with in order to form a group.

Most of our local groups were made up of the usual four members: a drummer, bass guitarist, rhythm guitarist and lead guitarist. Of these, one was the vocalist – unless a fifth member was included specifically for this purpose. His responsibility, apart from the obvious, was compèring the act, introducing numbers and making conversation during the inevitable breaks between each number.

Cash rewards were almost non-existent and in most cases hardly covered expenses; so with capital not forthcoming, most groups struggled along with very basic equipment. In some cases they had just one amplifier, even though each guitarist should really have his own. If no PA system was available the vocalist was in for a rough ride, trying to make himself or herself heard over the guitars, drums and crowd reaction.

Guitars of the time were expensive and not readily available to the average working teenager, other than on tick! It was therefore inevitable that many group members created their own, and although they were rough and ready, most were ingeniously made, and compared quite favourably with their expensive counterparts.

Uniform dress was optional, but again thanks to lack of finance most groups were not able to present themselves as they would have wished. As this was before the unkempt later '60s most groups were well-groomed young men wearing their best suit and tie.

Transport was non existent for most of the groups, and it was down to fathers and friends who had vehicles to transport them to their bookings. It was not unusual for local buses to convey members and their equipment in areas where there was much hardship.

Engagements were contracted by a group's members themselves and were nearly always referred to as bookings. The word 'gig' was not generally used, so I have used 'booking' in almost all cases. The same goes for the word 'band': in the early days a band was generally a dance band, and in the 1950s and early '60s the musicians I am describing were referred to as 'groups'.

Only a few groups had a manager (of sorts). Most information about where bookings were obtainable was passed from group to group by word of mouth and even by letter, as most families did not have a telephone.

Most groups tended to copy the popular numbers and discs being played throughout the rock 'n' roll world. Some performed them with outstanding accuracy; others tried and failed. As one popular number faded, the next was rehearsed and performed, until that too outgrew its popularity. Others were kept in the repertoire as they would never die, notably 'Shaking All Over', 'Whole Lot o' Shakin' Goin' On', 'Johnny B Goode', 'Sweet Little Sixteen', and the indestructible instrumental 'Apache'.

This was the 'World' of most of our local groups from the mid fifties to the mid sixties.

Who's Who

Included for all members of groups and other participants is a brief biography and details of their musical career. In most cases this is placed in the section relating to the group member's original group or band. In keeping with the era only original black and white photographs are used. In many cases, where careers continue after 1966 the biographies will continue until the present day – although there are no photographs from after 1966. Please note that some images are not as sharp as one would wish: for most people the only camera available was the old box type, with no flash. Some photographs are included as they are probably the only ones available of a particular individual. With the passage of time, some biographies (and photographs) are unobtainable – but names are still published.

While this book is primarily about rock 'n' roll music, in some cases skiffle groups that were popular in and around Bradford, especially in the mid-1950s, have been mentioned. This is because members of skiffle groups sometimes progressed to rock 'n' roll music or joined rock 'n' roll groups. It is also the case that from the mid-1960s, while traditional rock 'n' roll music was still being played, some groups began to incorporate R and B and soul music into their repertoire – and some of these latecomers are included, to show developments up until 1966 As an aside, it was becoming fashionable to move away from traditional rock 'n' roll group names and to use singular titles related to just about anything!.

It is of no concern if groups were good, bad or indifferent. All who were contacted or traced are included; after all, most, if not all, were striving for stardom or recognition. Even if they were involved in the scene only for a short time, they made their mark and deserve to be remembered.

Also included are individuals who contributed to the Bradford rock 'n' roll scene but were born outside the Bradford area. If, for example, two members of a group were born in Leeds and Halifax, and three in Bradford, details (if known) of the out-of-town members are included.

Any work of this type will always be incomplete to some extent, as it is well nigh impossible to document everything with total success. Inevitably some names will be missing as information has not been available or forthcoming. While every effort has been made to provide a clear and detailed study, there will no doubt be minor flaws, errors and omissions as well as the odd misspelt name. This is owing in some part to vague memories from over fifty years ago, more often to lack of research sources, and, of course, to the perils of secondhand information. It should be noted that all text by groups and group members is as written by those individuals, with no additions by the author.

Some astute readers will no doubt inform me of groups and group members whom I have forgotten or overlooked. For the first two years in which this book was brought together I endeavoured to contact as many groups as possible. This has been very successful, but some of those I tried to get in touch with did not reply. In the end I concentrated on the many who did contact me, who were enthusiastic and more than happy to be included.

This book is a tribute to musicians, group members and many individuals whose sweat, energy, skill, talent and dedication produced Bradford's rock 'n' roll music, which collectively gave so much pleasure to so many of us during those never-to-be-forgotten days of long ago.

Read on – Rock on!

PART ONE:
BRADFORD'S ROCK 'N' ROLL HISTORY

One of Bradford's iconic buildings, Kirkgate Market.

Two of the Woods' Music Shop assistants: Dawn Moss on the left and Linda Wilkinson pose on the shop counter, 1961. Behind them the new 45rpm records are being stored.

Chapter 1
BRADFORD IN THE 1950s AND '60s

Bradford is surrounded by a number of townships that all merge into the city we know today. Since 1974 Bradford has been enlarged to a metropolitan district, taking in Shipley, Bingley, Haworth, Keighley and Ilkley.

In the 1950s and early 1960s hardly anything had changed in Bradford's centre since before the war. It still had many fine Victorian buildings and, although smut-laden, they still showed quality and pride. Overlooking all were the beautiful parish church, Town Hall, St George's Hall, Mechanics' Institute, Swan Arcade, the Wool Exchange, the Alhambra, and the New Victoria Cinema (Odeon).

Shopping

Three large departmental stores dominated the town. Brown Muffs was on Market Street. This was where I first started work, giving me a stepping stone to other places of employment. On Manningham Lane there was the fine Art Deco building of Busby's, looking more like a glamorous ocean liner than a departmental store. This unusually styled building looked magnificent when lit up on winter evenings, especially at Christmas. Busby's was very popular with children at that time, with its wonderful Santa's Grotto, where a visit cost 1s. The third big Bradford store was the Sunbridge Road Emporium (later to become Sunwin House). It was a nice, open, clean store that had its own clientele and attractions, one being its escalator – the first in Bradford.

Among these stores was a variety of large and small shops, most established for many years and household names for generations of Bradfordians. For ladies the town centre bristled with fashion retailers: Lady of Fashion, Novello's, Clayden's, Marshall and Snellgrove, and the furriers Peter Brunskill and Kino's were very popular. Shoe shops catering for both ladies and men's shoes seemed to cluster in the Darley Street area, including Timpson's,

Barrett's, Stead and Simpson, Saxone, Dolcis, Freeman Hardy and Willis, Cable Shoes and Dr Scholl's.

The High Street names of Timothy White and Taylor and Boots were well established. Among the other chemists were Rimmingtons, and on Sunbridge Road Parkinson and Clark. Men's outfitters had prominent displays in Bradford. After all, it was still the world centre of the woollen industry. Montague Burton had three large shops, two in Tyrell Street, and one in Kirkgate. Other tailors of equal standing were Made to Measure, Alexandre's, Weaver to Wearer, John Colliers and O.S. Wain, the shop that for years had the monopoly in the hire of dinner suits. Around the corner on Bridge Street was Snowden's Outfitters, popularly known as Snowdens Corner. Dunne's, in Ivegate, was popular for its hats and caps, and Hope Brothers was a much-respected gent's outfitters in Lower Kirkgate next to the Talbot Hotel, famous for the statue of a hound above the door. If the outdoor person required special attire for walks on the moors, then Millets offered a whole range of clothing and accessories. Colletts, the gent's outfitters in Swan Arcade, catered for an upmarket clientele, and Starkies Outfitters, adjoining the Ritz Cinema, was very popular.

However, remembered by most Bradfordians is Lingards, not because the original building was destroyed by fire in 1940 or for its merchandise, but for the thrill of seeing the overhead cash containers at work. When you gave your money to the assistant, it was placed in a brass overhead container, which ran along wires to an assistant seated in a booth overlooking the counters. When a lever was pulled the container swooshed along the track, then shot back with your change and receipt.

Shops with a speciality were everywhere: Kendal's for rainwear and umbrellas, Chadwick's for leather goods, Taylor and Parsons for ironmongery and furnishings, while Bryer's in Forster Square were the leaders for the sale of fabrics. Molletts was a must for that new tiled fireplace when the Yorkshire range had to go. For the cyclist there was Baines in Lower Piccadilly, and two Halfords shops, which also catered for motor accessories. There was even a Catholic repository shop at the bottom of Sunbridge Road, which sold religious items from missals to rosaries.

For jewellery, Fattorini's was prominent in Tyrrel Street, although Mappin and Webb, Arensberg's, H Samuel, Minoah Rhodes and Fowler and Oldfields were very competitive. Choice ceramics, china, and glassware were sold at Jackson's in Darley Street, and Timms and Dyason provided the same quality goods from its own arcade in Town Hall Square. Dalbys was perhaps the only large antique establishment in the city centre; it was situated on the corner of Town Hall Square, facing the Crystal Palace (toilets). The windows of Dalbys were always filled with all kinds of china, jewellery, fine art and furniture. Christopher Pratt's on North Parade had been established on the same site for many years and was very popular for its high-quality furniture.

For the young rock 'n' roll teenagers, buying 45rpm records locally was no problem. Perhaps the best establishment for the top hits was Wood's Music Shop at the bottom of Sunbridge Road, which sold everything from sheet music to a variety of musical instruments. This was one of the first shops in the area to adopt the American method of selling records via a record booth. After

Musical Instruments of all types from Wood's
Woods
MUSIC SHOP
Sunbridge Road · Bradford
also New Street·Huddersfield

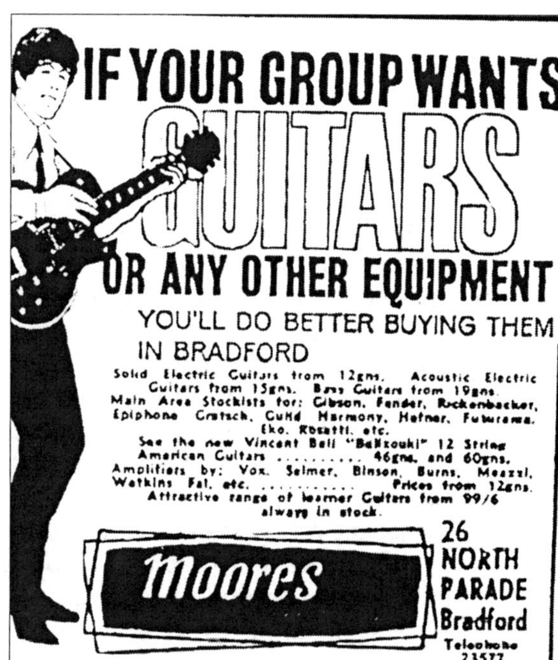
IF YOUR GROUP WANTS
GUITARS
OR ANY OTHER EQUIPMENT
YOU'LL DO BETTER BUYING THEM IN BRADFORD
Solid Electric Guitars from 12gns. Acoustic Electric Guitars from 15gns. Bass Guitars from 19gns.
Main Area Stockists for: Gibson, Fender, Rickenbacker, Epiphone Gretsch, Guild Harmony, Hofner, Futurama, Eko, Rosatti, etc.
See the new Vincent Bell "Bellzouki" 12 String American Guitars .... 46gns. and 60gns.
Amplifiers by: Vox, Selmer, Binson, Burns, Meazzi, Watkins Fal, etc. .... Prices from 12gns.
Attractive range of learner Guitars from 99/6 always in stock.
moores
26 NORTH PARADE Bradford
Telephone 23577

selecting a record you wished to hear, you were sent to a numbered booth, a similar size to a telephone box. You then listened to the record from a speaker in the booth as it was played on a turntable at the rear of the staff counter. The shop was managed by a very astute Richard Wood, and the selection of pop records was a priority – with business forthcoming from hundreds of youths. He was ably assisted by a young female staff, who also knew exactly what the teenagers wanted. Among them were the young Linda Wilkinson and Dawn Moss, as well as another teenager, Barbara, who later claimed fame with Dal and Dadio at the Gaumont ballroom, being on stage to sort the records selected by the patrons. She became the Della in Dal, Della and Dadio!

In the early 1960s Carl Gresham was manager of the Co-op record department, bringing his own style and professionalism to the job. Knowing what the teenagers wanted, he made the record department a very popular venue. Shuttleworth's on Darley Street, while a much smaller shop, always had a good selection of records – although the sale of sheet music was their speciality.

Teenage girls were starting to look less like their mothers in the latter part of the 1950s. Brightly patterned dresses with tight waists and wide skirts were popular, and effect that could only be achieved with a stiff starched petticoat. This style was suited to rock 'n' roll and jive dancing, in which the circle skirt swirled up, reflecting the energy of the dance, and in many cases showed their stocking tops, which was highly fashionable. Coloured patterned and pleated skirts made from a new fabric called Terylene were also worn for more casual occasions, and pullovers were becoming more popular for women. On top they wore scoop-necked blouses, cardigans, tight polo-necks or three-quarter sleeve white fitted shirts, often with a scarf knotted around their neck. These fashions had originated in America, but filtered into Britain in a slightly watered down form. Trousers followed men's fashion with narrow legs, but were usually tighter fitting. Jeans were also becoming trendy for casual wear. High heels were the order of the day with the circle skirt, and for more casual wear 'flatties' were most common. The most popular hair styles of this time were the pixie, beehive and bouffant (which needed a lot of backcombing), held in place with the ever dependable Bellair hair lacquer and a thousand clips!

In the early 1960s, although hairstyles were almost the same, hem lines had been rising since the end of the '50s, and by 1963 they were just above the knee. By the end of 1965 the newly christened mini-skirt really took off, and climbed 6in or more above the knee. Traditional stockings began to be replaced by one-piece tights in a range of ever more outrageous colours. These allowed women to wear the shorter skirts – which were considered incredibly shocking by some sections of society.

Fashion for men in the 1950s usually meant a trip to Burton's for a new suit, generally conventional in appearance and in a sober colour such as grey, black or navy. Suits were worn for nights out and for most social occasions, but casual clothes for men were also starting to make an appearance. A blazer or sports jacket with non-matching trousers looked less formal than a suit.

With the advent of rock 'n' roll in the mid-1950s male fashion was well catered for in Bradford, especially if you wanted 'with it' gear. Hargreaves Outfitters in Sunbridge Road offered a nice selection of frilled fronted shirts

Moore's shop window in the early 1960s.

MARIO

Gentleman's Hairstylists

Now has Two New Salons at Hustlergate and The Wool Exchange —Giving Top Service !

HAVE YOU TRIED IT YET ?

MARIO The Wool Exchange Bradford

Telephone Bradford 32135

The very popular gents hair-stylist Mario's, situated in the Wool Exchange following its move from its original site in Forster Square.

and string ties, and introduced the popular luminous socks (lime-green being their speciality), which brought a shake of the head and a frown from elderly people. Wallis Outfitters, at the bottom of Manchester Road, could also offer all the trendy rock 'n' roll ware, and was not as expensive as Hargreaves. There was quite an assortment of footwear, the most popular being crepe-soled shoes, sometimes referred to as brothel creepers, although a majority of teenagers still wore the standard leather shoes of the time. Well into the 1960s winkle-pickers with Cuban heels took over.

Most men wore a suit or a jacket of some kind and a shorty raincoat, taking the place of the large gabardine raincoat that most men seemed to carry over the arm even when it was not raining. The shorty raincoat guaranteed wet trousers on a rainy day, however!

In in the early 1960s the clean, Beatle-style mop-top haircut joined forces with these fashions to create a style so modern that it became known as the Mod movement. Simplicity was the order of the day: leather jackets were out, smart suits were in.

Also in the world of fashion, new hairstyles became the vogue for both men and women, especially with the advent of rock 'n' roll. It was in 1952 that the first unisex hairstylist in the city arrived. Hugo De Luca (1920–98), known as Mario, was a pioneering hairdresser who set up his business in the precincts of Foster Square station. He brought a vision to Bradford, and his hairdryer was a revolutionary styling tool. It was Mario who introduced the blow dry: not many people knew how to use the hairdrier in styling. Later his business moved to the Wool Exchange, when his brothers, who were also hairdressers, joined him from his home town of Naples. His wife Mary (1925–2011), who had met Mario when he came to Brighouse as a prisoner of war, was also part of the business. It was with the advent of rock 'n' roll, with the change of hairstyles and the business now well established, that it was became the favourite place for the Tony Curtis and DA styles for young teenagers. It was a little more than the usual 1s 6d for short back and sides, but well worth the extra shillings to have your hair washed and styled at Mario's. It was a must for the rock 'n' rollers of the time. (Mario passed away aged seventy-eight, and his business is still thriving.)

Near a Marks and Spencer, Woolworth's was in the centre of the Darley Street shops. It had individual counters with its own assistants and a wonderful central staircase with handrails of solid brass. From ping-pong balls to a pair of football boots, sporting enthusiasts had many shops to choose from. Among the popular ones were Sports and Pastimes in Market Street, Nutton's close to Forster Square, Carters, and Len Hutton (the Yorkshire and England cricketer) had a shop in Bridge Street for a short time.

Probably Bradford's best-known small shop, renowned for its marvellous meat pies and sandwiches, was Philip Smith and Son in Ivegate. It was advertised as the 'oldest pork shop in Yorkshire'. Pre-Christmas queues formed from early morning down Ivegate days before the event. A special favourite was a stand pie for Boxing Day. If the juice from meat pies happened to mark your clothes, then the dry cleaners Crockatt's, Martins, Smiths and Mercury, all in the town centre, were on hand with a two hour cleaning service!

Two local girls, Diana Winnard (later to become Mrs Derek Lister) and Jill, pose in the latest fashions for 1963.

One of the most enjoyable and interesting areas, away from the shops, was John Street's open air market. Built in 1931 on the site of Copper Quarry, it was surrounded by John Street, Westgate and Rawson Road. The market stalls were roofed and sold a wide range of items from pigeons to plates. The crockery salesmen held court, entertaining their audience by flinging tea services, dishes and plates in the air and catching the items with lots of clattering and drama. To watch this show was a treat for young and old alike. Much time could be spent wandering round, and for refreshments there were lots of cafés and snack bars around the perimeter. A favourite was the pea and pie stall that sold a plate of peas and a glass of Tizer for 3d.

In 1951 Bradford markets celebrated 700 years of their royal markets charter, which had been granted by Henry III in 1251. Market stalls were decked with bunting and flags, with special counter displays, and two Bradford trolley buses were painted with Royal livery and the dates 1251–1951 to celebrate the event.

There were many cafés and snack bars in the town centre, especially in Bradford's large indoor Kirkgate Market. In Darley Street there were also the quality shops of Silvio's and Betty's café. On Tyrrel Street were two well-known establishments. One was Collinson's Café, the coffee and grocer's shop. Its coffee roaster sent an aromatic smell wafting over the pavement into Tyrell Street, and the restaurant was famed for its three piece 'orchestra'. Next door was the Farmer Giles Milk Bar, which many parents advised their children not to visit as it had a reputation – of what, they did not say. It did, however, have a juke box installed in 1937: was that the reputation?

Regarding reputations, the New Inn on the corner of Town Hall Square and Thornton Road, an old coaching house, was well known as a den of iniquity. Similar notoriety was attached to the Old Crown and The Grosvenor in Ivegate, and the old Back Empress on Tyrell Street, which had a certain 'calling'! A place of leisure without this problem was The County, frequented by woolmen from all corners of the world on their visits to the Wool Exchange – as was Spink's Bar and restaurant. The Talbot Hotel had a 'Gentlemen's Bar'.

Bradford had its own speakers' corner: the large open car park next to the Ritz Cinema on Broadway. On Sunday evenings crowds gathered to listen to individuals, each with their own space , standing on boxes and talking about every subject under the sun, using the Englishman's privilege of free speech without fear of arrest. Communists proclaimed the doctrines of Marx, Lenin, Trotsky, and insults and jeers were often thrown at them from the crowd, the usual comment being, 'If it's so good in Russia why don't you go and live there'? Religion also came in for insults, as speakers for Catholics, Methodists, the Church of England and other denominations did their utmost to convince the onlookers of their faith. While some of the discussions turned into arguments, lots of laughter was always part of Bradford's speakers' corner. Most of the crowd left with laughter or a smile. Well, it was something to talk about at work the following day.

Transport

Bradford had always had a good transport system, with trams, trolley buses and West Yorkshire buses offering good cheap services. For most destinations,

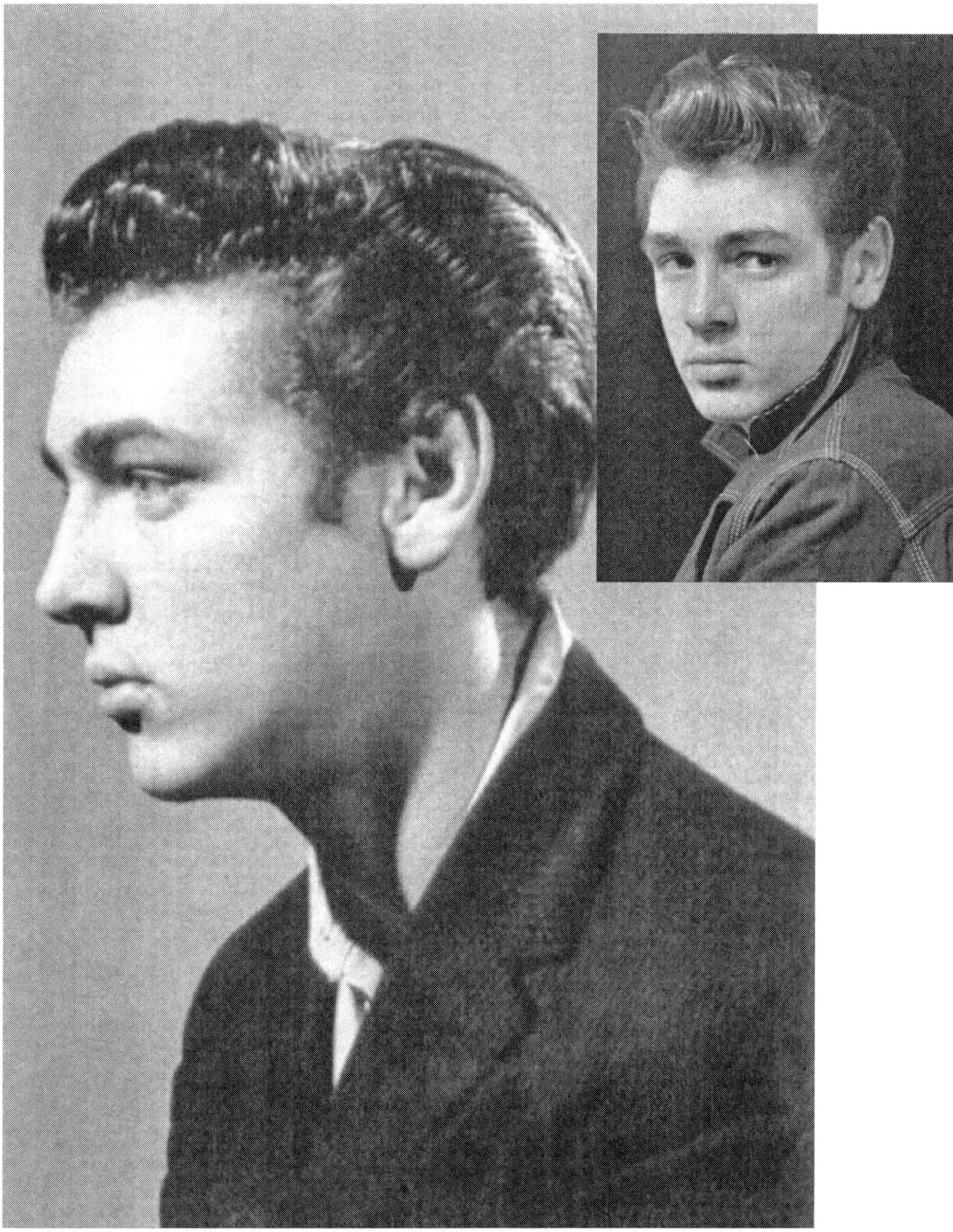

Local lad James Bordass epitomises the hairstyle of the time with an almost Elvis-like profile.

both local and far away, the town was provided with an excellent train service from Forster Square and Exchange station. Both stations could take you to any part of the country.

After eleven o' clock Bradford took on the look of a ghost town, as traffic diminished and everything came to a standstill. As most transport services finished at about this time, people could often be seen scurrying around Bradford centre every evening as the Town Hall geared up for the eleven o'clock chimes. Courting couples emerged from shop and warehouse doorways to catch that last bus. Many men had to walk home after seeing their girlfriend to her bus stop, especially if their last bus was from the other side of Bradford. This was quite accepted. If you were lucky and had some spare cash you could visit the taxi rank in Town Hall Square; otherwise it was the walk home. Women as well as men walked home after missing buses, either in groups or on their own, and it seems that hardly any trouble ever occurred. The most that people had to contend with was the occasional drunk.

Everyone wanted to be mobile, but few had money to throw about. Not many teenagers could afford the luxury of a car. While a few lucky ones had a motor-cycle, the alternative was the Italian-produced scooter, with much smaller wheels and engine. The most popular and famous makes were Lambretta and Vespa, the Italian 'wasp' earning the nickname of 'hairdryer' because of the distinctive side panels that covered the engine. The machines were a dream to customise, many sporting superbly artistic paint jobs and adorned with an excess of mirrors, lights and other paraphernalia. They were as much a fashion accessory or art form as a mode of transport.

It was also the Golden Age of the three wheeler bubble car in the 1950s and '60s. Some nifty little vehicles were produced for this market, and even the great BMW chipped in with its Isetta, a Heinkel look-alike. Heinkel and Messerschmitt bombarded Britain with their microcars. The Messerschmitt was a powerful little machine: its occupants travelled in tandem, unlike other bubble cars, which offered side-by-side seating. The standard steering wheel was similar to an aircraft joystick. Later Messerschmitt introduced a four wheeler version – a much speedier vehicle, with top speeds of over 70 mph. It did not sell well here because it was taxed at the more expensive four-wheeled motor vehicle rate. Its higher price was against it too: at just over £650 it could hardly compete with the new Austin Mini, which was launched in 1959 at the low price of only £425. End of story!

Employment

Most of the woollen mills were still fully operational, giving plenty of jobs to men and women, either in office work or in the mill itself, as liggers, doffers, combers, spinners and woolsorters. Plenty of office work was available for typists or clerical staff. Apprenticeships had to be served for mechanics, engineers and electricians, with large companies like English Electric and Croft Engineering prominent. There was always shop work as well. Jobs could be changed frequently. It wasn't unknown for someone to leave a job in the morning, look through the situations vacant column in the lunchtime edition of the *Telegraph and Argus*, and be working somewhere else in the afternoon.

Law and Order

Most members of the Bradford City Police Force (1848–1974) were local men who knew the area and its villains. The police were still respected, and in most cases a word was sufficient to stop any trouble. Of course there were occasions when people were rebellious, so there were times when actions spoke louder than words. The Riot Act could still be read, and capital punishment was still in some cases the punishment for murder. The police force had its headquarters in the Town Hall, complete with cells. At the rear, on Norfolk Street, was a building the third floor of which housed the Fingerprint Department. It was a dingy place, but its expertise was much sought after by other police authorities. Bradford City Police was one of the forerunners in fingerprint detection as early as 1903.

Changing Bradford

New housing estates were planned and built in the mid-1950s, designed to take people from back-to-backs and old terraced housing, which was now deteriorating. New estates like Holmewood, Delph Hill, Buttershaw and Woodside offered a paradise of open spaces, gardens and modern houses. At first most of these estates had no shops, no schools, no church or a pub, but there were excellent bus services so people could escape to their old familiar areas. For the great majority who moved to these estates it was a dream come true. People who had never had a garden took a pride in their lawns, flowerbeds and hedges, and while the children were small they enjoyed the freedom of these grassed areas. It was many years before the community spirit that had existed in those tiny streets they had left behind was forgotten.

(above) Linda Wilkinson with her first love, Irvin ('Smudge') Smith, the well-known drummer with The Dingos.

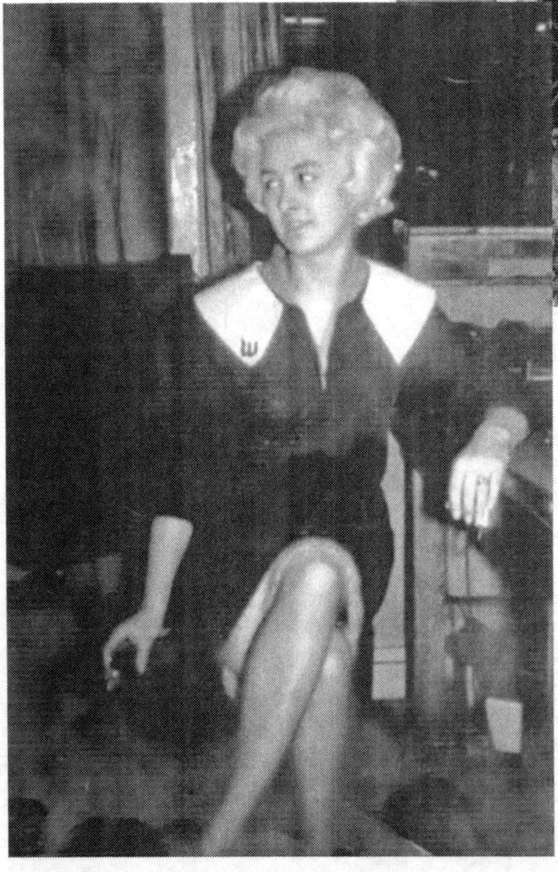

(left) Linda as a teenager in the 1950s and '60s.

Chapter 2
MEMORIES OF A DECADE

I am grateful to **Linda Wilkinson** for contributing this chapter.

I have been asked many times by today's young people what it was like to be a teenager in the late 1950s and '60s.

I was born in January 1944 and lived in Shipley with my loving parents. I owe my love of music to my mother: she sang all the old songs to me, and we were forever at the cinema watching all the musicals of the time.

I went to school in Bingley. My introduction to rock 'n' roll was in the very same cinema to which my mother took me as a child. I was fourteen years old and my cousin Maureen was two years older. She was great looking and all the boys were after her, so it was nice to hang out with her. I was skinny with not a lot of shape to my 4ft 10in frame, so no one really noticed me. Bill Haley's 'Rock Around the Clock' was the film we were going to see. When that music started to play, 'One, two, three o'clock, four o'clock rock', I thought my heart would burst; it was fantastic. That was when my whole life changed, and my mum's music was suddenly the past. I felt alive and ready for life in the '60s.

Leaving school at fifteen, I went to work in the wonderful Busby's department store on Manningham Lane in Bradford. I worked at first in the fashion department, where I met Barbara – who became a lifelong friend. After a while I went into the record department. At that time 78 records were just about gone and 45s were the in thing. I remember the last 78 record I sold was Adam Faith's 'What Do You Want?'. My favourite at that time was Cliff Richards 'Move It'.

During this time at Busby's, I had to fetch price tickets from what they called the ticket office. A young man called Irvin Smith worked there, and he was to be my next step into my time with rock 'n' roll. Irvin (Smudge) Smith was my first love; he was a couple of years older than me, born in 1942. When he asked if I went dancing at the Majestic ballroom in Bradford, I said I wasn't allowed to go into Bradford – just to the Lakeans in Shipley, with my cousin

Maureen, who by this time had taught me to rock and roll. Irvin told me he was a drummer in a band called the Dingos, and asked me if I would go to see the band the next Monday night.

Irvin introduced me to a very pretty girl called Mona Hurley, who was the girlfriend of Kenny Fowler, the lead guitarist in the Dingos. Mona lived in Allerton in Bradford. We became the best of friends, and later sang together with another top Bradford band, Mick Sagar and the Cresters.

I met the rest of the band and Garth Cawood, who was the manager. He was very dedicated and took great care to make sure all went well with the band. There was the great Malcolm Clark, who had a fantastic voice and could sing Orbison songs just like Roy Orbison; he was on rhythm guitar. Ian Bannister was on bass and Terry (Dadio) Moran on the piano.

For about a year Mona, Kenny, Irvin and I went everywhere together. While our boyfriends were on stage we proudly bopped to the music, keeping an eye out for all the groupies, life was great.

The band was thrown into a terrible state when Malcolm and Ian told Garth they were leaving to join Mick Sagar's band The Cresters. Poor Garth: how would he replace Malcolm with his wonderful voice? But fate moves in mysterious ways. They got a new bass player Stuart Sutcliffe and a new pianist, the unforgettable Spike O'Brien (Brian Holt). Irvin told me they were holding auditions for a new singer, as they had a gig the next Saturday night at the Alex Hotel in Bradford.

We all met at the Alex on the Saturday. Garth said he was very happy with Malcolm's replacement, because they had auditioned a multi-talented young man who could not only sing but could play any instrument, 'a right Sammy Davis junior'. Mona and I couldn't wait to see him.' Then in walked the cutest guy, only 5ft 3in, but so good looking and with gorgeous hair. Irvin said, 'This is Sammy.' He impressed us all with his great Elvis-sounding voice. He also sang one of my favourite songs, Conway Twitty's 'Mona Lisa' (Mona was dead chuffed). When she told me she fancied him, I laughed and said , 'Why don't you join us, Sammy? Don't sit on your own.' He was from Batley Carr, and he didn't know anyone. As Sammy recounts in his book *Penny Arcade*, we met again later.

Some time later Irvin and I broke off our engagement. We had been together for two happy years, but as you grow up your lives move on. He was and is a great guy. Irvin married about a year later and went to live in Australia, where his sister lived. I met him at a rock 'n' roll reunion in 1989 at the Pile Bar; he had his wife and two sons with him, and I was with my husband, Arnie Marriott, and my two daughters, Julie and Debbie. Irvin still plays his drums, and now lives in California.

Soon after Irvin and I split up Mona and Kenny also broke up. Mona and I continued to be friends, and still went to see the bands play at the Students Club and the Queens Hall. One night we got a lift to Doncaster, where the Dingos and Mike Sagar and the Cresters were playing. While we were at the gig we got chatting to a man called Steve Black, who was the manager of the Cresters. He asked if we knew of a couple of girls who could sing, as he wanted to introduce backing singers to the band because no one else had them. Mona and I looked at one another and smiled. 'Yes' was the answer. 'When do we start?'

We were told to meet at Richard Harding's recording studio in Bramley. It was so exciting: we couldn't believe we would be singing with Richard Harding, a fantastically talented guitarist. We were reunited with Malcolm Clark and Ian Bannister, and their heart-throb lead singer who all the girls swooned over: Mike Sagar.

Mona and I had been practising the songs all week in my bedroom and drove my parents mad. Many people of my generation will remember the dulcet tones of Mother shouting 'Turn it down!' Come to think of it, I've done the same with my children. Our first song was 'Hit the Road, Jack' by Ray Charles. When Richard played the recording back to us we were dead impressed: we had no idea it would sound so good.

We had our first gig on Friday night at a dance hall in Selby; this was a warm-up for a stage show in Wakefield on the Saturday evening. Mona and I had been shopping for stage clothes and made our entrance in black shimmy dresses, pink shoes (which we had painted with nail polish) and long pink beads. Oh, did we shake and shimmy to the music, we felt like pop stars: it was wonderful.

Saturday was to be the big one. When we arrived at the theatre it looked massive, and never having been on a big stage like that we were terrified. At the end girls were already at the stage door screaming for the bands, so we all sneaked out the front door with a guy called Shane Fenton and his band the Fentones, Mike Berry and a few others. Shane later became Alvin Stardust. We had a great night and all went well. I sang with band for about six months, I also sang with Lee Chevin and the Ravers for a short time and went out briefly with the lead guitarist Kenny Raper.

By this time I was working in the record department at J. Wood and Sons in Sunbridge Road, Bradford. I loved working here because it was the biggest and the best record shop in Bradford. I teamed up with a new friend called Dawn Moss, who also worked in the record department. Whenever there was a show on in Bradford all the top bands headed for Wood's, as this was where the in-crowd was.

One day a band called the Animals came in: they were on a show with the Nashville Teens. I remember asking Alan Price if he was an Animal or a Nashville teen, and he gave me a wink and said, 'I'm an Animal.' This was some show, as they were all supporting bands for a group you may remember, The Beatles. Sadly they didn't get to Wood's, but I did see them at the Gaumont. Wow!

A little tale about the first time I was asked for a Beatles record. A young man asked if we had a record by the Beatles called 'Love Me Do', and I replied, 'Who are the Beatles? I've never heard of them.' Then I took out a list of new releases and there it was, so we played it – and I thought, 'That's not bad. It could be a hit!'

I met and saw many great acts of the '60s. Gene Vincent walked off the stage when someone heckled him. I went to see the Rolling Stones at St George's Hall. Kiki Dee used to come into Wood's as did P.J. Proby and a funny guy called Wee Willy Harris. He always hung around trying to chat me up.

Derek Lister (aka Dal Stevens) was the DJ at the Gaumont and the Majestic dance halls, perhaps Bradford's most popular DJ of the time. He called weekly at Wood's for the latest 45s for his show. I also remember a very formidable and rather loud Mr Carl Gresham coming in to buy his records. I love him: he is one of our best friends today. Garth and Carl, as I remember, were kind of rivals in those days.

Well, that's it in a nutshell. I went on to marry and have two wonderful daughters, Julie and Debbie. Sadly I lost my husband Arnie in 2003 and Debbie in 2007, but I have gained two lovely grandchildren.

I am now proud to be married to Sammy King, whom I met at the Alexandra Hotel all those years ago: we have been friends all our lives. As we said before, fate moves in mysterious ways.

Chapter 3
LOCAL DANCE HALLS AND OTHER VENUES

In the mid-1950s modern ballroom dancers were well catered for in Bradford and the surrounding districts. However, when jive and rock 'n' roll arrived they had to change with the times and offer the new alternatives.

The new groups began to perform in varied places. Concert secretaries of working men's clubs booked them for lunchtime and evening sessions. They generally performed before or after the comedian, or stripper dependent on the type of club. If the group was successful word was passed around many other clubs, and further bookings were contracted.

Cinemas also asked groups to entertain their patrons during the intermission. This usually took place on a small stage just a few feet away from the screen. Any young teenagers who were present enjoyed this, but the older generation were often heard to state that they had only come to see the picture! This type of booking only lasted a couple of years, as it became obvious that 99 per cent of the patrons had come to see the film, and it did not produce any more customers.

Wedding receptions were not usually popular venues for the group members. Many guests were often more than merry with drink, and there were dire results. Drunk and incapable men and women who wished to sing or play an instrument could be loud and abusive, and to say no always caused problems – and in some cases fights. (When Dal Stevens and the Four Dukes played at a friend's wedding reception, for nothing, it resulted in a broken snare drum, a stolen guitar and general mayhem. Never again!) Open air galas and garden parties were in a similar vein. Troublemakers would be looking for a fight, especially if it were sunny and drink had been taken. It was not unusual to find that electric cables to the place where the group would perform had been tampered with. This kind of damage together with verbal abuse could result in chaos, and deterred groups from similar bookings. By and large groups made bookings like this in an attempt to become better known. Payment was usually about £4 or £5, to be split between four or five members.

Perhaps the most popular bookings were local dance halls. Bradford had many such in the 1950s and '60s. Some lasted a few years; others folded within a few months. Many will remember some of the following.

The Gaumont Ballroom

Built as part of the New Victoria Cinema project in the 1930s, the Gaumont ballroom was set with a central entrance in New Victoria Street across from the Allasio Coffee Bar and the Students Club. Up the steps and into the building, the ballroom was situated above the restaurant, overlooking Thornton Road. The ballroom had one of the finest sprung floors in the country. The resident band of the 1950s was the very popular Bert Bentley's Orchestra.

In 1960 the Gaumont ballroom had a new Sunday night rock 'n' roll evening entitled Big Beat Night, from 7.30pm to 10.30pm, admission 2s.On the opening night three local groups performed, namely Jo White and the Bluenites, The Ravers and The Tuxedos. Originally local groups performed, but pop stars were also booked on the Sunday evenings, the first one being Jess Conrad: admission was 4s 6d.

This all came about after a new ballroom manager had been appointed. Bradford-born Ray Moore (b. 1928) had been employed at Grattan Warehouse before making the break into Top-Rank management, securing the position of manager after only six months, such was his commitment to showbusiness, especially rock 'n' roll. Ray brought many pop stars to the ballroom, also giving the local rock 'n' roll groups many bookings and sometimes the opportunity to perform on the same bill as the pop stars. New innovations included jive, solo bop, fashion and rock 'n' roll competitions, with local celebrities presenting the spot prizes. His far sightedness and promotional skills were far in advance of his superiors. It is without any doubt whatsoever that it was Ray Moore who did more to promote the Bradford rock 'n' roll scene than anyone else at the time. However, in 1961 a new manager was appointed, and Ray left to take up a position with Kay's Catalogue. He retired in the 1990s and now lives with his wife Alice in Wibsey, Bradford.

So successful were the Sunday evenings that Ray introduced a DJ, namely your author, Derek A.J. Lister (also known as Dal Stevens of the Four Dukes). He also opened up the Wednesday night for rock 'n' roll. Both proved to be very popular and many stars appeared at that time, filling the Gaumont ballroom: Vince Eager, Dickie Pride, The Spotnicks, Heinz, Rob Storme and The Whispers, Wee Willie Harris, Cliff Bennett and the Rebel Rousers, Sounds Incorporated, Screaming Lord Sutch, Zoot Money and his Big Roll Band, Ricky Valance, Marti Wilde, Jess Conrad, the Karl Denver Trio and many others.

In 1961 Ray brought in Terry Moran (late member of The Dingos and the Blue Jays) as a partner for Dal, forming the well-known partnership of Dal and Dadio, later supplemented by Barbara from Wood's music shop: Dal, Della and Dadio lasted a few months. Barbara took requests, sitting at the end of the turntable with pen and pencil to write down the many requests – which seemed to triple, especially from the lads!

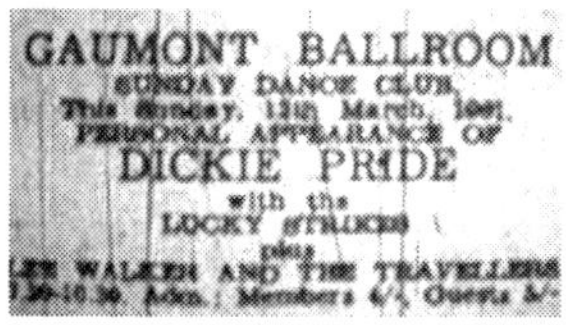

GAUMONT BALLROOM
SUNDAY DANCE CLUB
This Sunday, 12th March, 1961.
PERSONAL APPEARANCE OF
DICKIE PRIDE
with the
LUCKY STRIKES
plus
LES WALKER AND THE TRAVELLERS
7.30-10.30. Adm.: Members 4/-, Guests 5/-

The Gaumont ballroom, scene of many wonderful rock 'n' roll nights.

Ray Moore, manager of the Gaumont ballroom. It was Ray who built up a wonderful rock 'n' roll scene, knowing just what Bradford teenagers wanted.

DJ Dal Stevens at the Gaumont, 1961.

Diana Winnard, winner of the Gaumont's 'Miss Belair' competition, judged by Raymond 'Mr Teasy Weasy'.

Tony, the assistant manager, presents a £5 prize to Joyce Harvey, winner of the 'Miss Personality' contest, while runners up Sue (left) and Jean look on.

The Top Rank staff who kept the Majestic and Gaumont going during the early days of rock 'n' roll. Two managers are present: Ray Moore of the Gaumont on the far left, Laurie Lawrence of the Majestic on the far right.

In 1961 Bob Mitchell (b. 1932), from London, took over from Ray Moore. With the loss of Ray things began to deteriorate, as the new bingo craze began to take over and other nights at the Gaumont were restructured for its promotion. However, Wednesday and Sunday were still rock 'n' roll nights, with Bert Bentley's Orchestra surviving on Saturday evenings only.

It was about this time that Mr Lawrence, the manager at the Majestic, moved on; his place was taken over by Bob Mitchell, who was now running the two ballrooms. However, the end was in sight for the Gaumont. Towards the end of 1961 a new idea for Saturday night entertainment was proposed by Bob Mitchell. Bert Bentley's Orchestra would be on the bill together with an hour of jazz, with Benny Netherwood's Wool City Jazzmen, and with Dal and Dadio doing a couple of spots. In all it would be five hours of non-stop entertainment, all for 5s. As it was, things worked out quite well and, as with many new ideas, it appeared at first that it could be a winner. However, Christmas came and went and the crowds started to slip away, with disappointing Saturdays helping to sway the decision towards bingo. Sunday and Wednesday Big Beat nights were still going strong with capacity crowds, and while they did not offer top line groups, local talent was holding its own.

The end came a few weeks after Christmas. The announcement was short and to the point: the ballroom was closing, probably to promote bingo (which it did for a short while). Many loyal friends of the Gaumont were disappointed, but they knew they could continue at the Majestic ballroom. The closure caused little public consternation. The *Telegraph and Argus* did not even give it a mention: only many years later, when it was found to be in a dilapidated state, was it spoken of with nostalgia.

The last show was to be the Saturday Spectacular. This was much better attended, as some patrons had come for a last dance on that famous sprung floor. Benny Netherwood's Wool City Jazzmen had their time on the stage and Bert Bentley's Orchestra signed off at 11.30 pm, after which the DJ played out to the few dancers left on the floor. It was your author who was the last person to perform at the Gaumont ballroom in 1962, when he played out with the last number, Don Gibson's 'Sea of Heartbreak'. So the Gaumont ballroom passed into history.

At the time of writing there are still threats to demolish the New Vic/Gaumont/Odeon, a unique Bradford landmark. Bradford's councillors and outside consultants have still not learnt the lesson of the 1960s, and appear to be determined to destroy the city's heritage.

The Majestic Ballroom

'Goin' t' Maj?' was a very popular teenage question in the late 1950s and early '60s. Built as a cinema in 1914 in the Alhambra Complex, it was later known as the Morley Street Picture House. The cinema closed in 1956 and re-opened in 1957 as the Majestic ballroom, with the resident dance band of Billy Hey's Orchestra under a new manager, Laurie Lawrence (1914–71). Sheffield born, Laurie joined the RAF in the Second World War, serving as a flight lieutenant. He was shot down and became a member of the famous Caterpillar Club (a name given *to survivors who had been shot down)*. One of nature's gentlemen, it was he who gave many up and coming local rock 'n' roll groups the

The Majestic ballroom, where Bradford's teenagers danced the night away, 1961.

The Majestic, 1961. The manager Mr Lawrence organises another talent contest, while local girls look on with apprehension.

A rare photograph of an evening at the Majestic, 1962. The group on stage is Dave Arran (centre) with the Dakotas. The DJ at the back is Dadio.

1962. Dave Arran with the Dakotas at the Majestic. The drummer shares a joke with DJ Dal.

Emile Ford • Tornados • Ricky Valance
Mike Sarne & Wendy Richards • Jet Harris & Tony Meeham
Gerry and the Pacemakers • Brian Poole and the Tremeloes
Billy J Kramer and The Dakotas
The Honeycombs • The Hollies • The Viscounts
The Yardbirds • Screaming Lord Sutch • The Flintstones
Sounds Incorporated • Zoot Money and His Big Roll Band
The Spotnicks • Barron Knights • The Rocking Berries
The Fourmost • The Karl Denver Trio • Jimmy Crawford
Freddie Starr and The Midnighters
Nero and The Gadiators • Dickie Pride
Freddie and The Dreamers
Jess Conrad • Heinz • Billie Davis
Wee Willie Harris • Vince Eager
The Allisons • Shane Fenton and The Fentones
Joe Brown and The Bruvvers
Cliff Bennett and The Rebel Rousers • The Fortunes
Dave Berry and The Cruisers
Danny Rivers and The River Men • The Four Pennies
The Merseybeats • The Swinging Blue Jeans
The Bo Street Runners • Gene Vincent
Barry James • Rickey Baron
Rob Storme and The Whispers

Famous pop stars and groups who appeared at either the Gaumont or Majestic ballrooms between 1960 and 1965.

1000th. SPINNING ANNIVERSARY

THE Majestic Ballroom, Bradford, this week celebrated its 1,000th disc jockey session. Three nights a week, the resident D.J.'s, Del and Daddio spin the tops in pops.

Del is the name adopted by Derek Lister, a representative, who has been resident at the ballroom for the past three years. Derek lives at Ruffeild Street, Wyke, Bradford.

Daddio is the cool title taken by his friend, Terry Moran, a brewer's mechanic of Bright-Street, Bradford.

Just over three years ago both boys were hoping to make records—Derek with his own group and Terry with one of Bradford's best rock groups, the Dingoes, but their minds turned to introducing records rather than making them.

They still try a number or two now and again with visiting groups and say they enjoy it. Relaxation for them is spent in—playing more pop records!

Top liners

The Majestic has many top line groups booked to appear at their Monday, Wednesday, Friday evening Teenbeat Sessions. Freddie and The Dreamers are to play on Friday, October 4, and a package show featuring Shane Fenton and his group on Wednesday, October 9.

Next Wednesday—September 25——the grand finals of the Bradford Rock Group Competition will be held. Since April about 20 groups have taken part in the competition, and hoping to win first prize—£25—will be The Telecasters and Chad Wayne and The Cheesmen.

The *Bradford Telegraph and Argus* publicises the thousandth Dal and Dadio DJ session for Top Rank. This was a record at the time. A large cake was made to celebrate the event, and the cutting shows Dal and Dadio presenting the cake to Bradford Children's Hospital.

Freddie of The Dreamers struts across the ballroom floor to the delight of the audience.

Dal and Dadio, 1966. Two redundant DJs.

The Majestic ballroom, 1966. Gone are the dances and rock 'n' rollers.The groups and the teenagers have moved on and bingo reigns supreme.

opportunity to perform at the Majestic from 1957 to 1961, when he moved to Oldham. He was famous for booking the Beatles for £30 in Oldham, who became famous overnight before they were due to appear. The Beatles had to honour the booking.

The main entrance was situated half-way up Morley Street. If you walked through this entrance and turned to the right you went straight into the ballroom. On each side of the stage at the rear were tables and chairs. In the entrance hall steps took you up to a long balcony that encircled the dance floor and housed the soft drinks bar. Along the left-hand side of the balcony were more tables and chairs. In between there was a staircase that led down to the left-hand side of the dancehall. The capacity was 1,200 and most nights it was filled. At the back of the large stage stood a 2ft plinth with the DJ stand on it. The lighting was controlled by Bill the electrician, whose windowed box overlooked the drinks bar in the balcony. This was an excellent observation point to control coloured lights, starlight scenes and the large glitter ball, which gave a wonderful effect when the spotlight hit it. It was also an ideal lookout area from which to see any trouble that might occur in the large crowd.

In late 1959, with the popularity of rock 'n' roll and through the foresight of Mr Lawrence, the Majestic Monday nights were declared Teenage Nights. Local groups now had the opportunity to perform at a well-attended rock 'n' roll venue. Billy Hey's Orchestra still had the rest of the week for the usual ballroom dancers. However, with the Gaumont ballroom closing in early 1962 another two rock 'n' roll nights were added, Wednesdays and Fridays. Garth Cawood, who had been supplementing his time with The Dingos DJing at The Majestic, now passed it on to Dal and Dadio from The Gaumont. At the same time Mr Lawrence moved to Oldham and the former manager of the Gaumont, Bob Mitchell, took over.

Admission was 2s from 7.30pm to 10.30pm, with entertainment from the DJs and the guest groups for two half-hour spots. While the DJs had overall responsibility, control of the crowd was from another quarter, namely the doormen (not bouncers), all well remembered by the many patrons: the Scot Sandy, who was always looking at this watch at 10.30 pm; tall and elegant Jim, who was the spitting image of Sean Connery; and Laurie and the rest, making up a competent band of dinner-suited peace-keeping officers.

The rock 'n' roll nights at the Majestic were always attended to capacity and many of Bradford's own rock 'n' roll groups performed there, some for the odd night and others more regularly. A change of management took place again, with Bob Mitchell returning to the 'Big Smoke' and a temporary manager Carl Glass (b. 1934) Carl was a DJ's dream: being new to Bradford, for the next year he let Dal and Dadio run the rock 'n' roll nights – controlling advertising, choice of records and, even more beneficial, booking of any local groups. Carl booked many of the stars of the time, for example, Gene Vincent. Emile Ford, Eden Kane and Joe Brown, among others, much to the delight of Bradford's teenagers.

It was while the teenagers were enjoying these wonderful nights that the news broke that Carl, temporary manager for twelve months, was to move. It was a sad occasion for both the teenagers and Dal and Dadio. He took over from Mitchell at a bad time and helped to bring The Majestic name back into the limelight, well-known as a venue for many top groups and stars. It was hoped that someone of his calibre would replace him and build on his success. It was not to be.

Harry Radley (1925–197?) from Nottingham was the new manager, and within a couple of months things had drastically changed. His forte was bingo! Soon Billy Hey, his orchestra and his vocalist Jack would be no more, after many years of giving pleasure to the ballroom dancers. The teenage Wednesday night was axed, leaving only Monday and Friday, and about that time the popular Dadio departed, leaving Dal Stevens to perform for two nights. Just before Terry (Dadio) departed, Dal and Dadio had a special celebration after notching up over 1,000 DJ performances. This event was noted in the *Telegraph and Argus*, and they received a large iced cake, which they donated to the Bradford Children's Hospital. The total of 1,000, the paper omitted to say, included their many performances at the Gaumont, and their names were spelt wrong: Dal as Del and Dadio as Daddio.

Mr Radley's next step was to cut advertising in the *Telegraph and Argus*, and the purchase of records was drastically reduced. Many teenagers began to bring their own to supplement the DJ's collection.

The odd top pop groups like The Hollies and Gerry and the Pacemakers appeared, as well as some local groups. After The Hollies appeared Dal Stevens left, leaving Dave, a young amateur DJ, in charge until the Majestic finally closed to bingo in 1965.

The Majestic dance hall was later swallowed up by the Alhambra extension, where budding young actors and dancers went through their paces unaware that they were treading the same boards as the vibrant and colourful Bradford youth of the 1960s. It was a place where their hopes, fears and ambitions had been expressed as they danced away the laughter-filled hours, many meeting their future partners there. When the Majestic was filled to capacity on those rock 'n' roll nights the atmosphere was exhilarating.

I would like to pay tribute to the late Bert Bentley and his orchestra at the Gaumont Top Rank ballroom and the late Billy Hey and his orchestra at the Top Rank Majestic ballroom. They were two of the nicest gentlemen it was my pleasure to know. Soon, because of rock 'n' roll music, these popular dance band leaders were no more. I think they knew the writing was on the wall, even though they tried to include some upbeat rock 'n' roll numbers in their repertoire. In 1962 Bert's orchestra played its last numbers at The Gaumont, followed by Billy's orchestra at the Majestic in 1963.

During my time as a DJ I spoke with these gentlemen on many occasions about this musical transition. At no time were there any undue comments or envy expressed about what was taking place.

So it was that just as rock 'n' roll had taken over the ballrooms, it was in 1965 at the Majestic that I was in a similar position. Bingo had taken over rock 'n' roll.

Mecca Locarno Ballroom

When the Mecca Locarno ballroom opened its doors in Manningham Lane in September 1961, the dancing fraternity of Bradford was introduced to a new splendour and opulence. Rising from the ashes of the old Bradford Rolarena

The Locarno, 1962.

Alan Boyce, manager of the Locarno: one of nature's gentlemen.

Just as impressive at night: The Locarno, Manningham Lane, 1962.

Roller Skating Rink, it was the latest thing in modern ballrooms; in fact, it was one of the last purpose-built dance ballrooms to be opened in the UK.

From the elegantly named 'Ladies Boudoir' with its forty-five full-length mirrors and Georgian décor, to the gentlemen's 'Stag Room', offering electric shavers, hair-cream and free shoeshine, this was Luxury with a capital L. Two bands played, providing continuous music by changing over on the revolving stage. For patrons queuing outside on cold evenings, heat was provided by infra-red heaters in the canopy above the frontage, while the dance floor itself was maintained at a cool temperature by air vents discreetly placed around the raised edge. Above the dancers were 35,000 Italian-made light bulbs, which when lit on their own gave the impression of a starlight sky at night. The Bradford Mecca Locarno was the first ballroom in the UK to install this feature. Such was the prestige of this new ballroom that within a month of opening BBC Television broadcast the first of many *Come Dancing* programmes from the venue.

On opening it was advertised as 'Entertainment For Everyone' with Special 'Off The Record' dance sessions, 'Over 21' nights, Weekend Gala nights, Palais nights, and the Sunday Club. There were also to be Saturday matinee dance sessions and Monday midday 'Off The Record' sessions. Mecca Bingo was also introduced; patrons had to be members.

The general manager of the Locarno, Alan Boyce (1926–2006), was a well-respected gentleman who came from the Locarno in Bristol with a reputation that was absolutely first class. He was equally popular with the Bradford patrons. For many years the Locarno was very popular not only with modern ballroom dancers but also with rock 'n' roll teenagers. It was in competition with the Majestic, which in the early 1960s had held its own, but from the mid-1960s, when the Majestic was declining as a rock 'n' roll venue, most of its patrons visited the Locarno for its pop stage shows and artists. The DJ Mervyn Wood was very popular, as was the other budding DJ Carl Gresham, who had his own fan club. Some of Bradford's rock 'n' roll groups played at the Locarno, but this was rare: for most of its history it was dance bands and well-known artists that were the scene there.

It was ironic that on opening the Locarno introduced bingo in its weekly programme. As with similar dance halls/ballrooms it was this that finally took over in the 1970s. In the 1980s and '90s there were various changes in style and ownership, and in October 1993 Bradford entrepreneur and businessman John Pennington purchased the ballroom, now called the Maestro. He closed it, refurbished it, and reopened it as Pennington's Variety Club. It returned to its former glory and became one of the most popular nightspots in the north of England. In November 2003 the doors were sadly closed.

My first meeting with Alan Boyce was a few months after the Locarno's opening when I paid a visit to check out the Majestic's competition. I asked for him by name, introduced myself and said why I was visiting. Mr Boyce proceeded to show me round the building – offices, bars, dressing rooms and back stage. I was impressed! It seemed that he had done his homework as well, and knew all about the Majestic and the 'very popular' DJs Dal and Dadio (his words). After this meeting we became firm friends, so much so that he gave me a free pass. I took the opportunity to see various pop stars and groups who appeared there, like The Searchers and the Temperance Seven. During a visit in 1964 Alan asked if I would like to be the full-time DJ at the Locarno. The offer was very tempting, but I declined as I still had loyalties to many friends and patrons of the Majestic.

The Gaiety

This was perhaps one of the best known of Bradford's pre-rock 'n' roll dance halls for modern ballroom dancers; its heyday was in the late 1940s and '50s. Opened in 1947 and situated above Burtons Tailors on Tyrell Street, it was a hive of activity, with big bands and swing music. The loud music could be heard through the open windows in Tyrell Street and beyond on hot summer evenings. Not many, if any, local rock 'n' roll groups appeared here. The Gaiety was demolished in the 1960s.

The Textile Hall

The Textile Hall opened in 1915 in Westgate as a social centre and dance hall as well as headquarters of the Yorkshire Society of Textile Craftsmen. It was mostly used for many years by the popular and well-known Les Garrett Dance

The twist, Textile Hall style, 1963.

On the right, above Burton's, was the popular Gaiety ballroom. When the windows were open the loud dance-band music could be heard in Tyrrell Street and beyond.

Band, for works dinner dances, other local functions and dance classes. In the early 1960s it became a very popular venue for many of the smaller pop show tours, with Heinz, Tommy Bruce, Vince Eager, Wee Willie Harris and Sammy King and the Voltaires. Some local rock 'n' roll groups also appeared from time to time, in addition to the resident band.

Milton Rooms/The Europa

Situated above a row of shops at 45 Westgate, close to Lumb Lane, the Milton Rooms was a popular small dance hall in the early 1950s. For a time it had a reputation as troublesome and down market. In the late 1950s it was modernised and changed its name to The Europa: many local rock 'n' roll groups played at functions here. It was also used for ballroom dancing and rock 'n' roll lessons. In the 1980s it was taken over by toe-tapping pensioners, who renamed it The Harmony.

The Kings Hall and the Queens Hall

These two dance halls were situated within the Windsor Baths complex and were popular for many years well into the mid-1960s. Both, although independent, were very spacious and could accommodate many patrons. However, the Kings Hall was really the Windsor Baths swimming pool: when it was required for dancing a sprung floor was placed over the pool. Few people realised what was waiting below as hundreds of feet pounded the boards. The independent Queens Hall was surrounded by a large

The Kings Hall and the Queens Hall.

balcony and could be opened into the Kings Hall to make a really large venue. Many local groups played at the Kings and Queens, especially for firms' dances, and it was very popular for the university ball. In 1968 the Queens was taken over by Bradford College Students Union. The Kings Hall no longer opened for dances and reverted to full-time use as the Windsor Baths.

The Co-Op Hall

Situated in Southgate off Thornton Road, this was one of the many dance halls used for private functions, with resident band Haydn Robinson and the Dunedin Players. With a beautiful stage and PA system, its central position also made it very popular for theatrical shows and exhibitions connected with its adjacent Emporium (Cooperative Society store). In the 1950s, with the advent of rock 'n' roll, from time to time it tried to introduce rock 'n' roll sessions with local groups. However, with too many other local rock 'n' roll venues and the demise of private functions, it closed in the 1960s and was demolished.

The Somerset

Situated at 11 Idle Road, this was one of the first rock 'n' roll disco venues, which came to prominence in the mid-1950s before the central dance halls of Bradford had changed from dance bands to rock 'n' roll nights. For early rock 'n' rollers the Somerset was the place to go. The venue was very small (two bedrooms knocked into one over the shop), and you had to climb a flight of steps to reach the two small rooms where boys and girls 'bopped' and rock 'n' rolled. The music was supplied by gramophone records played by the person who was running the club or by a hired DJ. Mick Judge, late of the Jurymen, was an accomplished DJ there for some time in the mid-1960s. Sometimes a local skiffle group and the odd rock 'n' roll group performed, but because of the size of the room this was not a success. Despite its lack of space it was always a well-attended venue.

The Queens, Idle

Another of the early rock 'n' roll venues, this was a rather small place. It had very subdued lighting but a fair amount of volume from a speaker: there was no DJ, records being played on a large radiogram in the corner of the room. The room was always packed and very hot, humid and sticky, but it was a very good evening for the cost of 1s. It was managed for a short time by Garth Cawood.

Tudor Dance Hall

This was situated behind the Engineers Public House at the crossroads at Dudley Hill; it was the Tudor Café in the daytime. The tables and chairs were moved to make room for dancing on Saturday nights. This was the idea of a young entrepreneur, Garth Cawood, in 1957. The highlight of these Saturday nights was a demonstration of ballroom dDancing by Garth's mother Dulcie Burton and her partner Ernest Page. It was during this time that Garth developed and introduced his system of DJ-ing: it is therefore conceivable that

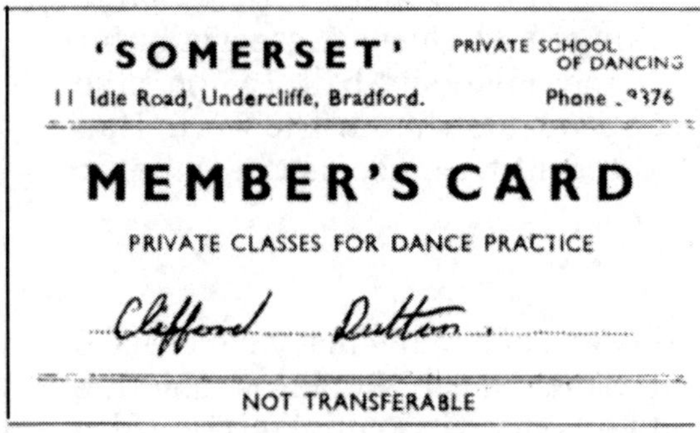

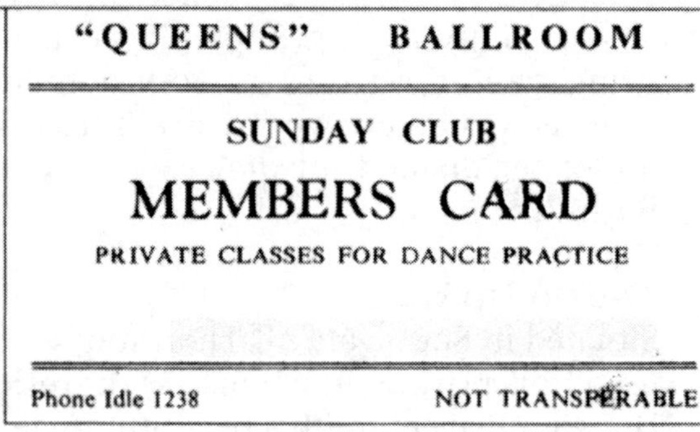

he was Yorkshire's first DJ. Some local groups played at the ballroom, and it was at this time that Garth joined the Dingos – who had played there.

The Top Twenty Club

In Idle, on the outskirts of Bradford, from 1964 to 1967 was this very popular rock 'n' roll venue. It was managed by Garth Cawood as DJ and compère. Many local groups appeared here, as also did many of the Top of The Pops stars of the 1960s: Lord Sutch and the Savages, The Kinks, Tom Jones and a host of other stars. When Billy (Wicherly) Fury visited the Top Twenty he often visited his uncle, Ernest Wicherly, who was the landlord of the White Bear pub over the road.

The Dungeon

In 1964 The Dungeon at 85 Westgate was opened. It was meant to be like a 'cellar club' although it was on the ground floor: it became famous for its blacked-out windows. Run by Readmore Productions, it was very popular as a venue for local rock 'n' roll groups, supplemented by many of the star groups of the time. These included Long John Baldry and his supporting band Bluesology, with a very young pianist still using his original name Reginald Kenneth Dwight (later Elton John). The Hoochie Coochie Band also appeared, with Rod Stewart as a group member. It was during this time that Carl Gresham was the resident DJ.

Ideal Ballroom

Formerly the Ideal Cinema, this was transformed into a ballroom in 1934 by Bert Shutt with his wife Edith. Officially the Ideal ballroom, it was affectionately known as Bert Shutt's. Situated at Bankfoot, it was very popular in the 1940s and '50s: the décor and furnishings were of high quality and it was very spacious, with a large mirrored ball hanging from the ceiling. Many resident bands and orchestras played here, but it did not adapt as well as some

The Ideal ballroom at Bankfoot, always referred to as Bert Shutt's.

other Bradford dance halls to the advent of rock 'n' roll. Some local groups played here in the late 1950s, but they were not successful. Adverse publicity followed the 'Battle of Bankfoot' in 1955 (see Teddy Boys chapter) and it never regained its popularity; it was one of the earliest ballrooms to close and reopen for bingo, in 1962. After the decline in bingo's popularity it finally closed in 1983.

Fountain Hall
Fountain Hall was situated in Fountain Street close to John Street Market. From the 1950s it was very successful, particularly for serious ballroom dancers, with the resident Stanley North Band. The venue was also very popular for local staff dances, but it was not noted as a rock 'n' roll venue and in 1974 it closed. In 1975 it reopened as Gatsby's.

Lakean Ballroom
This very popular venue in Shipley was founded in 1941 by Tommy Kean (1921–2000) with his wife Edna Lake; they put their surnames together to form its name. After a few different locations, it was in 1946 that it settled in new

Proprietor : T. KEAN Phone : Shipley 55317

LAKEAN BALLROOM

BRIGGATE

SHIPLEY, YKS.

24th, March. 1960.

Dal Stevens Esq,
47, Ruffield Side,
Delf Hill,
Wyke,

Dear Mr Stevens,

Thank you for your letter regarding your Rock 'n' Roll Group namely Dal Stevens and The Four Duke's.

At the moment we are only engaging groups to play on Friday evenings and have already made bookings to the end of April, if however you will let me know if you are available to accept engagements on Friday evenings and your fee required for two short sessions of twenty minutes duration I will try and give you a booking at some future date.

Yours faithfully,

Tommy Kean

Tommy Kean's ballroom in Shipley was known as the Lakean ballroom. It was popular with dancers of all ages. Friday evenings were especially for guest rock 'n' roll groups. Dal Stevens was offered a booking some months hence, such was the popularity of this venue.

premises in Briggate. They went on to teach generations of ballroom dancers: both Tommy and his wife were professional dance instructors. In the rock 'n' roll era groups played here on Friday evenings, as an alternative to the ballroom dance venues.

While the dance hall venues mentioned above were perhaps the most popular from the early 1960s, other lesser-known venues also opened. They were advertised in the local newspaper, and although some are remembered to this day others are long forgotten. They include the following.

The Mojo Club, in the Market Tavern, was open from 1963 until 1969. In 1964 the first independently run music club opened: the Little Black Fat Pussy Cat, in Millergate. The same year saw the opening of the Coffin Club at 35 Ivegate and also the Hole in the Wall Club at 49 Godwin Street. This was a café during the day and in the evening a regular teenage spot for discos and live music,until it closed in 1969.

Between 1964 and 1970 the Heartbeat Club (Silver Blades, Little Horton Lane), had many discos with some live music. In 1971 it reopened as Annabella's. For a few short months between 1964 and 1965 the Flamingo Club at 8–9 Walmer Villas was opened. Run by Mike Sagar of The Cresters and his wife Glenice, it was a mixture of discos, gambling and dining. It also hosted a few of the local groups.

Other clubs included the Romantica Club, on Godwin Street from 1964 until 1966. The Witchbarn Club at 8 Manor Street opened in early 1965. In the same year at 2 Manor Street the Top Hat Club opened, holding regular discos between 1965 and 1966. The Lyceum Rainbow Club on Wardley Drive, off the top of Leeds Road, was opened in the early 1960s by the Hammond brothers. The Lyceum was a cabaret venue, with the usual chicken-in-a-basket meal, that put on stars like Tom Jones and Dusty Springfield. In the 1970s the Lyceum changed its name to the Talk of Yorkshire. In 1966 the newest club around town was the Penny Farthing Club, at the Ritz building on Charles Street; it changed its name to Scamps in the 1970s.

During the mid-1960s the music scene was changing rapidly and rock 'n' roll music was very quickly being supplemented by new music, trends and dress, hence the opening of many of these clubs. Did any of Bradford's original rock 'n' roll groups play at any of them? It is highly probable that some did.

The Alhambra Theatre

From when it was built in 1914 the Alhambra had been the venue almost entirely for theatre and pantomime, and occasionally in the 1950s for nude revue shows. However, in the late 1950s entrepreneurs could hire the theatre for local talent contests. One such took place in late 1959, with the attractive title Aim for Fame.

Similar to *Opportunity Knocks*, it was for many contestants a short cut to stardom, or so it seemed. Contestants mingled and queued down Morley Street before auditions. They were male and female singers, performing everything from opera to pop, with an assortment of magic acts, jugglers, dancers and many would-be comedians. For many of Bradford's local rock 'n' roll groups it was an opportunity to perform at the Alhambra in front of (hopefully) a large crowd.

Each evening the local talent appeared, culminating in a grand final on a Saturday night – to win £25 for the first prize, £15 for the second and £10 for the third. Who was judging this remarkable contest? Someone famous? A television celebrity, or a movie star? It was none of these. Just like *Opportunity Knocks* the winners were chosen by audience applause only. This inevitably meant that all the contestants brought friends and relations along when they performed. This of course swelled the box office receipts and brought financial success to the organisers, if not to the contestants – who were appearing free of charge!

Two of the groups in the final were the The Dingos and the Rhythm Rebels, who were well organised and very professional. At this time they both outclassed the other groups in the final, including Dal Stevens and the Blue Jays. However, one contestant shone above all others: a young girl in her thirteenth year who had a tremendous voice and talent. Her name was Pauline Matthews. In a packed house Pauline (later Kiki Dee) was the winner! The Dingos were second and the third prize went to another of Bradford's up and coming young female vocalists, Josie McCann.

Chapter 4
LEARNING TO DANCE

Rock 'n' roll is an infectious rhythm popular with pupils of all ages. The rhythm creates a certain type of body movement. The dance has many forms. When no regular foot pattern is used many people call it Le roc. Many 'natural' dancers use this form of rock 'n' roll. Mostly self taught at the time, many teenagers adopted their own style and all sorts of variations were to be seen at the dance halls. In most cases the girls had the edge and could gyrate and swing to any of the rock 'n' roll music, at the same time following their male partners' own style. In the mid 1950s it was a learning curve for most of the teenagers as there were really no dance studios that taught rock 'n' roll: modern ballroom dancing was still the vogue.

Many parents sent teenage daughters to the few dance academies in Bradford to learn ballroom dancing, to give them confidence. However, teenage boys were not as enthusiastic, although some reluctantly took part. The most popular schools were Gledhill's in Westgate and Ashworth's School of Dancing in Manchester Road. With the advent of rock 'n' roll both of these establishments, like the others, began to include it in their repertoire.

Smart lads,one and all: Jackie Binns and friends. Back row, left to right: Billy Kilmister, 'Buck' Henry, Terry Dalby, T. Wilson. Front row: Bob Dyson, Bob Lorenz, Rob Green, Jackie Binns, Buck Ryan.

Chapter 5
DOORMEN: DANCE HALL PEACE-KEEPERS

For many years until the rock 'n' roll era Bradford dance halls had an assortment of men, some in a full-time capacity, others part-time, to act as peace-keepers when patrons got out of hand. The word bouncer was first used in an English newspaper in 1883, the word meaning 'chucker-out'. However, in the dance halls of the 1950s and '60s the name doorman was still used. It seems a pity that the doormen of yesteryear are generally overlooked, as without these gentlemen in dinner suits many dance halls would not have functioned so well.

It was still a time when most men wore suits, and most doormen were dressed to a high standard, resplendent in double-breasted dinner suits with white shirts and bow ties. A certain ability to defend oneself was required, and sometimes doormen as well as troublemakers could be injured. However, in most cases a few choice words from the doorman would be enough to avoid a fracas.

The Gaumont ballroom had a variety of such men, two of whom were very popular with the young teenagers, namely Aubrey Stead and Ken. Both were reliable stalwarts who could be relied on in any situation, always looking very smart and alert in their dinner suits. Both were ex-King's Own Yorkshire Light Infantry Second World War veterans and one of them, if not both, had received a Military Medal for Gallantry. Aubrey was small and stocky, but for his stature strong and dependable; he could handle himself diplomatically or physically. Ken was a little taller but again stocky, with an old-fashioned quiff and a slightly broken nose, a result of once being the boxing champion of his regiment. You would want both these gentlemen on your side, whatever the situation. A quick call over the microphone ('Doormen to the floor') brought these two peacekeepers to the scene – problem solved!!

The Majestic ballroom also had its peacekeepers on rock 'n' roll nights; again they were very popular with the teenagers. There was Sandy the Scot, who was everyone's friend. He was always looking at his watch at 10 30 and asking the DJs to wind up, shouting, 'Come on, Dal, get a move on, I wanna gi' home.' Like most people he had a bus to catch. Tall and elegant Jim was the spitting image of Sean Connery, and always seemed to have a bevy of young beauties around him. Laurie was another good-looking peacekeeper: it seemed that the Majestic had more than its fair share of good-looking doormen! Again, the slightest hint of unrest and the same message from the DJs went over the microphone. Within seconds the doormen would converge on the trouble from all sides, confidently sorting out the problem before it got out of hand.

There were many doormen in and around Bradford looking after dance halls and other venues, and trouble was rare. At the Majestic and Gaumont ballrooms there was a no alcohol policy for teenagers, just soft drinks, and after the dances most of the teenagers just wanted to get the last buses home: everyone needed to be up for work in the morning. In my five years as DJ at the Gaumont and Majestic, any serious trouble was minimal. The following was about as serious as it got. Dadio and I were on the DJ stand at the Gaumont when a big fracas developed. A knife was thrown at the DJ stand during the mêlée, and stuck in the backdrop about 2ft from Dadio's head. Surely we weren't that bad! Once, again at the Gaumont, I was physically threatened by a drunk. During a break I was at the soft drinks bar when a stocky Scots guy came up and threatened me, because (he said) I had not played his girlfriend's record request. At this point the two doormen, Aubrey and Ken, arrived, picked him up and threw him out. I thought no more about this until 10.30pm when, as we were closing, the manager Ray told me that my 'friend' was hanging about outside, promising he would get me on the way out. Ray said not to worry as he was getting a taxi and would see me home. The minute the taxi pulled up outside I was rushed down the steps presidential fashion with my raincoat over my head, surrounded by Ray, Aubrey and Ken. They literally threw me into the taxi. As we sped away I noticed my Scots friend cowering in a doorway I had visions of another confrontation, but found out later that he had been in town on holiday.

One notorious Bradford character who only occasionally showed his face at dances was Jacky Binns. Jacky's reputation went before him. He had had a few skirmishes with the police, and as this was common knowledge people trod warily when he was around, giving him a wide berth. I could sense when he arrived at the Gaumont. A hesitant quietness would fall over the dance hall as the tall wiry figure of Jacky emerged at the back, probably with a couple of well -known henchmen. On the few times he paid us a visit he never caused us any trouble, although you could see the apprehension on the faces of the doormen.

On one occasion Jacky appeared while the group was playing, and as Dadio and I were acquainted with him we were asked to join him and his beautiful girlfriend at his table. During the course of our conversation the young lady kept interrupting Jacky and pestering him for a soft drink. Jacky's retort was thunderous. 'F... off when I'm talking to my mates!' We laughed about it later, as it reminded us of some Al Capone type with his moll in downtown Chicago. This was Jackie's style, but there was also another side to him. On one occasion a fight developed outside the Allasio coffee bar across the road from the Gaumont. Two young thugs were giving a policeman a hard time, eventually striking him a blow that rendered him unconscious. Jacky witnessed what had happened and collared the two culprits, who then set about him. In the meantime police reinforcements from the Town Hall arrived and, disregarding the two lads fighting Jacky, waded into him and hauled him away. Luckily, before Jacky was charged the injured policeman had regained consciousness to point the finger at the real villains.

Chapter 6
TOP FIFTY NUMBERS PLAYED AT THE GAUMONT AND MAJESTIC

'Nutrocker', B Bumble and the Stingers
'Baby Sifting Boogie', Bobby Angelo
'Runaway', Del Shannon
'I Remember You', Frank Ifield
'Whole Lot of Shaking Goin' On', Jerry Lee Lewis
'Newcastle Twist (Who's Chicken)', Lord Rockingham's XI
'Cotton Fields', The Highwaymen
'Drumming Up a Storm', Sandy Nelson
'Walk On By (Wait on the Corner)', Leroy Van Dyke
'Picture of You', Joe Brown
'Multiplication', Bobby Darin
'Happy Birthday Sweet Sixteen', Neil Sedaka
'Shout', Lulu
'Halfway to Paradise', Billy Fury
'Take Good Care of My Baby', Bobby Vee
'Shakin' All', Johnny Kidd
'Apache', The Shadows
'Peggy Sue', Buddy Holly
'Sweets for my Sweet', The Searchers
'Glad All Over', The Dave Clarke Five
'Twist', Chubby Checker
'Living Doll ', ', Cliff Richard
'Speedy Gonzales', Pat Boone
'Breaking Up is Hard to Do', Neil Sedaka
'Blue Moon.', The Marcels
'Summer Holiday ', Cliff Richard
'5.4.3.2.1', Manfred Mann

'The House of the Rising Sun', The Animals
'I Get Around', The Beach Boys
'Sweet Little Sixteen', Chuck Berry
'New Orleans', Gary U.S. Bonds
'What'd I Say', Ray Charles
'Bits & Pieces', Dave Clarke Five
'C'mon Everybody', Eddie Cochran
'The Wanderer', Dion
'Shazam', Duane Eddy
'Sherry', Four Seasons
'How Do You Do It', Gerry and the Pacemakers
'Telstar ', The Tornados
'You Really Got Me', The Kinks
'Let's Jump the Broomstick', Brenda Lee
'It's Late', Ricky Wilson
'Just One Look', The Hollies
'Dream Baby', Roy Orbison
'Twenty Four Hours from Tulsa', Gene Pitney
'Five Foot Two, Eyes of Blue', Shane Fenton
'La Bamba', Richie Valens
'Be-Bop-a-Lula', Gene Vincent
'Rhythm of the Falling Rain', Cascades
'The Locomotion', Little Eva

The prolific hits of the following stars were played at least two or three times a week: Elvis Presley, the Everly Brothers, Cliff Richard, Buddy Holly, Little Richard, The Beatles and the Rolling Stones.

Chapter 7
COFFEE BARS: THE FROTH AND THE FURY

After the war, British families holidaying in France and Italy would have had their first taste of espresso coffee made in Gaggia machines, a far cry from the bland brown liquid served at home. Britain's first Gaggia arrived in 1952, and helped fuel the explosion of coffee bars in London. By 1960 there were about two thousand UK coffee bars. For a generation of teenagers rebelling against the traditional pub and teashop, the coffee bar provided a welcome alternative. The beauty of these places was that they were cheap and informal. You bought your coffee or an orange juice and you made it last. Nobody bothered you so long as someone from the party you were sharing a table with went to the counter occasionally to order another drink. Usually frothy coffee was the main request, but sandwiches were also available. The two in Bradford that were longest established were the Allasio and the Olympus.

The Allasio was situated on New Victoria Street, facing the Gaumont ballroom entrance and a few yards from the popular Students Club. Opened in 1957, it comprised a small restaurant on the ground floor and a coffee bar downstairs. The owner and manager was an Italian by the name of Costa. Surprisingly the restaurant cooked and served mostly English meals: as holidays abroad were few and far between for the English, most foreign cuisines had not yet been tried. Because of the large student population (mostly art students), the coffee bar with its formica tables and frothy coffee attracted young students and rock 'n' roll fans alike. Costa applied for a music licence, hoping to install a juke box, but this was refused owing to the small size of the coffee bar and because it was too close to the restaurant upstairs.

The Olympus was situated a few doors from Seabrook Fisheries up Great Horton Road. Like the Allasio it was well patronised, being owned and run by Cypriots who had a flair for this kind of business. The coffee bar was situated on the ground floor, with seats and tables close to the entrance. A small flight of stairs led to the rear of the building, giving more table space: the counter ran the full length of the room. Again, rock 'n' roll patrons of both the Majestic and Gaumont flocked there, with the usual contingent of students.

While other coffee bars opened later it was these two that achieved the best reputation.

When Screaming Lord Sutch appeared at the Gaumont ballroom in 1961, when I was the DJ, he invited me to the Allasio restaurant for a meal before the show, and said he would pay. How it transpired I shall never know, but I ended up paying the bill of 17s 6d, a small fortune in 1961.

Chapter 8
EXCEL RECORDS

Most of Bradford's local groups, with or without talent, wanted to make a record, but only a few succeeded in obtaining a recording contract with one or other of the London-based recording companies. Bradford had its own recording studio, however, which was affordable and was used by all the local budding pop stars. This was Excel Records at 49 Bradford Road, Shipley; the proprietor and recording technician was Mr F. Thistlethwaite. The building had a shop frontage. Upstairs there was a former lounge, with the ceiling and walls covered with egg boxes to improve soundproofing. It was a cosy studio. In one corner of the room was a large control panel fronted by a thick glass window, behind which the proprietor could control the sound of the recordings.

The records were all 78 rpm, old style, thick, with metal centres. The cost for the A and B sides was £1 for the master and 10s per copy.

Mr Thistlethwaite and Excel Records are to be thanked for helping local groups to record their songs for posterity some fifty years ago.

To add a personal note, my group Dal Stevens and the Blue Jays made one such recording with Excel Records in late 1959, 'Whole Lot of Shakin' Goin' On' and 'Why Must I be a Teenager in Love'. At home one Saturday morning, while I was playing 'Why Must I be a Teenager in Love' on the radiogramme, the coalman called to be paid. Thinking it was the radio, he commented, 'Don't they play some bloody rubbish on the radio these days?' I gave him his money and agreed.

Stan Pearson on the left from the *Telegraph and Argus* with pop star Vince Eager.

Mike Priestley. This sixteen-year-old rocker rose to become one of Bradford's most popular journalists with the *Telegraph and Argus*. This photo was guaranteed to be admired by many rock 'n' roll girls.

Chapter 9
PERSONALITIES

During Bradford's rock 'n' roll era the local *Telegraph and Argus* had very little or no coverage of the local skiffle and rock 'n' roll groups. There were no columns or features dedicated to their talent. The very popular package pop shows at the Gaumont Theatre , with top line pop singers and groups were always well covered, mostly by the newspaper's very knowledgeable and erudite theatre critic, Peter Holdsworth (1930–1994). Peter's impression of Buddy Holly's show in Bradford on his first UK tour became part of Bradford's folklore: 'Unless they had previously read the lyrics I would have defied anyone in the audience to tell me 70% of the words which issued from the lips of this foot-stamping, knee-falling musician. Where in earth is show business heading?' So wrote the clearly unimpressed Peter Holdsworth in March 1958. But the public had a different view of the iconic bespectacled singer, who died on 3 February 1959. However, no one was better qualified to tell the story in his book about the Alhambra *Dome of Delight* (1989) with great authority and perhaps more important, great affection. In doing so he illustrated not just the history of one theatre, but also an important part of the history of Bradford. He was a gentleman!

There was only one early *Telegraph and Argus* correspondent who sought out and wrote features about the local groups, and that was Stanley (Stan) Pearson (b. 1933). Born in Allerton, Bradford, Stanley was educated at Bradford City High School and joined the *Telegraph and Argus* aged fourteen. He spent over forty years with the newspaper and became a most respected golf journalist. In his spare time Stan did freelance work for the world's oldest weekly music newspaper, the *Melody Maker* (1926–2000) between 1955 and 1972. Also during those years he wrote a pop music and jazz column based on the Yorkshire scene for the old *Daily Herald* national newspaper. Because he was 'moonlighting' again, he had to do this under the pen name of Fred Armstrong! When he retired there was no need to keep the secret any more, so at last the world knew who Fred Armstrong was!

With his notepad and pencil Stan wandered into the Majestic, and Gaumont ballrooms on various rock 'n' roll nights and wrote snippets about who was who in the local groups. On most occasions these were published in some small way in the *Melody Maker* and the *Daily Herald*. Whether any success came from this is hard to tell, but Stan served a purpose when no other journalists were interested. Serious, with a wonderful sense of humour, he was a credit to his profession who saw the chance to promote local talent. A good friend of Dal and Dadio, he always made the same record request, The Shadows' instrumental 'Apache'. Stan still has that sense of humour. Retired, he lives in Menston with his wife Sandra.

Stan was key to Kiki Dee's success, as he recounted to me in 2011:

> I often think that even Kiki Dee, who was quite young at the time, may not know how she got her first step up into show business. I believe she worked at Boots in Bradford and lived at Bankfoot. I was there when she won a small talent contest in the city, but had no contact with her afterwards. Indeed, to this day I have never physically met her.
>
> The following Sunday afternoon I was working in our front garden at Ascot Avenue, Horton Bank Top, when a couple came walking up the road and stopped at our front gate. 'Are you Stanley Pearson'? the husband asked, and when I said 'Yes' he introduced them as Mr and Mrs Matthews, the parents of Pauline. He went on to say he was an old friend of Don Aldred of the *Telegraph and Argus* and had asked him how to get someone in the record industry to listen to Pauline. Don replied, 'Stanley's your man.' He gave Mr Matthews my details.
>
> Now, through Bradford band leader Les Garrett, Ken Macintosh and the *Melody Maker* I had got to know Walter Ridley the A&R manager of HMV Records in London very well, so I gave the Matthews Walter's phone number and rang him personally on Monday. The Matthews fixed up to take Pauline down to London for the audition, and the day afterwards Walter rang me to say he had been very impressed and would be signing her up. The rest, as they say, is history. Incidentally it was Walter Ridley who changed her name to Kiki Dee after signing her up.

It was some time before Bradford's rock 'n' roll generation had their own *Telegraph and Argus* journalist. Mike Priestly (b. 1944), born in Undercliffe. It was 1968 before he joined the *Telegraph and Argus*. From that date for the next forty years, besides his other journalistic commitments with the newspaper, he wrote many features about former Bradford rock 'n' roll stars, until his retirement in 2008. Many owe much to his journalistic comments and features about talented group members of that era. Mike is married to Maureen, his childhood sweetheart, and still lives in the Bradford area.

Robert Dewhirst (Radar): Solo Bop Champion

Solo Bop: what does that conjure up? This was a style purely for the male dancer. He jived or bopped on his own, with legs gyrating and bouncing about, with the occasional splits thrown in, usually accompanied by a fast instrumental number. Most ballrooms and dance halls banned this derivative of rock 'n' roll because of the problems it could cause if physical contact was made with the more conventionally dancing couples. This rule applied at both the Gaumont and the Majestic, but from time to time Dal and Dadio gave the solo bop enthusiasts a five minute spot to dance on their own, with no danger of colliding with anyone else.

The lads really enjoyed this, just as everyone else did by watching them. In Bradford everyone's favourite solo bopper was Radar. To this day he is remembered by many, and was known and loved by everybody. He was about 5ft 6in tall and was always smartly dressed in a dark suit with 14in trouser bottoms, the usual thick crepe-soled shoes, and a white shirt with a narrow dark tie. He had a round boyish face with short dark brown curly hair. Radar was an unassuming lad of the times blessed with a very nice disposition.

Radar was generally the instigator of the requests for the solo bop spot, and when he was in action everybody crowded round to watch his unique style. Needless to say, he won a prize every week; even if there was not a competition or a spot prize then the DJs would invent a reason: some said it was strange how Radar seemed to have a birthday every other week. Just a mention of his name over the microphone was met with resounding cheering and clapping. Radar was unique, and was perhaps the ultimate solo bop star of Bradford.

Radar (Robert Dewhirst, b. 1941) went on to be employed with Bradford Council. Retired now, he lives in Heaton with his wife Jean.

Everyone's favourite icon of Bradford's solo bop.

Popular radio and television DJs from top left: Kent Walton, Don Lang, Josephine Douglas, Pete Murray. David Jacobs, 'Old Mate' Brian Matthew, Cathy McGowan, Jack Jackson, Alan 'Fluff' Freeman and Barry Alldis.

Chapter 10
TELEVISION AND RADIO POP SHOWS

Initially television of the mid-1950s and early '60s only offered programmes for young children and the older generation. While radio did cater for teenagers with some pop programmes, television offered nothing until the powers that be woke up to the fact that something had to be done for the youth of the day.

Everything changed in 1956. All in black and white, with the average television screen only 12in, ITV set the scene with the wonderful title *Cool for Cats* (1956–61). This was introduced by an ex-208 Radio Luxembourg announcer Kent Walton (Kenneth Walton Beckett, 1917–2003). With a cultivated transatlantic accent, picked up in Bomber Command while serving with a Canadian air crew as a wireless operator, and a charming manner, it was perhaps he more than any other DJ of the time who is remembered by most of the rock 'n' roll generation. Later he became very popular as the 'Voice of Wrestling', introducing the *World of Sport* Saturday afternoon ITV wrestling programme.

In 1957 the BBC joined the competition with *Six-Five Special* (1957–8) introduced by a local Halifax-born lad Don Lang (Gordon Langhorn, 1925–92) who also sang the well-known introduction theme. Also compèring this very popular pop show was local Huddersfield born girl Josephine Douglas (1925–88) and the ever youthful Pete Murray (b. 1925). Surprisingly, it only ran for eighteen months, but it is probably the one that is most remembered.

ITV came up with *Oh Boy* (1958–9) presented by newcomers to the pop scene Tony Hall (b. 1926) and Jimmy Henney (1922–98). Again, it was a very popular programme with a host of top pop stars and groups, but it only ran for a few months and was almost immediately followed by *Boy Meets Girl* (1959). In 1959 the BBC came up with *Dig This* (1959), a well-known phrase of the time. This programme was dropped after only three months and was followed by *Drumbeat* (1959); again this was not a successful show.

In the meantime ITV came along with *Wham* (1959). It seemed that 1959 was a year for trial pop programmes that did not do too well. As ITV seemed to be running out of ideas, the BBC finally won the pop race by introducing what was possibly the best of the rest: *Juke Box Jury* (1959–67). This ran for eight years under the charming, softly spoken David Jacobs (b. 1926). A panel of four celebrities chose whether a record would be a Hit or a Miss. Incidentally the original theme was 'Juke Box Jury' by Ozzie Warlock and the Wizards. This was replaced by the more familiar 'Hit and Miss' by John Barry.

In 1961 ITV introduced *Thank Your Lucky Stars* (1961–6), which was perhaps one of their best programmes. It covered many stars and groups and was introduced by various popular presenters, the most popular being Brian Matthew (b. 1928). In 1963 ITV introduced *Ready Steady Go* (1963–6), presented by an up-and-coming 19-year-old Cathy McGowan (b. 1945) and a slightly older co-presenter Keith Fordyce (1928–2011). However, this show, like *Thank Your Lucky Stars*, closed in 1966.

It was 1964, and the BBC could do no wrong with the all-time favourite *Top of the Pops* (1964–2006), which ran through five decades of music and styles. The programme was originally to have run for a few weeks, but this turned into forty-two years. Most DJs and presenters in the pop world appeared on this wonderful programme.

And what about radio? The BBC had the only radio programmes for pop music from 1955 until 1964 (excluding 208 Radio Luxembourg). The ones that were popular during the rock 'n' roll era stood the test of time and are well remembered, if not for content then for the DJs and presenters who became household names. There were many such programmes, and here are a few.

Record Roundabout (1948–77) was hosted by bandleader Jack Jackson (1908–78). His shows included recorded comedy clips interspersed with music of the day, including rock 'n' roll. He went on to broadcast on Radio 2 from 1971 to 1977. Jackson's lightning cuts between comedy and music have been described as an inspiration to succeeding generations of DJs. Jack Jackson was affectionately known as the daddy of all disc DJs during his brief spell (nine months) on Radio 1.

Pick of the Pops (1955–72) began as a pop record segment during late Saturday night music shows. The first presenter was Franklin Englemann (1908–72), closely followed by Alan Dell (1924–95), David Jacobs and Don Moss (b. 1930). In 1962 a Top Ten was introduced when the show was moved to Sunday afternoons with Alan Freeman (1927–2006). From 1961 Alan Freeman made 'At the Sign of the Swinging Symbol' by Brian Fahey famous by using it as the theme tune to *Pick of the Pops* and later for his Saturday rock shows. *Pick of the Pops* was renamed *Top 20* when Alan left the show in 1972, but the original name was resurrected in 1989 when he recalled charts gone by on Radio 2.

Saturday Club (1958–69) followed on from the success of the short-lived 1957 series *Skiffle Club*. Brian Matthew (b. 1928) was the compère of this two-hour 'experimental teenage music show'. He chatted with guest artistes in the studio and introduced their live performances often before they had established themselves as recording stars. Almost every pop star in Britain appeared on the programme, which was always broadcast live. Keith Skues (b.

1939) took over on the first Radio 1 show in 1967, and although it completed 500 editions on 4 May 1968 it was axed on 18 January 1969. Since April 1990 Brian Matthew has hosted the popular *Sound of the Sixties* show on Radio 2, playing requests for 1960s records. The theme tune is the Shadows' 'Foot Tapper'.

Easy Beat (1959–67), a pop music show on Sunday mid-mornings, was launched in 1959. Originally produced and compèred by Brian Matthew, the show regularly featured Kenny Ball's Jazzmen, the Johnny Howard Band, Laura Lee, Tony Steven, Danny Street, guest artistes and BBC top tunes. It was later introduced by Keith Fordyce (1928–2011). When Radio 1 was launched in 1967, the show remained for a few months under the new title *Happening Sunday*.

Go Man Go, featuring David Ede (b. 1926) and the Rabin Band, was one of radio's flagship lunchtime pop music shows during the late 1950s and early '60s. It consisted typically of the band's renditions of songs from the current pop charts together with set pieces showcasing the impeccable jazz and swing credentials of the musicians. Each week saw the appearance of at least one guest artist or group from the charts. Listener requests and dedications were encouraged ('on a postcard only, please') and the show was linked by a resident compère. Several compères were used throughout its long run, including such personalities as jazz guitarist Diz Disley (b. 1931), *Pick of the Pops* compère Alan Freeman and BBC staff announcer Don Moss.

208 Medium Wave: Radio Luxembourg

From the mid-1950s well into the '60s Radio Luxembourg's *Top Twenty Show* each Sunday evening between 11pm and midnight was listened to by thousands of teenagers. Although boasting one of the most powerful transmitters in the world, it needed much re-tuning – but this did not detract from listening to the full Top Twenty, finishing just before midnight with the week's number one. There was always something in that hour that you would enjoy. It seems that almost everyone listened to and enjoyed Radio Luxembourg's *Top Twenty Show*.

It was perhaps Australian-born Barry Alldis (1930–82) who more than any other radio DJ is remembered for hosting the *Top Twenty Show* between 1958 and 1966. With a pleasant voice that always sounded enthusiastic, he built up a considerable following in Britain. For many listeners, Barry Alldis *was* Radio Luxembourg. His two well-known catchphrases were 'Your DJ, BA,' and 'Whether at home or on the highway, thanks for tuning my way.' During my six years as a DJ with Top Rank I tried many times to emulate Barry Alldis, all to no avail!

Pirate Radio

As rock 'n' roll was on the wane in the mid-1960s, the introduction of pirate radio brought a whole new dimension. Offshore pirate radio started in Scandinavia in 1958; and was copied in Holland in 1961. Outside national waters it was completely legal to broadcast, thanks to a loophole in the law. In 1964 Radio Caroline took to the air as the first offshore pirate radio in the UK. It played twenty-four-hour music and adverts, revolutionising radio for teenagers. It helped break several new artists and gave airplay to many who had never been heard on the BBC. The disc jockeys, who spent a fortnight at a time on the vessel, became minor celebrities, and were feted by teenagers.

However, Radio Caroline, and those pirate stations that followed, roused the wrath of the government. There were questions in Parliament, as they were draining too much of the BBC's audience and the pirates were making too much money. It took until 1967 before the law closed the legal loophole, and on 15 August the pirates were put out of business.

Chapter 11
SKIFFLE

Skiffle developed in the mid-1950s as a blend of folk song with an up tempo jazz and rock rhythm: it is happy and spontaneous. It gave the working classes a chance to start their own bands, and skiffle groups were formed in virtually every town and village across Britain. At the height of the craze there were probably more people playing skiffle than listening to it. Skiffle didn't require training or qualifications, and best of all it could be played on improvised instruments, such as your mother's washboard and a tea-chest bass (a tea-chest and a broom handle!). An acoustic guitar improved the group's sound, but you only needed to learn a few basic chords from Bert Weedon's *Play in a Day*.

Although some have described skiffle as a British form of rockabilly, its more immediate line of descent was from traditional jazz and American folk music. It was probably the influence and personal tastes of one man, Lonnie Donegan, with his long series of hits, that inspired a generation of teenagers to play skiffle. Why did it end? Quite simply, skiffle was no match for rock. Electric guitars could twang, the bass could rumble and drums could twitch it all along. Rock was new (or so it seemed) and the real raw music of rebellion.

Skiffle faded but it served its purpose, kick-starting the careers of so many hopefuls and forming a transition from the adult music of the 1950s to the rock 'n' roll that dominated the 1960s. Many teenagers went on to form their own rock 'n' roll bands.

1960—61

THE STUDENTS' CLUB

(Proprietors: P. J. P. Dennehy Ltd.)

6 NEW VICTORIA STREET · BRADFORD 1

Tel. Bradford 28002

MEMBERSHIP Nº 1553

In April 1964 the music scene was changing and so was fashion. Many of those in the photograph were fans of the Majestic,the Students Club and other new venues springing up around the city. This picture was taken in New Victoria Street, in the old car park at the rear of the Allasio coffee bar. Back row, left to right: John Pajac, Roy ?, Jennifer Mann, Pauline Matthews (Kiki Dee) with handbag, Laramie ?, Barry Lee, Mick Bedford, Eddie Savage, Val Hardman, -?-, -?-, -?-, Mary Wilde, 'Little' Brian, 'Stony Tony', Susan ?. Front row: Tony ?, Eddie Messenger, Cilla Black lookalike Janet Kirby.

Chapter 12
STUDENTS CLUB

It was in 1957 that the Students Club opened, the city's first dedicated jazz venue. During the five years of the club's existence, while predominantly a jazz club, it was also popular as a rock 'n' roll venue.

The club was in a basement of J. Walton Ltd, Newsagents on New Victoria Street. It was the idea of Mike Lamb, who was 24 and worked for the family firm of fruit and vegetable sellers at St James' Market. Peter Dennehy, aged twenty-five, was his working partner: he worked for Bradford Corporation in the vehicle licensing department. They decided that Bradford desperately needed a proper jazz club, and pinched the idea from The Cavern in Liverpool, which was a jazz club at the time.

The entrance to the club was through a black front door with large wooden studs set in it. At the bottom of the stone steps, under a stone-vaulted roof supported on iron columns, there was a stone-flagged dance floor and a similarly constructed stage. It was very spacious. A few red bulbs and a white lighted alcove were supplemented candles stuck in bottles on about two dozen iron tables: these and the whitewashed walls gave a very 'with it' atmosphere. The windows, which were high up, opened partly onto the pavement outside the newsagent's – so that the music sailed into the evening for passers-by to enjoy or dislike.

The club membership reached 4,000 at one time, thought to be the largest in the UK. It wasn't for students only: members' jobs included wool merchants, bricklayers, engineers, clerks and shopworkers. Members were drawn from every town in the West Riding.

The club was not licensed, so members nipped out to Viv's Bar, underneath the Majestic Hotel at the bottom of Manchester Road. Pass-outs, coloured dye hand stamps, were very hard to forge.

Saturday night was the most popular, opening at 8pm and usually closing at midnight. Later all-night sessions ended at 7.30 in the morning. There are

Outside the Allasio coffee bar, 1964. A fashion display – with turned-up 'winkle-pickers'. Left to right: 'Stoney' Tony, -?-, Eddie Messenger, 'Little Brian' and John Pajac.

On the corner by the belisha beacon, below the shops, was the Students Club.

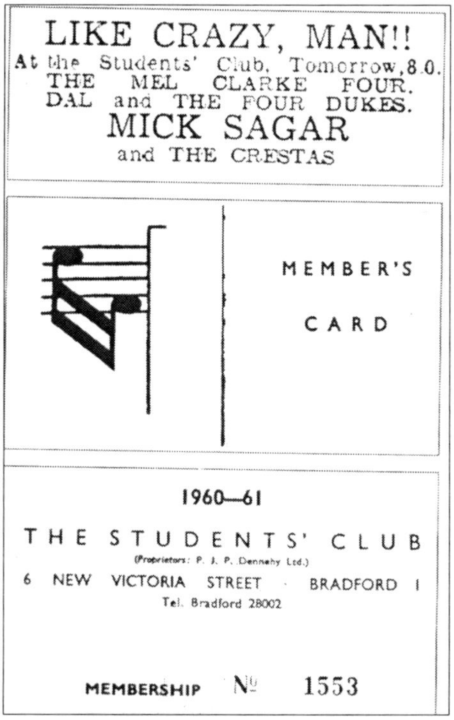
LIKE CRAZY, MAN!!
At the Students' Club, Tomorrow, 8.0.
THE MEL CLARKE FOUR.
DAL and THE FOUR DUKES.
MICK SAGAR
and THE CRESTAS

MEMBER'S CARD

1960—61

THE STUDENTS' CLUB
(Proprietors: P. J. P. Dennehy Ltd.)
6 NEW VICTORIA STREET · BRADFORD 1
Tel. Bradford 28002

MEMBERSHIP No 1553

Jay Walton's, Queen Victoria Street. The doorway close to the belisha beacon was the entrance to the Students Club, which was situated in the large cellars beneath the shop.

many conflicting accounts about which famous jazz musicians played there, but the true list of who actually performed is lost in time.

Local skiffle, blues and up and coming rock 'n' roll groups, such as The Cresters, The Dingos, The Dakotas, The Crusaders, Dal Stevens and the Four Dukes, the Mel Clark Four, played at the students club on Thursday nights, which were devoted to rock 'n' roll. The Students Club had a fantastic atmosphere, and most that played there enjoyed the occasion, despite only receiving 30s per group. Sometimes as many as three local groups were on the same bill. Sometimes a mediocre local group performed first, proudly dressed in their mix and match best suits, with one amplifier and a small hand mike. A group like the professional Cresters would follow, impeccably dressed, with half a dozen Vox amplifiers and the rest. It was then that some groups realised how mediocre they were – but it was all part of the game.

The Students Club was a remarkable achievement. Moya Pollard, Mike's fiancée, was secretary, and Joan Kilshaw served soft drinks behind the bar, helping to run the club in a professional and positive way long before the 'traddy-pop boom' of the 1960s. Mike Lamb continued in the music business for many years, managing bands and arranging bookings for other venues. He now lives in a cottage a few miles outside Skipton, which he shares with Moya.

For many years it was rumoured that the murals painted on the walls of the Students Club were the work of David Hockney. However, during an interview in 2005 Mike Lamb said that 'they were painted in 1957 by impecunious art student John Seaton who drank tomato juice for his lunch, and that was his payment'.

Chapter 13
TEDDY BOYS

The British Teddy Boy subculture was typified by young men wearing clothes that were inspired by the styles of the Edwardian period. The group got its name after a 1953 newspaper headline shortened Edward to Teddy and coined the term Teddy Boy (they were also known as Teds). Teddy Boys started in London in the 1950s and rapidly spread across the UK, soon becoming strongly associated with American rock 'n' roll music. It was the first youth group in England to be differentiated as teenagers, thus helping to create a youth market. Teddy Boys made it acceptable for young people to care about how they looked and to dress purely for show, instead of only having work clothes for Sunday best. Young people's disposable income was increasing during the post-war years, thereby making this possible.

The US film *Blackboard Jungle*, with the introduction of Bill Haley's 'Rock around the Clock' in the opening sequence, marked a watershed in the United Kingdom. When it was shown at local cinemas the teenagers in the audience began to riot, tearing up seats and dancing in the aisles. It was stated that in most cases it was Teddy Boys who began to riot, but their involvement was often exaggerated in the popular press. After spending £20 to £30 on an outfit, when wages were probably no more than £3 10s a week , who would contemplate rolling around in the gutter, fighting or ripping seats out of a cinema?

Bert Shutt's Ideal ballroom, Bankfoot, had always been popular, but received some bad publicity in the mid-1950s after events that became known as the Battle of Bankfoot. This took place on the night of Saturday, 26 November 1955.When the battle finally ended, after a police baton charge, three teenage girls had suffered knife wounds and seventeen Teddy Boys had been arrested. At the height of the riot, a crowd of more than 200 people was milling about outside the Ideal ballroom, and the road was blocked to traffic.

The trouble began inside the dance hall, part of a feud between Bradford and Keighley Teddy Boys. Police were called when about a dozen youths began

James Bordass with a mean James Dean look.

James again, looking a bit more Elvis.

fighting on the balcony. It was in the aftermath of this that three girls, who had the misfortune to be in the wrong place at the wrong time, received knife wounds – one in the wrist, one in the arm and the third in the back. The dance hall was cleared and police reinforcements were summoned, but by the time they arrived trouble in the street had escalated. A large crowd gathered, clearly unappreciative of the police presence. Soon it was not only Teddy Boy against Teddy Boy, but Teddy Boys against twenty police officers – who were hopelessly outnumbered. The fight that followed was so fierce that helmets were knocked in and uniforms were damaged. Staffs had to be drawn before order could be restored and the road was reopened to traffic.

At one point several arrests were made and drunken youths were put into a police van. A roar went up from the crowd, and youths charged the van in an unsuccessful bid to release the prisoners. When the seventeen arrested youths appeared in court the following Monday, three were given short prison sentences for offences, including being drunk and disorderly and for behaviour likely to cause a breach of the peace. A further fourteen were fined and bound over. So ended, the Battle of Bankfoot. The proprietor of the dance hall, Bert Shutt, later said he had been warned in an anonymous telephone call that there was trouble brewing among the Teddy Boys, and had taken steps to prevent 'what might have been a very serious situation'.

Teddy Boy clothing consisted of long drape jackets, usually in dark shades, sometimes with velvet collar and pocket flaps, and high-waisted drainpipe trousers, often showing brightly coloured socks. Favoured footwear was chunky brogues: large crepe-soled shoes, often suede (known as brothel creepers). A high-necked loose collar and a white shirt, a narrow 'Slim Jim' tie and a brocade waistcoat completed the ensemble. These clothes were mostly tailormade at great expense and paid for through many weekly instalments. Preferred hairstyles included long, strongly moulded greased-up hair with a quiff at the front and the sides combed back, to form a DA (duck's arse) at the rear of the head. Another hairstyle was the Boston, in which the hair was greased straight back and cut square across the nape.

Teddy Girls adopted a style similar to Teddy Boys, with items such as drape jackets, hobble skirts, long plaits, cameo brooches and straw boaters or coolie hats. Later they adopted the American fashions of toreador pants, voluminous skirts and hair in ponytails.

There was nowhere for Teddy Boys and other teenagers to go except the occasional coffee bar that had real espresso coffee machines and a jukebox, where you could hear most of your favourite music for a tanner. At the dance halls in Bradford the resident bands slipped in the odd tune among the standard ballroom dances. Frustrated young musicians, tied down by years of waltzes, fox trots and medium quicksteps, found that youngsters came alive when they jazzed it up.

Saturday night dances suddenly became a mecca for the town's youths. At the beginning Teddy Boys could get into Saturday night dances without any trouble from the door staff, but once inside their outfits stood out like a sore thumb. Round and round went all the stuffed shirts with their ladies in pre-war frocks, gliding gracefully across the floor. Musicians went through the standard numbers as if they were asleep. Then they started a quickstep, and in one corner a group started jiving, then another. The ballroom dancers looked on in horror and kept a wide berth, leaving more room for the youngsters to join in. Then, suddenly, the band woke up. The next number was faster, the jiving more flamboyant. Soon the staff started getting complaints. Who let those youngsters in? This scene was enacted all over Bradford in the mid-1950s.

The council and older population were suddenly confronted with youngsters who wanted change. Who was it who decreed that Teddy Boys would not be allowed into dances? It soon became a compromise between the authorities, dancers and the bands that there was a half-hour session for jiving only. These sessions became longer, and the bands began to play more numbers from the hit parade, including rock 'n' roll. Soon drainpipes were becoming the standard, and acceptable within the dancing fraternity – as were the Teddy Boys and Girls. With more dance venues opening in Bradford and other cities from the mid-1950s onwards, at last they had somewhere to jive, relax and above all show off their fashion.

As with all fashion movements, something else always comes along. In the late 1950s Italian suits with short jackets, narrow trousers and the famous winkle-picker shoes soon took over, and within a short time the Teddy Boys and Girls were few and far between. Some of the old guard survived, however, and kept faith with their fashion well into the 1960s. By then, however, most had disappeared into history.

I never had the inclination to be a Teddy Boy, but I secretly admired the style and those who had the courage to dress and look the part. My only concession was 16in trouser bottoms. My father blamed the decline in the woollen industry on such as me and thousands of other teenagers!

Only once did I wear the full Teddy Boy regalia. In 1956 I had just completed my basic training in the army at Aldershot and had a twenty-four hour pass. It was too far to travel home, and anyway I was on stand-by to go to Cyprus. I had thought of a visit to Aldershot, but I had no suit and it was nearly always impossible to pass inspection in uniform at the guard house. Rescue came when I met Peter Speight in the next barracks. Peter and I had been in the same class at St Patrick's, Westgate. He had recently returned from Cyprus, been home on leave and brought his suit back with him. Telling him of my predicament, he asked if I wanted to borrow his suit. Great, I thought – until he showed me his outfit, a pale blue Teddy boy suit with all the accessories. Well, needs must, and he kindly loaned it to me. Two hours later I walked into the guardhouse to show my twenty-four hour pass. The provost sergeant (a real hard-case veteran of Arnhem) took one look and burst out laughing. Within a few minutes all the provost staff had arrived and joined in the joke. Still laughing, the provost sergeant signed my pass and waved me on through the gate.

I was pulled up a few dozen times in Aldershot by MPs and SPs (RAF police), each asking for my AB64 ID card. They laughed too! The problem was that while the suit was perfect, with its long jacket and 14in trouser bottoms, finished off with large brothel creepers, my hairstyle made me quite ridiculous: it was a really over the top short back and sides army haircut, with a tuft of hair on top not unlike a Mohican. I could only be a squaddie or a deserter.

Having had enough of being public enemy number one, I returned to camp. On my return the provost sergeant and staff went into hysterics again. Still laughing, the sergeant admitted that he had only signed my pass and let me out as it was odds on I would be arrested and returned with a military escort. I thanked Peter, and said how great it had been. His only comment was that the outfit did not really match my army haircut. Needs must!

Chapter 14
TWANG BANG BOOM AND ZOOM: THE KIT

I am grateful to **Geoff G. Chew** for contributing this chapter.

This is not meant to be a definitive guide to the kit that was available to us in the 1950s and '60s, rather a recollection of the equipment I knew and aspired to.

The year was 1957 when I watched the flickering black and white images on our TV set of Elvis Presley performing 'All Shook Up', an experience that left an indelible impression on me, both visually and musically. Shortly afterwards I saw an advert in *Exchange & Mart* extolling the benefits of owning a 'Tommy Steele' guitar, and so it was in the fullness of time (it seemed like an age) the aforementioned guitar fell into my eager hands. What a disappointment! It was half the expected size and, horror of horrors, manufactured from plastic and virtually impossible to tune. If this was not bad enough, worse was to follow. After I retired to bed, my dad decided to try his hand at playing the instrument and, giving up in frustration (as I had), had leant the guitar against the sofa and in front of the storage heater. In the morning I found to my dismay that the heat had warped the neck so that the strings stood proud of the fingerboard by about an inch, rendering the guitar unplayable. Even the Tommy Steele motif had slid out of place!

Fortunately, on hearing my tale of woe our next-door neighbour presented me with a banjo, admittedly without a resonator and with only four of its five strings intact – but at least it gave me an opportunity to learn the rudiments of 'Peter Gunn'. This continued until I finally saved enough money from birthdays and Christmases to purchase my first electric guitar, in late 1959. This was a £12 Zenith from R.S. Kitchen in Leeds, with a Höfner pick-up attached to the base of its fingerboard. The jack lead was hard-wired and was only 6in, which meant there was no way I could escape from the amplifier.

Through financial necessity the amplifier was home-made, courtesy of the school boffin – one George Herbert Christopher Peters – who, between swotting for his exams, had his head firmly wedged in the pages of *Practical Wireless* magazine. On completion he informed me that the amp was based on a push-pull Baxendall circuit, a fact I long suspected! The need to house the wizardry in a cabinet was answered by gutting one of my dad's old radio sets and screwing in a new 10in speaker, which seemed huge at the time, topped off by a smart new brass handle. The transformation was complete. It was not exactly magnificent, but at least my attempts at instrumental solos on the likes of The Ramrods' 'Riders in the Sky' and 'The Packabeats' 'Gypsy Beat' could now be heard above the rhythm accompaniment supplied by my eager colleagues.

Before long I felt the need for an amplifier with more visual appeal, increased volume and a tremolo unit. This took the form of a Watkins Westminster in blue and beige, and was quickly followed by a more efficient guitar. Limited financially, but desperate for a solid model, I bought a Hofner V3 with Bigsby tremolo arm.

As my band, The Senators, grew in stature and the occasional gigs became more frequent, my savings increased accordingly. This enabled me at last to fulfil my dream of owning a salmon pink Fender Stratocaster, like Hank Marvin's, and the obligatory VOX AC 30 amplifier.

Later, as musical styles changed and The Shadows lost their appeal, my salmon pink Strat was superseded by versions in white and then pale blue, before I eventually opted for a cherry red Gibson ES 335.

Guitars

The early skiffle-style Spanish guitars, with their plywood bodies, tail-piece and steel strings hovering over a substandard action, produced a thin sound totally at odds with the vibrant music they claimed to represent. The only alternatives were the more expensive cello-style arch-topped guitars with spotted 'f' soundholes. Owners quickly added pick-ups, prompting manufacturers (including Hofner, Levin, and US firms Gibson, Gretch, Guild and Epiphone) to incorporate either one or two pick-ups with integral volume and tone controls.

More expensive than these were the semi-acoustic electric guitars that even outpriced their counterpart solids. Most popular were the Gibson ES 330 and the 335 (345 and 355 stereo models). They also provided a host of jazz-based models too numerous to list. Gretch touted their Tennessean, Country Gent, Anniversary (mint green) and their flagship White Falcon. Guild promoted their Starfire model. The alternative on offer to the less affluent was the Höfner range starting from £11, with the Congress, Senator, President, Committee and their 335 look-alike Verithin. For the wealthy, strictly purist acoustic guitarists could invest in the likes of Martin, Taylor, Ovation and the later Yamaha and Takemini. Harmony listed some semi-acoustic models, such as the Meteor, Rocket and the Silvertone. Kay, National and Dobro were also held in high regard by those who preferred to go unplugged.

Solid bodied guitars grew in popularity, enabling cheaper variants from £22 and upwards to become available, bearing names such as Futurama,

Colourama, Framus, Fenton Weill, Vox (pre-Phantom models), Rosetti and Echo. Needless to say, everyone aspired to the more expensive Burns Black Bison and Sonic models, but above all others they desired the US Fender Stratocaster – price 164 guineas – or its stablemates the Telecaster Jaguar and Jazzmaster. Rickenbacker produced a range of solids and semi-acoustics to set pulses racing. Fender's main US rival, Gibson, produced solid bodied guitars such as the SG, Junior, Standard and the Special. Its Les Paul range, priced in excess of £200, offered the Studio, Standard and Custom models, complete with their Humbucker, with two or three pick-up variations. I owned a three pick-up model, but it failed to produce the Hank Marvin sound I craved so it went back. Other contemporary models with more unusual design features were produced by firms such as Danelectro and Travis Bean.

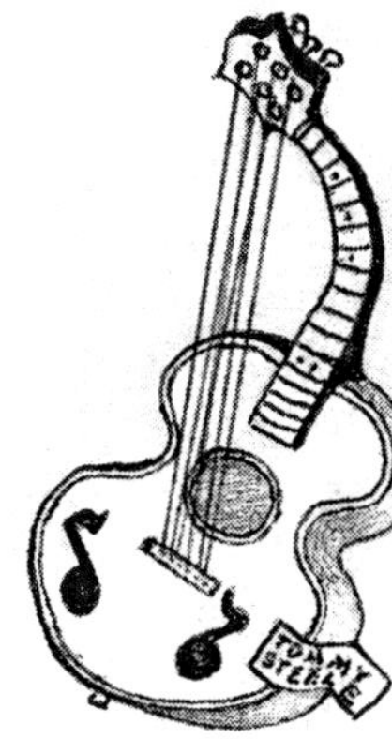

With the advance of technology a demand for new sounds increased, and before long guitars were augmented by an assortment of gadgets. The basic echo and reverb units were joined by treble boost, fuzz boxes, wah-wah and overdrive pedals.

Bass Guitars

The precursor of the electric bass was obviously the cumbersome double bass, followed for economic reasons by the tea-chest bass when skiffle became popular. With the advent of the electric guitar and amplifiers a louder bass sound became necessary, hence the birth of the electric bass guitar.

Leo Fender was at the forefront of its inception, designing the Precision Bass – a single pick-up instrument with one volume and one tone control. He also produced a bass version of the Telecaster, both soon followed by the Jazz bass. This model featured an off-set body shape that improved the balance when hanging from a shoulder strap, and a neck that narrowed more significantly towards the head. Two pick-ups, two volume controls and one master tone control gave it a more versatile range than its predecessors. A less popular Fender model was the Duosonic Music Master six-string bass.

Gibson's offerings were the EB2 and Epiphone Rivoli semi-acoustic bass guitars, along with Rickenbacker's very expensive solid bodied stereo-wired bass.All the above were well out of the price range of most aspiring young bass players, who opted instead for the more modestly priced Vox and Futurama solid bass guitars. The better Burns Nu-Sonic was also to prove popular. Höfner had a unique design with their 'violin-bass', as used by Paul McCartney. Unfortunately these designs needed larger amplifiers and speakers to handle the depth of sound; but with the introduction of ground-breaking transistor amplifiers with their improved treble the balance was soon redressed.

Amplifiers

Maximising the sound of our guitars depended on the amplification: the more powerful the better! The earliest models came via Selmer-Truvoice, and their valve amps. The basic Little Giant, retailing at £14, led to the larger treble and bass 50 watt heads with separate cabinets to hold the Goliath 18in speaker. Watkins offered a range of less powerful but nevertheless exotic models, while Bird was one of the first companies to supply large amps with built in reverberation units.

Rated higher than these were products made by Jennings Musical Industries. The Vox AC30 twin range of valve amplifiers were much sought after, followed later by the Beatles-endorsed 50/100 watt solid state transistor amplifier heads. Seeking a slice of this lucrative market, Fender soon began importing their own amplifiers, also valve based, but unlike their UK rivals these emitted a cleaner sound.

The majority of the amplifiers I have mentioned generated an output of between 30 to 100 watts. By the mid-1960s Marshall, Sound City, Park, Matt (later to become Orange) and WEM (formerly Watkins) were producing powerful 100 watt models, and became brand leaders.

Microphones

In the late 1950s and early '60s vocalists often plugged their mics into one of the guitarist's amplifiers, sometimes enhanced with the echo effect. The early mics were often the Grampian moving coil variety, which tended to sound very trebly, but these were soon superseded by the Reslo ribbon-type mics, closely followed by Shure, Beyer, Telefunken, Calvec and Sennheiser.

Echo Units

The earliest 'echo chambers' were the Selmer-Truvoice upright model and the more flexible Watkins Copycat, both of which employed a replaceable endless tape-loop. They were later eclipsed by the sophisticated Dynachord Echolette, Shaller and the Vox Cliff Richard Reverb echo units. Top of the range were the disc-styled Baby Binson and the larger Echorett II models

Drums

The first basic kits catering for the modern sound came from manufacturers such as Gigster, Broadway, Olympic and John Grey Autocrat, along with the British brand leader Premier. Premier didn't have the prestige of the more expensive US makes like Ludwig, Slingerland, Gretsch, Ledi and Rogers, or the

innovative stainless steel shells of the (French) Asba kits. German manufacturers were Trixon and Sonor.
Early cymbals were made of turned brass-coloured tin-and sounded like it. Other makes were the Zyn and the even better Super Zyn, but if you wanted the best then you bought the Turkish hand-finished Zildjan or Swiss Paiste cymbals.

Keyboards
After the guitar-based groups came the piano combos. A piano was a very difficult instrument to transport, so the only alternative was to look for venues that had a keyboard – but these were few and far between. This opened up an opportunity for portable electronic organs and keyboards such as the Vox Continental, Italian Farfisa, the Bird Duplex and Wurlitzer organs, the Hohner Pianette and the classic Fender Rhodes piano.

If you wanted an organ, and could cope with the size, weight and transportation, the Hammond, with its separate speaker cabinet, was the one to have. The cabinet housed a Leslie Rotary speaker, giving it that unique sound. The less well-off could have a Höfner Bandmaster harmonica!

Transportation of all this kit invariably meant relying on parents or friends with vehicles, and on many occasions public transport, but many bands resorted to hire-purchase to obtain a van such as a Commer, Bedford or Ford Thames 15cwt. I well remember an experience with my own band, The Senators, when we had to resort to the bus. The venue we were trying to get to was the Burley Miniature Rifle and Social Club. We hid with our equipment behind a wall next to the bus stop, while one of the guys held his hand out to request the oncoming bus to stop. When it drew up, we all piled onto the bus, much to the annoyance of the conductor and driver. Without such tactics they would have swept by.

Chapter 15
DEL SHANNON (1934–90)

It was early February 1990. I was in Leeds paying a visit to Graham Harrison, who is an authority on and friend of the late Buddy Holly's Group, The Crickets. During our conversation he left the room to answer the telephone, returning a few minutes later to say that someone wanted to speak to me. Picking up the phone, I heard a voice with an American accent. 'Hi, Dal, this is Bobby Vee. Graham tells me you were a good friend of Del Shannon. I'm sorry to tell you that Del committed suicide yesterday at his home in Canyon County.'

After Del Shannon hit the jackpot with 'Runaway' the hits would not stop – all featuring the distinctive falsetto that undeniably identified them as Shannon releases. Probably more than most he paid due respect to his original catalogue, performing them accurately and not merely chucking them into hurried medleys or, even worse, hamming them up with ad-libs. Del boy was still sharply dressed and still very rock 'n' roll. What a tragedy his death was.

I first met Del Shannon in 1963 when he was appearing at the Gaumont Theatre. My position as Top Rank DJ at the Majestic ballroom entitled me to go back stage at the many package shows held at this venue. I was standing just off stage in the wings behind the curtain when Del, who was finishing his act, ran off the stage towards me and said, 'Shall I go back for an encore, sir?' I said, 'Yes', and pushed him back onto the stage. This happened three times – and we had never even met. Later it transpired that he thought I was the stage manager, and while it was accepted that he would do an encore, the well-mannered American was asking me if it was OK.

Later we met when I was asked along with two girlfriends to a press supper at the Victoria Hotel. Surprisingly a firm friendship began. During our conversation it transpired that like me he was an avid 78rpm record collector, and he asked if I could obtain certain old records for him. This I was able to do over many months, and we had frequent phone conversations and exchanged many letters as I pursued them.

Del Shannon gave this autographed picture to my mother after his stay at our house at.Delph Hill. 'Mrs Lister – love ya! Del Shannon.'

In late 1964 Del was appearing locally in a package show, which he invited me to. Towards the end of his performance, knowing my mother was a fan, he asked out of the blue if he could meet her. This would necessitate a very late evening's visit, but I told him I would phone to warn her she was about to meet her number one pop idol. She didn't believe me, and suggesting I should ask him to stay. The show was almost at a close when I told him this, thinking there was no chance. But without hesitation he said yes, although he would have to clear it with his tour manager as they were booked into the Victoria Hotel. His tour manager asked me a few questions, but then said it was no problem.

It was 11.15 pm and a taxi was waiting (costing me 3s 6d). Off we went to my home on Delph Hill Estate, Wyke. The taxi rounded the corner of Ruffield Side and there was my mother standing waiting in the doorway on a very cold windy night. They greeted each other like a mother and her long-lost son, with hugs and kisses: at one point I thought she was about to faint. My dad was looking through the front window, with an obvious question mark above his head: 'Who's our Derek bringing home now?' For the next hour, in the front room, Del told my mother and me absorbing stories about his life (my dad, having to be up early for work, had disappeared to bed). It was around 1.30am when I showed Del to my bedroom: I had to sleep in the small boxroom. I don't know what time my mum was up, or even if she went to bed, because the next morning laid out on the kitchen table for breakfast were the best china and cutlery.

Del's tour manager had asked him to return by 10am at the latest, and time passed very quickly. Del and my mum were again all hugs and kisses, and there were tears in her eyes as my mum said goodbye to him. He left a publicity photograph on the kitchen table, with a message: 'Mrs Lister, Love Ya, Del Shannon'.

Arriving at the Victoria Hotel, the tour manager met us and asked Del if all was well. He replied that he had had a great time. I would have loved to have publicised this very unusual event, but his manager asked me not to! Now it can finally be told that Del Shannon slept at 47 Ruffield Side, Wyke.

Del was very active until his premature death. His letters to me were misplaced some years ago, and the only autograph I have is the one he gave my mother. He was a good friend and a fine upstanding young man with impeccable manners, calling me 'Sir' even though I was younger than him.

It was on 8 February 1990 that Charles Weedon Westover (Del Shannon), aged fifty-five and suffering from depression, committed suicide with a .22 rifle at his home in Saddleback Road, Canyon County, California.

Gene Vincent. A good friend, he never found out how my trick with the pencil was done.

Chapter 16
GENE VINCENT (1935–71)

Gene Vincent was in a class of his own! We all have our own definition of what makes a star. Many artistes I met and introduced to were undoubtedly stars of the rock 'n' roll era: big stars, household names, even internationally famous. One of these was Gene Vincent. After five years in the navy, he had suffered a mishap that would alter the course of his life. While walking across the naval base he was struck by a staff car, which inflicted multiple fractures to his left leg. In later years he often attributed the injury to a motor-cycle crash or a bullet wound sustained in the Korean War. Later Gene received further injuries to his leg and pelvis in the same car accident that killed Eddie Cochran, thus necessitating the use of calipers.

Gene was a favourite of mine from my army days, his music accompanying my many travels. His biggest hit at the time was 'Be-Bop-A-Lula' – which must have been special, because even my mum could be heard humming along while she was doing the ironing: perhaps not many mothers were as square as we thought. Gene appeared at the Gaumont Theatre Package Show in 1961, and that was the first time I saw him. I was impressed, but the majority of the audience were not, particularly during a number that was a favourite of his but not of the fans, namely 'Somewhere Over the Rainbow', sung not as a rock number but as a flowery ballad, which of course it was originally intended to be. Whether Gene was using painkillers that night I do not know, but his performance was not up to standard. A section of the crowd began to heckle and taunt him as he groaned and sweated in his black leather gear, legs akimbo, unable to conceal his metal caliper. He endured the insults bravely to the end, and then departed the Gaumont stage with some applause from loyal (and embarrassed) fans. Because of the audience's reaction to Gene's performance it was quite difficult to get back stage to meet him, but in my position as a DJ for Top Rank I won through and was ushered into his presence for a few minutes. He kindly gave me a signed photograph, but I did not savour the moment because of the tense atmosphere that surrounded him and his manager. It was not possible to ask the many questions I had, so I wished him well and left.

Two years later Gene Vincent was to be our guest star at the Majestic. His backing group in the old days had been The Bluecaps, but on this UK tour he was to be accompanied by Sounds Incorporated, most of whom I knew and was good friends with from their many previous visits to the Gaumont ballroom. Monday night was the date, and as usual I was at the Majestic in the afternoon, ensuring everything was in order, and back again by six o'clock. The usual queue four deep wound its way crocodile-style down Morley Street and then disappeared around the Alhambra corner: because of the publicity I knew we would have a capacity crowd of nearly 1,500 people. Humorous catcalls greeted me as I walked up to the entrance. As I entered, Sounds Incorporated were already well on the way to having set up all their equipment. It was nice to be remembered by this very talented group, and we decided that Gene would have just one live spot on stage that night, at nine o'clock for an hour.

I proceeded to the dressing-room to change, and when I opened the door I was confronted by Gene Vincent himself perched on a chair sipping a coke. He had very curly black hair and, in keeping with most of the American stars of the time, a permanent suntan. There was also an enigmatic quality about him. 'Hello,' I said. 'I'm Dal Stevens, the DJ here at the Majestic.' 'Hello, sir,' he replied. Just as I had hoped he was a real gentleman, and for the next thirty minutes we chatted amicably. Who would have thought five years ago, as I had sat watching him in the Jane Mansfield film *The Girl Can't Help It*, that I would be seated in his company being referred to as either 'Dal' or 'Sir'. When my colleague Dadio came on the scene he was treated likewise.

Needless to say the show was a tremendous success. Gene did his spot until ten o'clock, one sweet hour of 'Shake, Rattle and Roll'. As I had introduced him, Dadio brought him off – accompanied by rousing applause from many hundreds of teenagers crowding round the front of the stage. These had been moments for listening, not dancing.

When the group had left the stage Dadio and I finished off the last hour. The crowd built up around the stage doors, and we took the many autograph books down to Gene to sign. 'No problem, happy to do so' was his reply.

It was 11.30 pm before the area was clear enough for him to leave. Thinking he would be accommodated at the Midland or Victoria Hotels, we were surprised to find that he and Sounds Incorporated were booked into the Castle Hotel at the top of Albion Street, off Westgate. Dadio and I were asked if we would like to join them for a drink, so we all went up to the Castle. With glasses charged we passed the time away exchanging experiences of the pop scene. During our conversation I remember an old gentleman sitting on a stool at the side of the bar asking who the 'Yank' was. 'Gene Vincent,' I retorted, 'the American pop star', my voice trembling with humility. 'Oh,' was the reply, as he quickly re-adjusted his glasses and returned to his racing paper.

Around 2.30am the little group was down to Gene, Barry Cameron and Alan Holmes, of Sounds Incorporated, with Dadio and me. For some time I entertained Gene with one of my old party tricks, which consisted of breaking a pencil in half with an old one pound note. Many pencils were broken during the early hours of the morning. This had Gene fascinated, and I performed this trick many times as he pleaded with me to explain how it was done. Somehow I never got round to telling him.

It was at dawn that I said farewell to the great star. We met again a few times later, the last time in 1970 when he was in a package show: he was just one of many stars in the lower order. I was talking to Cliff Bennett, who was on the same show with the Rebel Rousers, when suddenly a door opened behind me and I was grabbed around the neck. A voice shouted, 'Hey, Dal, you never did show me how to do that pencil trick' – and then Gene Vincent was gone, overwhelmed by screaming fans.

The ravages of time and accidents took their toll. After a few years sliding down the scale, Gene Vincent was just climbing back up when he died of heart failure at the age of thirty-six in 1971.

PART TWO:
BRADFORD'S ROCK 'N' ROLL GROUPS

The 789 Skiffle Group soon progressed to rock 'n' roll and changed their name to the Delph Boys. Left to right: Brian Leake, Keith Artist, Brian Foster, Tony Gribbin.

The Delph Boys. Left to right: Tony Gribbin, Keith Artist (bending down to pick up his drum sticks), Brian Leake, Brian Foster.

THE 789 SKIFFLE GROUP/THE DELPH BOYS

skiffle /rock 'n' roll

In 1956 a group of local lads from Wyke decided to form a group using the basic skiffle equipment. The line-up of the 789 Skiffle Group was Brian Leake, vocal/rhythm guitar, Tony Gribbin, vocal/rhythm guitar, Keith Artist, washboard, and Brian (Fozzy) Foster, tea chest bass. As was usual in those times it was one of their parents' homes that was used for practice; in this case it was Brian Foster's house on the Delph Hill estate. Venues played were the local working men's clubs and the surrounding districts, notably the Crown Hotel, Wyke, New Roadside Working Men's Club, Wyke, and Odsal Social Club, Odsal Top.

After a time it became obvious that skiffle was becoming outdated and the new exciting era of rock 'n' roll was emerging. Despite this they carried on with the same line-up, but changed the group's name to the Delph Boys.

They entered a skiffle group contest at the Gaumont Cinema, hosted by Jim Dale. The Delph Boys won their heat on the Tuesday night but were pipped at the post on the Friday night final by The Sidewinders. For the competition they had added another guitarist, Jack Narey. Jack played in a dance band and was able to add some fancy solo work that they hoped would give them an advantage. Also in the line-up for the show was Tony's girlfriend Marion on the washboard, to give the group a more visual appeal, and Keith was playing a borrowed snare drum and brushes. They soon progressed to rock 'n' roll, but all to no avail: within a year the group was waning, and in 1960 the Delph Boys broke up, each going their separate ways.

Tony Gribbin (b. 1939) vocals and rhythm guitar

Tony was born in Bradford; he and his family lived on the Delph Hill estate, Wyke. He was educated at Carr Lane Primary School in Wyke and Belle Vue Grammar School. After leaving school Tony was employed in the grocery trade, including driving a Lyon's Stores mobile shop, during which time he played vocal/rhythm guitar with the 789 Skiffle Group and the Delph Boys. In May 1960 Tony, aged twenty-one, was one of the last conscripts to be called up for National Service, serving the RAOC at Bicester between 1960 and 1962. It was while there that he and other musicians formed a dance band, which played in the NAAFI for the princely sum of 15s each every Thursday night.

After demob in 1962 Tony played with small dance groups, among them a country and western group known as the Big D Ramblers, but this was short lived: when he purchased an electric organ from Wood's in Sunbridge Road and took lessons from their tutor, the guitar took a back seat.

After thirty years as a paint sales representative with Johnstone's paints from 1970 to 2000, Tony is now retired. He still lives in Wyke with his wife Marion. In 2010 they celebrated their golden wedding anniversary.

I knew Tony from the mid-1950s as I also lived on the Delph Hill estate. He was a good friend and a reliable musician, and it was he who helped with the formation of the Four Dukes by introducing me to the drummer Keith Artist.

Brian (Fozzy) Foster (b. 1940, Bradford) tea chest bass
Brian played with both the 789 Skiffle Group and the Delph Boys.

Brian Leake (b. 1940, Bradford) rhythm guitar and vocals
Brian played with both the 789 Skiffle Group and the Delph Boys. He was employed with BBA (British Belting and Asbestos) of Cleckheaton.

Jack Narey (b. 1937, Bradford) guitar
Jack played with local dance bands. He was employed at BBA.

Keith Artist (b. 1941, Bradford) washboard and drums
After playing washboard with the 789 Skiffle Group and the Delph Boys, Keith became one of the north's most proficient rock 'n' roll drummers. (see profile)

ALAN KNIGHT AND THE CHESSMEN
rock 'n' roll

It was in the winter 1962 that a Bradford entrepreneur, Mrs Miller from Bolton Junction, decided to form a 'super group'. With this in mind she got together four local lads: Roger Davis, lead guitar, John Whalley, rhythm guitar, Harry Hunsworth, bass guitar and vocals,Ken Hickey, drums, and Alan Lodge, vocals. Alan became Alan Knight, hence the name of the group.

They all had good experience with other groups, and it was therefore not surprising that they soon had a good repertoire of rock 'n' roll music. Practice took place at 'Ma' Miller's house in Sefton Grove, and it was not long before they were playing at the usual local venues: they performed many times at the Majestic ballroom as well as the Mecca Locarno on Manningham Lane, and a variety of pubs and clubs throughout Yorkshire. Two other regular bookings were the Victoria dance hall in Keighley and the Riley Smith hall in Tadcaster.

Perhaps their main claim to fame was when they travelled to London, having been invited to play at the 2i's Coffee Club in Old Crompton Street in Soho (there are photos to prove it!). This was their jewel in the crown – appearing on the small stage from which the likes of Tommy Steele and many others went on to make it to the top.

Soon it was back to reality. Ma Miller's enthusiasm seemed to dwindle and they parted company. Help came from Carl Glass, the popular assistant manager at the Majestic, who volunteered to manage them. Carl's many connections soon came up with many bookings.

It was now late 1964: two years had passed and the group had been exceptionally popular, but things were to change very quickly, Alan Knight left, and his place was taken by the very experienced Ronnie Thornton, formerly Chad Wayne of the original Chessmen. The bass guitarist Harry Hunsworth also moved on and his place was taken by Derek Nuttall. A name change was on the cards, so they reverted to the early 1960s and recreated the Halifax group name Chad Wayne and the Chessmen. They were soon back in the top ten of local groups, being booked again at many venues. In 1965 they auditioned for an agent who was looking for groups to work in Germany, and they were offered a residency at the Stadt Wien Club in Kaiserslautern. This

Local Bradford lads play at the famous 2i's coffee club, London. Left to right: Harry Unsworth, Alan Knight, Ken Hickey, John Whalley, Roger Davies.

On stage at the 2i's coffee club. Left to right: Ken Hickey, John Whalley, Alan Knight.

Another angle at London's 21s coffee club: John Walley, Alan Knight and Roger Davis.

Chad Wayne and the Chessmen rock 'n' roll at the Halifax Ideal Home Exhibition,

The Chessmen on the same bill as Joe Brown at the Imperial Ballroom, Nelson, Lancashire. Left to right: Chad Wayne, Ken Hickey, Roger Davis, Joe Brown, Derek Nuttal; and the group's driver Eric also gets in on the act!

resulted in drummer Ken Hickey leaving to join The Crusaders; his place was taken by Sowerby Bridge drummer Pete Vernon. Off they went to Germany with a girl singer called Tina – who was part of the deal. Once they arrived she left them to join up with an American musician! There was no publicity, and during the day they had to give out flyers throughout the town. They played seven hours every night, and things went from bad to worse: they ended up working for accommodation and food only. The experience was something they never really recovered from and within a few months of returning home in 1966 they had disbanded.

Alan Lodge aka Alan Knight (b 1942, Batley) vocals
Alan left the group in early 1965.

Ken Hickey (b 1947, Bradford) drums
See profile.

Roger Davis (b. 1942, Bradford) lead guitar
Roger lived in New Cross Street, and attended Marshfield Junior and Highfield Tong schools. In 1957 he signed on in the Junior RAF until 1961. In 1962 he joined Alan Knight and the Chessmen as their lead guitarist. From 1965 he continued under the new name Chad Wayne and the Chessmen, and was part of the group that went to Germany

In the 1970s Roger's career continued with a few 'normal' jobs in music, his most successful outfit being Simplicity, the first to be signed for Yorkshire's TVs own record label, York Records. For this label they recorded the theme tune for Hughie Green's *Sky's the Limit* TV show.

From the '80s onwards Roger became more involved in agency and management, working for the Bradford club owner Dave Simpson, then later with his own company, which specialised in comedy and the after dinner market .

Roger is the agent of one of Britain's most loved comedians, Johnnie Casson, who was also one of the 1960s and '70s great local rock 'n' roll drummers. Still as busy as ever, song writing, playing with fellow musicians of the 5 Oaks Skiffle Group, which he was part of in the late 1950s, and still at the helm of a successful agency, Roger lives in the Halifax area.

John Whalley (born 1942, Bradford) rhythm guitar
See the Del-Fi's.

Harry Unsworth (b. 1938, Bishop Auckland) bass guitar
See the Del Fi's.

Ronnie Thornton aka Chad Wayne (b. 1942, Halifax) vocals
Chad was originally with a Halifax group called The Sundowners. When Alan Knight left, Chad came in with the Chessmen, and was with the group until it disbanded in 1966.

Derek Nuttall aka Duke Everest (b. 1940, Halifax) bass guitar and vocals
Derek took over from Harry Unsworth, and was with the group until it disbanded.

Pete Vernon (b. 1940, Sowerby Bridge) drums
When Ken Hickey left Pete came in at the last moment for the trip to Germany, and was with the group until it disbanded.

Allan Holdsworth aged twenty, 1966.

Dave Arran and the Crusaders: a publicity photograph at Sheffield Ice Rink, backing Jess Conrad. Left to right: Cliff Dutton, Dave Arran, Ken Hickey, Allan Holdsworth.

ALLAN HOLDSWORTH
pop musician

Allan Holdsworth was born in Idle, Bradford, in 1946. Encouraged by his grandfather (an amateur musician), as a young lad Allan became very proficient with the guitar, and aged sixteen began to play in local club-based groups in the region, honing his future guitar skills.

In 1962 Allan joined Margie and the Sundowners, and in 1963 formed Black Diamonds. However, this group split because they got no bookings and had no transport. In March 1964 he joined Mick Judge and the Jurymen, and was with them from June until September, when they went to Butlin's for the season. In 1965, having left the Jurymen, Allan started guitar classes for young teenagers, at the same time becoming a member of The Crusaders. He played locally as well as going on tour with them to Germany.

In June 1966 Allan worked at the Mecca in Bradford with the Graham Warner Band, and later that year joined the Dave Allan Collection (ex-Crusader). In September Allan married Angela. In April 1967 he played his final week with the Dave Allan Collection, and around this time his daughter Lynn was born.

In 1968 Allan was back with the Graham Warner Band at the Mecca, and in 1969 he formed his first serious band, 'Igginbottom, with mates at his parents' house on Thorpe Edge estate. They did a regular Monday night residency at the Old Oak Tree pub near Kirkstall in Leeds. In June of that year they recorded a LP entitled *'Igginbottom's Wrench*. In July they were playing at the famous Ronnie Scott's in London, and at about this time *'Igginbottom's Wrench* was released. In August the group played at a guitar festival for a month, but in November they broke up.

At the beginning of the 1970s Allan joined Glen South's Magic Roundabout (based in Sunderland), and was with them when they moved to the Manchester Ritz ballroom in 1971. In 1972 he left the group, and went to London at the request of Ray Warleigh (sax and flute). Later he was invited by Pat Smythe (piano) to join him in the Tubby Hayes Quartet to make a TV commercial. Around this time Allan recorded his first BBC radio *Jazz Club*, in which he played the guitar and also a violin, which he had bought for £3 and learned to play just four months earlier.

Also in 1972 Allan played with Ian Carr's Nucleus and recorded the LP *Belladonna*. Back at Ronnie Scott's he supported Barney Kessel, John Williams, the classical guitarist, and Flamenco guitarist Paco Pena. Later that year the BBC asked Allan to represent them at the Montreux Jazz Festival.

Allan's career went from strength to strength in the world of modern jazz, and he became a world-renowned virtuoso guitarist and composer. He has released ten studio albums and played many different styles of music over a period of four decades, but is best known for his work in jazz fusion. It is ironic that this Bradford guitarist, despite being widely regarded by fans and fellow musicians as one of the twentieth century's most prominent and extraordinarily innovative guitarists, with his own trademark sound, is hardly known in his home town.

A long way from Thorold House, Thorpe Edge, Idle, Allan has lived in California since the early 1980s.

THE BEATNIKS/THE BEAT SQUAD

rock 'n' roll

In 1960 a young Keighley rock 'n' roll group came to the fore, The Beatniks. The line-up consisted of Roger Manton, rhythm guitar and vocals, Richard (Ricky) Hardacre, lead guitar and backing vocals, Michael Pickles, piano and vocals, Barry 'Bones' Swaine, bass guitar, and Derek Heaton, drums. They played at all the usual popular venues in and around Bradford, Keighley, Halifax, and for the next eighteen months built up quite a following. Then in 1961 members of The Beatniks and local group The Presidents merged, to form the Beat Squad – which consisted of Linda Russell, vocals, Bruce Russell, bass and vocals, Roger Manton, rhythm guitar and vocals, Ricky Hardacre, lead guitar and vocals, and Ted Earl, drums and vocals. Not many groups of the time could count every member as a vocalist!

In the early days the Beat Squad worked mostly in dance halls, on the 'Derek Arnold presents' circuit. They supported many of the up-and-coming acts of the day, including Jess Conrad, Vince Eager and the Big Three (one of Brian Epstein's Liverpool bands). They also supported a group called Alvin Lee and the Jaybirds. Alvin Lee went on to appear with his band Ten Years After at Woodstock.

They worked with many of the Bradford groups including The Cresters and the Del-Fi's. In 1962 the Beat Squad turned professional and went on to tour American bases in France. They worked in Verdun, Orleans and Toulon, spending a month on each base. At the end of the summer Ricky and Roger left the group to go to university, and the Beat Squad became Linda Russell and the Keymen.

Roger Manton (b. 1944, Keighley) rhythm guitar and vocals

Roger left the Beat Squad in 1962 to go to university, where he gained an art degree. He later became creative director for Saatchi and Saatchi, and was art director on several TV ads, including the famous blue jean advertisements.

Richard (Ricky) Hardacre (b. 1943, Keighley) lead guitar and backing vocals
Ricky gained an electronics degree and became sound engineer for Yorkshire Television, working on *Emmerdale*, *Countdown* and many other shows.

Michael Pickles (b. 1944, Keighley) piano and vocals
Michael later became an airline pilot for South African Airways.

Barry (Bones) Swaine (b. 1946, Keighley) bass guitar

Derek Heaton (b. 1942, Keighley) drums
Always fond of the outdoors, Derek became a gamekeeper!

Linda Russell (b. 1942) vocals
See Linda Russell and Bruce.

Bruce Russell (b. 1939) bass guitar and vocals
See Linda Russell and Bruce.

Edward (Ted) Earl (b. 1940) drums
See The Presidents.

The Beat Squad take a rest during a break at Keighley's Central Youth Club, 1961. Left to right: Richard Hardaker, Bruce Russell, Linda Nixon, Derek Heaton, Roger Manton.

THE CARAVELLES

rock 'n' roll

The Caravelles gained popularity from the early 1960s. All local lads, the line-up consisted of Dave Barraclough, lead guitar, Mike Berry, bass guitar, Dave Marshall, drums and Roy Woodrow (stage name Roy Sharon), vocals. Soon the group was playing at many local venues, including The Majestic and Gaumont ballrooms and the Students Club.

Mike Berry's father was concert secretary for Bolton Woods Liberal Club and knew many other local concert secretaries, so it wasn't long before the group had plenty of bookings, mainly in the Bradford, Leeds and Spen Valley areas. The great demand for the group was also due to Dave Barraclough's father Herbert, who managed The Caravelles throughout their existence.

Soon they acquired a singer called Lorraine Burns, who added a certain amount of glamour. With Roy, the group had both male and female singers up front.

A good selection of dance halls was added to the venues at which they performed, including the Gaiety on Tyrell Street, the Gaiety dance halls in Dewsbury and Batley, and the Textile Hall in Bradford. One of the best places they played was the American base at Menwith Hill, near Harrogate, where they entertained the troops – who had dances regularly, inviting many nurses from Harrogate and Ripon. The base had everything inside that perimeter fence: it was the first time that any of the group members had eaten a chilli or blueberry muffins with blueberry ice-cream.

Roy left the group after a while, but it carried on as The Caravelles with Lorraine with many bookings in Yorkshire and the North East. The money was better but it was further to travel. It was at about this time that Roger Wells, rhythm guitarist, joined them, as did his brother Jack on bass guitar.

In 1963 Lorraine left the group, and Sharon Vaughan (also very glamorous) took her place, and the group continued to be successful – its name changing to The Caravelles featuring Sharon Vaughan. In 1964 Mike Berry left and went to France, his place being taken by Pete Newlove. Roger Wells, the rhythm guitarist, also left at about the same time, to be replaced by the popular

Brendan Crowe, late of Mick and the Tornados. With the new line up, they won the coveted Wharfedale Trophy for the best group in Yorkshire in July 1964; the competition was held at Ilkley swimming baths.

Sharon Vaughan parted company with the group in 1964, to join The Strollers. A new singer was introduced, Frances Ann Robertshaw (her stage name was Carolanne), and the group continued to be successful in this form until she departed in 1965. The same year Dave Marshall moved on. Another female singer was appointed in 1965: fifteen-year-old Mary Smith. For over a year the group, with Mary (now named Vicky Lee) and Shirley Middleton (aka Lynne Tracy) on backing vocals and as compère, they took the North of England by storm, so much so that they ordered a new van from C.D. Bramhalls of Bradford. Gold in colour, this had all the comforts of home – and an illuminated sign on top showing the name Caravelles.

Still managed by Dave Barraclough's father, the group continued to obtain well-paid bookings, and it looked as if they would make it to the top. This was not to be, however, and in late 1966 the group disbanded.

Roy Woodrow aka Roy Sharon (b. 1942, Bradford) vocals
Roy is believed to have moved to Blackpool later.

Roger Wells (b. 1942, Bradford) rhythm guitar
Roger played with The Caravelles from the early days until he left to join Lorraine and the Baht'ats (1964–5).

Jack Wells (b. 1945, Bradford) lead guitar
Jack played with the Caravelles from the early days until he left to join Lorraine and the Baht'ats (1964–5)

Dave Barraclough (b. 1942, Bradford) lead guitar
See Vince Wayne and the Falcons

Dave Marshall (b. 1944, Plymouth) drums
See Vince Wayne and the Falcons

Mike Berry (1945–2008, Bradford) bass guitar
Mike was born in and lived at Mafekin Terrace, Shipley. He attended Frizinghall Junior School and Beckfoot Grammar School in Bingley. He was the first to say that he was not a model student: he regularly played truant and went off fishing. His first employers were Hanson's Butchers in James Street Market. His father was on the committee of Bolton Woods Liberal Club, where local groups used to rehearse. Mike loved to listen to them, and his main ambition was to play in a group.

One day, when The Caravelles were rehearsing, they mentioned to Mike that they were looking for a bass player. Without hesitation he jumped at the opportunity and said he could play bass – and he was in. They didn't know that he didn't have a bass guitar, let alone a clue how to play one. He went home and persuaded his dad to buy him a bass guitar, a Hofner Blonde Archtop, for 15 guineas, and then taught himself how to play it. Within a couple of weeks he

The Original Caravelles 1961: left to right Mike Berry, Roger Wells, Dave Marshall and Dave Barraclough.

Sharon and the boys jump for joy during their break at the Holme Wood Social Club.

had became quite proficient, and this was complemented by his good looks and similar image to Heinz (a popular recording artist of that time). Mick even dyed his hair blonde to complete the resemblance.

Mike was soon a respected member of the group, and remained with them until 1964 when he left the Caravelles to go to France, later returning to join Lorraine and the Baht'ats. Later he formed his own band, the Mike Berry Sect, which reunited him on stage with Sharon Vaughan (his wife). Another name change brought Sharon Vaughan and her Brothers. They toured the clubs, attended the City Variety Clubland Awards and also did a summer season at Butlin's in Pwllhelli. Yet more name changes came to pass, and they became the Bobby Gee Three and Rivington Pike.

After a while Mike decided he had had enough of being on stage. Deciding to change direction, he began to work backstage as a sound and lighting technician. Over the next few years he worked on many shows, including *The Rocky Horror Show* and David Soul's England tour, and with Michael Ball, Simple Minds and Danny La Rue. Mike's proudest moment was when he accompanied The Bachelors to the Royal Command Performance and met Her Majesty the Queen.

Mike owned his own business Vox Lumiere, then joined forces with 3D Productions, later leaving to work for Pro Audio. After a few years he returned to his passion of performance and joined a country band named Palomino. Sadly he became ill and passed away in 2008. Mike Berry was an enthusiastic beginner who went to the top, and is much missed by Sharon, his family, many friends and artists he met over the years.

Lorraine Burns aka Lori Wells (b. 1942, Bradford) vocals

Lorraine sang with the Caravelles from 1962 until 1963 before forming her own group in 1964, Lorraine and the Baht'ats. This survived until 1966, after which she changed her name to Lori Wells and joined a new group: Lori Wells and the Brothers. She continued with them for some years, performing in Egypt and for a season on the *QEII*. Later, with the help of the famous Leeds agents ATS, Lori did lots of TV work both as an actress and singer, and appeared many times at Batley Variety Club. Now retired, she lives in the Huddersfield area.

Sharon Holt aka Sharon Vaughan (b. 1942, Bradford) vocals

Sharon was born in Bright Street, Listerhills, and attended Carleton Street Junior School. Around this time she attended the Queeny Romas Dance School in Ash Grove, which kick-started her singing and dancing career. She went to Princeville Secondary School, and left aged fifteen, going to work at the shoe shop Saxone in Darley Street. After two years she left to make boiler suits for AIS (Allied Industrial Services) in Lidget Green.

Later Sharon became involved with local youth clubs, and it was at one of these in 1962 that some of her friends were trying to form a rock 'n' roll group. She was asked if she would care to join them as a singer, and although reluctant at first she soon conceded – and changed her name to Vaughan..

A few bookings followed, and as girl singers were thin on the ground Sharon was soon in demand. In 1963, as Lorraine Burns was leaving The

Sharon Vaughan joins The Caravelles, now called The Caravelles featuring Sharon Vaughan, 1963. Left to right: Dave Barraclough, Roger Wells, Sharon Holt, aka Sharon Vaughan, Dave Marshall, Mike Berry.

The Caravelles pose in a back street off Whetley Hill, while curious onlookers wonder which famous group is in the area. Left to right: Mike Berry, Dave Marshall,Roger Wells, Dave Barraclough.

Caravelles, she was asked to join them. It was a step up for her – and the group's name changed to the Caravelles featuring Sharon Vaughan. Her first appearance with them was at Low Mill Lane Club in Keighley, by which time she had met the bass player, Mike Berry, who was to be her husband. She was working during the day and with the band at night, and loving every minute.

In 1964 Sharon left The Caravelles to join The Strollers, and then in 1968 worked with her husband's group the Mike Berry Sect, travelling to night clubs in South Yorkshire and the North East. In 1969, as Sharon Vaughan and the Brothers, she spent a season at Butlin's. The group also worked at Batley Variety Club, and topped the bill in Liverpool with Lonnie Donegan.

It was soon back to the local clubs with a new group, the Bobby Gee Three, and then she joined an all-girl band called Flame as vocalist. They became very popular playing at Foo Foo's Palace in Manchester. Their most unusual engagement was on an oil rig in the Orkneys. They were locked in a room until they were due to go on stage, and as soon as they had finished they were rushed into a boat and back to land.

After finishing with Flame, Sharon decided to give bands a break and began to help her husband Mike with his light and sound business. After a while she decided it was time to have a 'proper job' and became a carer for the elderly in several local nursing homes. However, after an accident she had to give up this caring profession.

Now retired, Sharon still lives in the Bradford area with her family, spending her leisure time on the computer and listening to country music.

Frances Ann Robertshaw aka Carolanne (b. 1946, Bradford) vocals
Frances lived in Buttershaw. She spent a short time with The Caravelles, as the Caravelles with Carolanne, from 1964 until she left in 1965 to join the newly formed The Hornets with Carolanne, which folded in 1968 .She later married Paul Young of The Hornets, and in 1970 they emigrated to the USA.

Peter Newlove (b. 1943, Bradford) bass guitar
Peter joined The Caravelles when Mike Berry left in 1964. He left the group in 1965, and became part of the Hornets and Carolanne until they folded in 1968.

Brendan Crowe (1944–85) rhythm guitar
Brendan joined the group in 1964 after Roger Wells left to join Lorraine and The Baht'ats (see Mick and the Tornados)

Mary Smith aka Vicky Lee (b. 1949, Bradford) vocals
Mary lived in the Princeville area., She attended Princeville Nursery School and, after a move to Buttershaw, Farfield Junior School. In 1960 the family moved to Girlington, and Margaret was educated at Princeville Secondary Modern School. During her early school years she started singing lessons, and she was soon singing in public alongside her singing teacher in a choral group.

Leaving school at fifteen, Mary was employed at Woolcombers head office at Daisy Bank, training as a comptometer operator. In 1964, still enjoying singing, she was auditioned for a pop group of sorts called ARCs, who were resident at The Junction pub in Baildon. The audition was a success, and she

CLUBS
SOCIALS
CABARET
DANCES

The Caravelles

The North's Premier Vocal and Instrumental Group

featuring Sharon Vaughan

STATION HOUSE
GREAT HORTON
BRADFORD 7

Manager:
H. BARRACLOUGH
Tel. Bradford 74007

From 1965 until 1966 this was The Caravelles' new line-up, and their new Commer van. Standing, left to right: Shirley Middleton, aka Lynne Tracy, Dave Barraclough, Mary Smith, aka Vicky Lee, Malcolm Bradshaw. Front: Robin Hemmingway.

A new line-up: The Caravelles with Lorraine. Left to right: Jack Wells, Roger Wells, Lorraine (Lorraine Burns), Dave Marshall, Dave Barraclough.

took the stage name Marianne. Beginning to be noticed as a quality singer by other groups, she was invited to join The Caravelles, a chance she jumped at – now renamed Vicky Lee. Mary continued with The Caravelles until they disbanded in late 1966.

In December 1966 Mary formed a duo with Malcolm Bradshaw, who had been a replacement bass player in the last few months with The Caravelles. Calling themselves the Two Ms, they were quite successful on the club circuit and even brought in their own drummer for a while, Colin Sullivan of Cullingworth. All went well until April 1968, when they disbanded.

Mary continued to work at Woolcombers in the sales and purchase department and in other establishments until she retired in 2009. In rock 'n' roll circles she is still remembered for her vocals and her versatility. She lives in the Fairweather Green area of Bradford with her husband Jack, a keen member of West Park Bowling Club and enjoying retirement.

Len Fox (b. 1942, Bradford) bass guitar

Len took over from Pete Newlove in 1965, but was with The Caravelles for only a short while before bass guitarist Malcolm Bradshaw from The Meteors replaced him.

Shirley Middleton aka Lynne Tracy (b. 1946) backing vocals and compère.

Shirley worked as a hair stylist in salons in Bradford city centre, and joined the new Caravelles in 1965. When Shirley left the clubland scene she moved to live in Morecambe.

Malcolm Bradshaw (b. 1946, Bradford) bass guitar

Malcolm followed Len Fox. See Toni Star and the Meteors.

Robin Hemingway (b. 1946, Bradford) drums

Robin replaced Dave Marshall in 1965. See Toni Star and the Meteors.

A change of scenery for two of the lads from The Chillas. Left to right: Les Atkinson, Richard Jennings.

JOHN. LES. TERRY. TONY. RICH.

- THE CHILLAS -

Pops. Ballads and Beat.

All Enquiries: Mr. A. Bradley.
144, Lister Avenue, Bradford 4.
Tel: Bradford 681516 & 681652.

THE CHILLAS
rock 'n' roll

In 1963 some young teenagers with an average age of fifteen got together to form a rock 'n' roll group. There was nothing remarkable about this, as the same scene was being re-enacted all over the UK. They were Richard Jennings, vocals, Les Atkinson, rhythm guitar and vocals, John Verity, lead guitar, Terry Bainbridge, bass guitar, and Tony Bairstow, drums. The only experienced musician was fifteen-year-old John Verity, who had spent a short time with The Crusaders.

It was Richard Jennings and Les Atkinson's idea to start a group when they both attended Princeville Secondary School and lived in the Listerhills area. Les had had a guitar for his birthday, and after a few bleeding fingers he was quite good. When it came about that three lads from the Allerton area wanted a lead singer and guitarist, Richard and Les met them – and The Chillas had arrived.

They practised at a church hall on St Mary's Road by the children's hospital, specialising in music from The Kinks, Rolling Stones and The Beatles. They looked around for transport so they could travel to venues, and a butcher from Oak Lane with a Morris 1000 van agreed to pick them up and drop them off for a modest sum. It was no surprise that they could all fit in a small van, with equipment, and with a large butcher as the driver!

The venues played were all around the Bradford area, with an assortment of the usual pubs and clubs, including the Princeville Working Men's Club, the Railway Club, the Odd Fellows on Manchester Road, and even the Catacombs in Huddersfield on one occasion. Like many groups, with transport costs and musical instruments on tick, at the end of most evenings not much was left in the kitty.

Probably the best booking the group had was at the Towers Hall Cinema, Manchester Road, one Saturday afternoon, which had a special showing of the new Beatles film 'Hard Days Night'. With a ready-made audience of screaming teenagers who had come to watch The Beatles, The Chillas played the Beatles number 'Hard Day's Night' during the interval. The noise and the screaming for The Chillas was what it was all about – stardom at least for a few minutes.

Reality returned as they made their way home, with the sound of their teenage audience ringing in their ears. The Chillas would soon be no more, but they made a contribution and a small impact in 1963–4.

Richard Jennings (b. 1948, Bradford) vocals
Richard lived in Hollins Street, off Thornton Road. He attended St Andrew's Junior School and Princeville Secondary Modern School. He became a butcher's apprentice, but a year later had joined British Gas. During 1963–4 he was vocalist with The Chillas, and went on to join Gary Lane and the Rockets from 1968 to 1969. Richard took voluntary redundancy from British Gas in 1997 and finally retired in 2009. He still lives in the Bradford area, Oakenshaw, with Linda, his wife of over forty years, and spends lots of his time with his grown-up family and four grandchildren. An avid biker, he thinks nothing of covering 100 miles a day on his Suzuki 1400.

Les Atkinson (b. 1948, Bradford) rhythm guitar
With Richard Jennings, Les formed The Chillas.

John Verity (b. 1949, Bradford) lead guitar
See profile.

Tony Bairstow (b. 1948, Bradford) drums
In 1965 Tony joined the Five Leighs, and was with them until the group was dissolved in 1966.

Terry Bainbridge (b. 1949, Bradford) bass guitar
In 1965 Terry joined the Five Leighs, and was with them until the group was dissolved. From 1966 until 1968 he was part of the Soul System. From 1969 Terry was two years with Fresh Garbage. In 1971 he became a member of Pilot and finally in 1974 spent a short time with Jed's Blues Band.

CHRIS AND THE DELTICS/FOUR U FOUR

rock 'n' roll

Chris and the Deltics started out in 1962 as a skiffle, country and western group called Jessie and the James Boys, with Dennis Raynor, Ron Short and Roy Atkinson. Their music was outdated, so something had to change. Within a few weeks the group was completely reorganised, with Dennis Raynor, rhythm guitar, Roy Atkinson, bass guitar, Robert Ayres, lead guitar, Dave Potts, drums, and Ron Short their manager. The group invested in Futurama's guitars from Moore's, at North Parade in Bradford, and the drummer bought a very secondhand set of drums once used by the Temperance Seven. A new name had to be found, and that was supplied by Ron Short. He was a railway signalman, and chose Deltic as this was a large diesel locomotive of the time – and he liked the name. Dennis Raynor had always wanted to be called Chris, and as he was the lead singer the group's name was chosen.

With Ron's management skills they were soon playing throughout West and South Yorkshire and in many pubs and clubs locally, including the Prince Arthur on Sticker Lane, the Black Bull in Denholme, the White Horse in Wibsey and the salubrious Kings Head in Westgate, as well as many in Leeds, such as the popular Star and Garter in Kirkstall. In 1963 they played at the famous Birkenshaw Agricultural Fair, although this was quite a shock for a group with limited amplification.

Early in 1964 Dave Potts left, and his place was taken by the experienced drummer John White. At around the same time the lead guitarist Robert Ayers left. John Raywood, originally from Goole, joined in his place.

In 1964 there was a setback that could have had serious consequences. At Stump Cross near Northowram their van hit a lamp standard by the junction of the Bradford, Halifax and Leeds roads. The lamp was demolished and the vehicle was a write-off. Luckily there were no serious injuries, other than to Roy Atkinson, who was thrown through the windscreen (this was pre-seatbelt days), causing a perforated ear drum and a week in hospital. All the instruments were thrown out of the van when the back door was flung open, and although the guitars were in cases they were all damaged in some way. The local council made them pay £120 for a new lamp standard and £20 for repairs. The rigours of the pop world!

The group's popularity continued well into 1965. John White, the drummer, moved on to be replaced by Paul Robinson, and John Raywood also left. Alan Bennett, a good keyboard player, and female vocalist Mary 'Misty' Maddison were recruited, to give some depth.

In 1966 they had an average of ten bookings a month, most of them at top venues, including Haddon Hall in Leeds, the Adelphi Hotel in Harrogate, the Silver Blades ice rink in Bradford, the White Swan in Pontefract and the American airbase at Menwith Hill. Over this period the name of the group changed to Four U Four. However, in September 1966 the diesel had run out, and the group was no more.

Roy Atkinson (b. 1948, Bradford). bass guitar

Roy attended Tyersal Secondary Modern School. Leaving school aged fifteen he became an apprentice motor mechanic. In 1962 he became a founder member of The Deltics, and formed the Chapter Two Duo with ex-Deltic member Dennis Raynor for four years until 1970.

After a short spell with car audio equipment he went on to spend many years in the car audio industry. With not long to go until retirement, Roy is now back with his music partner Dennis: they call themselves The Deltics and play at many local venues. Roy has been married to Barbara for over forty years and still lives in the Wrose area of Bradford.

Dennis (Chris) Raynor (b. 1947, Bradford) vocals and guitar

Dennis lived in the Swaine House of Bradford and attended Swaine House Boys Junior School and Tyersal Secondary Modern School. Leaving school at fifteen, he became an apprentice electrician. He was a founder member of The Deltics, remaining with the group until it disbanded in 1966 .He continued for the next four years with Roy Atkinson as The Deltics.

Dennis later moved to the Sheffield area before settling in Doncaster with Kathleen, now his wife for over forty years. Although he has retired, he is playing on the rock 'n' roll circuit with Roy again. The Deltics are back

Robert Ayres (b. 1946, Bradford) lead guitarist

Robert lived in the Wrose area. He was with The Deltics as an original member from 1962 until 1964. He left because his family was moving from Bradford.

Dave Potts (b. 1947, Leeds) drums

Dave attended Leeds Grammar School. He was an original Deltics member from 1962 until 1966.

John Raywood (b. 1947, Goole) lead guitar

John attended Pasture Road Infants', Alexander Junior and Goole County Secondary Modern schools in Goole. Leaving school aged fifteen, he worked at Goole shipyard in a riveting team. Having learnt to play the guitar, he was with a group at school called The Playboys, playing lead. Not having a vocalist, they only played instrumentals, but after acquiring a bass player and a vocalist they

Early days at the King's Head, Westgate, 1963. Left to right: Ron Atkinson, Robert Ayres, Denis (Chris) Raynor, John White.

The Deltics busking in the mist of Sticker Lane. Left to right: Dennis (Chris) Raynor, John White, John Raywood, Roy Atkinson.

Chris and the Deltics: the 1964 line-up. Left to right: Roy Atkinson, John Raywood, John White, Denis (Chris) Raynor.

A publicity photograph of sorts after the accident at Stump Cross, Northowram, in 1964, on view at the station house, Idle. Front row, left to right: John Raywood, Barbara Short, Denis Raynor, Roy Atkinson. Rear, on top of the van: John White.

changed their name to Odean and the Odd Ones. Moving with his family to Bradford in 1964, within a few weeks John had joined Chris and the Deltics. His time with them lasted for only a few months, while he was working at the Manningham Railway Shed in Bradford.

A few years later he moved to West Sussex where, now retired, he lives in Littlehampton with his partner Sandra.

John White (b 1944, Farsley near Leeds) drums

'Big' John White was educated at Wellington Road and Hutton Secondary Modern schools. He left at fifteen and became an apprentice motor mechanic. A self-taught drummer, he soon established himself in the local pubs and clubs, and for a while he was resident with Eddie Smith on piano at the Oddfellows Arms in Harrogate Road, Bradford. He also played with the Carl Barrie Duo at the Prince Arthur in Sticker Lane and later at the Park Hotel in Park Lane, Bradford.

Early in 1964 he joined Chris and the Deltics, playing through some of the group's best days until he left in late 1965. From 1966 for a few years John played with the Mel Clarke Four, and also filled in with residencies and different organists at most of the working men's clubs in the district until 1986, when he gave up playing.

Now retired, John lives in Ipswich with his wife Yvonne. His hobby is a loft full of model railway – which keeps him out of mischief!

Paul Robinson (1947–71, Holmewood, Bradford) drums

As an up-and-coming drummer it was Paul who took over in late 1965 when John White moved on. Paul played throughout 1966, and was there at the end when the group folded in September 1966. Paul went on to play with Midnight Train during 1966–7, with the nickname Paul 'Reany' Robinson.

Alan Bennett (b. 1948, Bradford) organ-and keyboard

Alan lived in Wrose. He was an excellent keyboard player with The Deltics from 1965–6, having been brought into the group to give it some depth. He later emigrated to Canada.

Mary 'Misty' Maddison (b. 1948) vocals

Ron Short (1935–2005, Landour, India) manager and stand-in drums, banjo and guitar

Ron's father was serving in the British Army (Green Howards) when his son was born. Later, Ron attended Hutton and Great Horton schools. It was during his National Service days, also with the Green Howards, that he became interested in theatre and music. Leaving the army in 1955, he became a member of the Bradford Gilbert and Sullivan Society. However, with the advent of skiffle his attention changed to bluegrass and country music, and he was soon a competent guitarist, banjo player and drummer.

It was Ron who instigated both Roy Atkinson and Denis Raynor to form Jessie and the James Boys, with Ron playing drums. Such was his enthusiasm that he stood guarantor for both Roy and Dennis's first Futurama guitars. With the advent of rock 'n' roll the James Boys rode out of town and Chris and the Deltics was born. Ron was a signalman for British Rail and it was he who renamed the group. He was formally the full-time manager, but from time to time stood in on guitar or drums. Ron managed the group until it disbanded in 1966, and later encouraged Dennis and Roy to form their popular and successful Chapter Two Duo. Ron, who was married to Marjory, sadly died in 2005, aged fifty.

Every Bank Holiday the group families all meet up for a reunion in Filey, a tradition that Ron started. This carries on as a tribute to a well-loved family member, without whom Chris and the Deltics would not have existed.

Ron Short, without whom the Deltics would not have existed.

CLAY MARTIN AND THE TRESPASSERS/THE GREAT PACIFICS WITH RITA

rock 'n' roll

Paul Hornby and Allan Davies were the founders of Clay Martin and the Trespassers. In 1959 they were both aged fourteen and living opposite each other when they formed a skiffle group, consisting of a tea-chest bass and acoustic guitar. Playing at local church halls and youth clubs as The Trespassers, they were joined by Steve Clayton, drums, Barry Clay, lead-vocals and Kevin ?, rhythm guitar. Their musical style changed from skiffle to rock 'n' roll. The Trespassers became quite popular in the next few months, playing at pubs, working men's clubs and local dance halls such as the Majestic, the Gaumont and the Queens at Idle. It was during this time that Barry Clay changed his name to Clay Martin, and the group became Clay Martin and The Trespassers.

Following the usual arguments, Barry Clay left and was replaced by Rita, a singer who was somewhat older than the other group members. The group changed its name to the Great Pacifics with Rita. Although they were very popular, things were never quite the same, and the members went their separate ways in August 1963.

Paul Hornby (b 1945, Bradford) lead guitar and vocals

Paul attended Carleton Grammar School. In 1959 he was an original member of The Trespassers, playing lead guitar and vocals. After the group broke up he did not continue with any other group, and later joined the fire service.

Steve Clayton (b 1946, Bradford) drums

When the group disbanded it is thought that he did not continue to play with any local groups.

Barry Clay aka Clay Martin (b. 1946, Bradford) vocals, lead guitar and vocals

Some time after the group disbanded he joined a group called Tic, Tack, Toe.

Kevin ? (b. 1946, Bradford) rhythm guitar and vocals
When the group disbanded it is thought that he did not continue to play with any local groups.

Allan Davies (b 1945, Bradford) bass guitar and vocals
See The Royalists.

Practice in the garden for one of Bradford's youngest groups. Left to right: Paul Hornby, Steve Clayton, Barry Clay, aka Clay Martin, Kevin ?, Allan Davies.

CLIFF AND BRENDA WITH THE DOMINATORS

rock 'n' roll

It all began in the front room of 5 Newhill Close, on Parkside Estate, in about 1960. Two friends, Malcolm Husband and Eric Holt, purchased guitars and decided to learn to play them with the help of the popular Bert Weedon guitar book (play in a day). The Shadows were all the rage at the time, with their 'Apache' chart topper, so these two young men had a lot to live up to. A helping hand to keep the beat was provided by Malcolm's brother Dennis, using his mother's pans and wooden spoons as a drum-kit. Similar scenes were enacted all over the UK!

After a polite request from Malcolm's mum, practice sessions were moved to his sister Marjorie's house in Little Horton Lane. As time progressed it was decided to form a group, and his mum and dad supplied Dennis with a drum kit from the Grattan catalogue, and a Selmer amplifier was purchased from Harmony House in Morley Street (weekly payments, of course). Much practice was required, and with the addition of bass guitarist Bernard Brophy a recognisable group began to form.

Practice now took place at Sedbergh Boys Club in West Bowling, with the stipulation that they perform at the club (free of charge) at the Friday dance night. Even now the group still had no name. Then a club member who was a singer (of sorts), Cedric Ludlum, and Brenda Husband, sister of Malcolm and Dennis, joined the group as vocalists, with Cedric naming the group Los Angeles and the Four Tombstones. This name only lasted one booking, at Bolton Youth Club.

A complete reassessment came when the excellent vocalist Cliff Martin joined the group. Finally, with Cliff Martin, vocals, Brenda Husband, vocals, Malcolm Husband, rhythm guitar, Eric Holt, lead guitar, Bernard Brophy, bass guitar, and Dennis Husband, drums, they were named Cliff and Brenda with the Dominators.

The group's name was synonymous with the Bradford rock 'n' roll scene in the early 1960s. They moved to The Fountain pub for rehearsals and, following

Early days at Princeville Working Men's Club. Left to right: Cliff (hidden), Dennis Husband, Malcolm Husband, Kenny Fowler, Steve 'Red' Williams (bass) hiding behind Brenda.

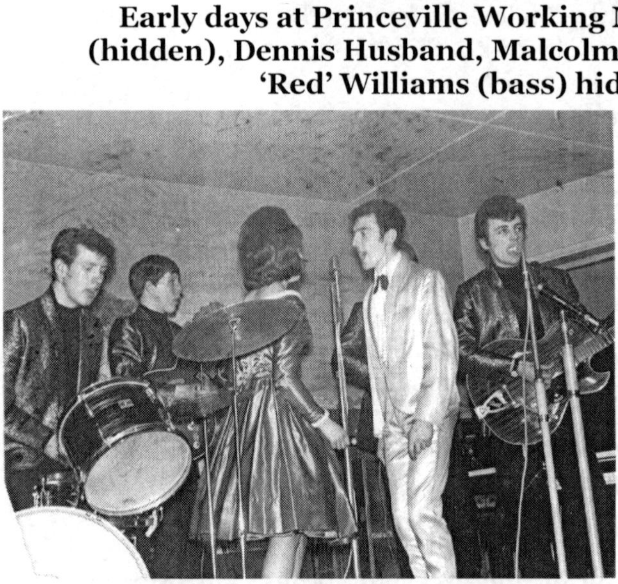

Left to right: Dennis Husband, Malcolm Husband, Brenda, Cliff, Kenny Fowler. This time Steve 'Red' Williams hides behind Cliff!

Practice night for Cliff and Brenda with a new Dominators line-up. Left to right: John ?, Dennis Husband, Paul Young, Cliff, Malcolm Husband, Brenda.

auditions, were soon performing on the popular working men's club circuit in West Yorkshire. They also had regular bookings at many local dance halls, including the Majestic in Bradford and the Mecca Locarno on Manningham Lane, where they had a regular monthly spot.

Until 1963 they were among the most popular groups in the area, commanding a large following and fan club. It was around this time that lead guitarist Eric Holt left, to be replaced by the ex-Dingo Kenny Fowler. With Kenny the group's music changed to incorporate the Mersey Sound, with Chuck Berry and Chet Atkins numbers added to the repertoire.

Sadly young and much-respected bass player Bernard Brophy suddenly died. His place was taken by the popular Steve (Red) Williams, formerly of the Mel Clarke Four. Back on the usual circuit the group was a tremendous success, and began to venture over the border into Lancashire working men's clubs, where they enjoyed many top bookings.

Come 1966 and bass player Red decided to leave. The same year Brenda and Cliff married and set up home in East Bowling. Kenny Fowler also left, his place being taken by lead guitarist Mick Brook. At the same time Paul Young replaced Malcolm Husband on rhythm guitar. It was one of those transitional periods which most groups went through, when they had to decide whether to carry on or disband. With the advent of new music and personnel the group soldiered on for a short while until 1968, when it finally folded. Cliff and Brenda with the Dominators is still remembered with affection.

Brenda Martin née Husband aka Brenda Martine (b. 1945, Bradford) vocals

Brenda lived on the Parkside estate, and when she left school she was employed as a wages clerk. In 1966 she married fellow group member Clifford Martin; they lived in East Bowling. Brenda continued in the music world after her time with The Dominators and today as Brenda Martine, she continues to sing around the Bradford area.

Clifford (Cliff) Martin (b. 1942, Bradford) vocals

Cliff married Brenda Husband in 1966. He was a club steward in the Bradford area for over twenty-eight years, and is now retired.

Malcolm Husband (1943– 78, Bradford) rhythm guitar

Malcolm lived on the Parkside estate. Brother of Brenda Husband, he spent his career as a van driver.

Dennis Husband (b. 1947, Bradford) drums

Dennis lived on the Parkside estate. Brother of Brenda and Malcolm, Dennis was a butcher by trade. He later joined the Royal Marines, leaving in 1993 with the rank of sergeant major, after which he joined the police and became a law instructor. Dennis is now retired and lives in Devon.

Eric Holt (b. 1943, Bradford) lead guitar

Eric left The Dominators in about 1963.

Bernard Brophy (1944–63, Bradford) bass guitar
Bernard lived in Haworth Road.

Kenny Fowler (b. 1940, Bradford) lead guitar
See The Dingos.

Steve (Red) Williams (b. 1942, Shipley) bass guitar
See the Mel Clarke Four.

Mick C. Brook (b. 1942, Bradford) lead guitar
In 1968 Mick emigrated to South Africa.

Paul Young (b. 1943, Bradford) rhythm guitar
In 1969 Paul emigrated to America.

COLIN HOUGHTON
drummer

Colin Houghton (1943–90) was born in Bradford and was a self-taught drummer. From an early age Colin was in demand from by young up-and-coming local groups. Aged sixteen he joined Mel Clarke's group, then known as the Unknown Four; its name soon changed to the Mel Clarke Four. For the young Colin this was two years of learning the trade, which gave him confidence and the opportunity to show that he was a gifted drummer.

In July 1960 Colin was invited to join the new group The Cresters, with Mike Sager. It was a good move, as three months later in October they were in the EMI studios at Abbey Road in London recording 'Deep Feeling'. The following day Colin was in hospital in Leeds for a long-awaited heart operation. Several weeks later he was required for a publicity photo session, and such was his commitment to the group that he asked to be discharged from hospital early, going straight to the photographic studios even before going home. He returned to The Cresters in December 1960, obliged to Kenny Gough for sitting in while he was in hospital recuperating. Kenny, another well-known Bradford drummer, had previously played permanently with The Cresters,

In the meantime 'Deep Feeling' had been released and even voted a hit on *Juke Box Jury*. However, the record failed to live up to its expectations (see The Cresters). The group was still semi-professional, thereby limiting their engagements to the North of England. They turned professional in late 1961, putting their daytime jobs on hold – Colin giving up his job with a transport company. Now able to play venues nationwide, during 1962 they had a booking almost every night, mostly at dance halls and clubs, and occasionally supporting top pop stars.

Early in 1963, during a dreadful winter, Colin was beginning to be disillusioned with the low wages, incessant travelling and arguments. They had played the TV *Jimmy Young Show* in Bristol and arrived home one Sunday morning in February, expecting a few days' rest, as there were no gigs until the following weekend. But no! Manager Steve Black insisted that they should turn up the next day to rehearse with new bass player John Harding. By now Colin had lost enthusiasm, and could not be bothered to turn up – his place being taken by Johnny Casson.

The most Colin ever earned in one week was £19! Usually the group incurred tremendous expenses, with agent's and manager's commissions, road manager and van costs, accommodation, expenses, stage wear, publicity, maintenance of musical instruments, and so on. What was left could be shared – equally.

Colin filled in with a few local groups for a while, including The Crusaders, and returned to his career with a transport company until he passed away in 1990.

In 1989 I visited Colin's home in Eldwick for information for my original Bradford rock 'n' roll book, *The Golden Years*. He was so enthusiastic that he wrote over fifteen pages about his years with the Cresters. There was so much detail, but at the time a lack of space meant that I could not use it. Most of the information about the Cresters in this book is from those fifteen pages. Colin had not been well when I saw him, and it was a short while later that he passed away – never having seen my book.

Colin was one of those people who it was a pleasure to know and to have as a friend. With a life-threatening illness he performed with the best on what can only be described as probably the most stressful and energy-sapping of instruments. His contribution has been overlooked in the past – but not any more.

Colin Houghton was one of Bradford's finest drummers, with charisma to match.

THE CRUSADERS

rock 'n' roll

One of Bradford's most prolific groups in the early 1960s was The Crusaders. As with many other groups a few personnel changes took place, but they maintained their professionalism and popularity.

Originally formed in 1960 by Clifford (Cliff) Dutton, rhythm guitar, Norman Sutcliffe, bass guitar, Kenny Rhodes, lead guitar, Keith Artist, drums, and Dennis (Duane) Oliver, vocals. These well-groomed young men soon became a well-established and popular group. Guitarist Trevor Calloway was also associated with the group in its early days, but his apprenticeship took preference. They played at many local venues, working men's club circuits for private functions, the Majestic and Gaumont ballrooms, the Mecca ballroom, Queens Hall, and many out-of-town venues, including the Winter Gardens, Morecambe, Sedbergh dance hall, Cumbria, RAF Leeming and the Imperial ballroom, Nelson (as support group for Jess Conrad and Sounds Incorporated). For a while they had Pauline Matthews in the line-up, before her star career as Kiki Dee. The Crusaders were the first group to play in the mess at the American army base at Menwith Hill, Harrogate, on a Friday night. They performed from 8pm until midnight, and as there was no other music on the premises they only had a ten minute break every hour – lots of sweat and repeated numbers! Later a juke box was installed, which made appearing there much easier.

In late 1962 Dennis Oliver left and was replaced on vocals by Dave Arran. In 1963 Norman Sutcliffe also left, leaving Dave Arran to play bass guitar as well as sing. Now the group was called Dave Arran and the Crusaders. With their new member, time was spent working on new material in a rehearsal room above a garage in West Bowling.

Back on the road they soon found themselves back in demand six or seven nights a week. They were all working in full-time jobs, and it was beginning to take its toll. They would work at a club in Newcastle, get home at 2am, be up for work at 6.30am, get back home at 5pm, then be off again! Keith Artist had had enough and he left, to be replaced for a while by Colin Houghton (late of

In late 1959 The Crusaders arrived, although this format would only last a short time. Left to right: -?-, -?-, Steve Calloway, Cliff Dutton.

The 1960 Crusaders line-up that would be constant for many months. Left to right: Keith Artist, Dennis Oliver, Kenny Rhodes, Cliff Dutton, Norman Sutcliffe.

The well-known drummer Colin Houghton joins Dave Arran and the Crusaders

In late 1963 drummer Ken Hickey joined The Crusaders. Back row, left to right: Ken Hickey, Dave Arran, Cliff Dutton. Front row: Laurie Baxter (manager, roadie and fixer), Kenny Rhodes.

Left to right: Kathleen Milton, Steve Calloway, Diana Swanson. Steve was one of the 1959 Crusaders foursome.

Cliff Dutton at the Trichter Bar, Stuttgart, 1964. It was Cliff who more or less invented The Crusaders and held them together from 1959 into the late '60s, his name being synonymous with the band.

The Cresters) until a superb and very young drummer named Ken Hickey took over, and brought stability to the group.

The agent for whom the Crusaders worked sometimes, Owen Hammond, told them that there was a German agent coming to Bradford to book bands for Europe. His auditions at Holme Wood Club were packed out. Owen worked a miracle by explaining to the agent that the group had its own rehearsal room, so could he come across and see them. They soon had their gear set up in record time at the room in West Bowling, and when the agent turned up it took just two songs before they were booked for Germany in June 1963. There was now a four-piece line-up: Cliff Dutton, rhythm guitar, Kenny Rhodes, lead guitar, Ken Hickey, drums, Dave Arran, bass guitar and vocals. To appear more modern they dropped 'Dave Arran' from their name and called themselves simply The Crusaders.

In all they spent three very good years working in Germany and in between, back in England, they carried on with the working men's clubs and fitted in a summer season at Butlin's, Filey. Kenny Rhodes, lead guitarist, did not make the second trip to Germany, and they were lucky in finding a replacement in Allan Holdsworth. When Allan left, after twelve months, his place was taken by another future legend, John Verity.

The group continued into the 1970s and '80s, called Collection, and with many different members later on.

Clifford (Cliff) Dutton (b. 1938, Bradford) rhythm guitar

Clifford was born in Upper Castle Street and was educated at St Stephen's Primary School and Woodroyd Secondary School. Leaving school in 1953, he was employed by the British Railways Motive Power Depot at Low Moor, Bradford. In 1956 he was called up for National Service and served in the RAF. Leaving in 1958, and with rock 'n' roll taking over the music scene, he decided he wanted to be part of it.

Cliff was a gifted self-taught musician, and it was not long before he was excelling as a rhythm guitarist. Having watched some local groups perform, in 1960 he decided to form a group, and soon had gathered around him some local talent that was equally enthusiastic. Thus The Crusaders came on the scene.

For the next seven years, with the usual change of musicians, Cliff brought to prominence, at home and abroad, a name that was well respected in the music world. In 1967 the group's name was changed to Collection, and they played well into the 1970s and '80s. Some of his many friends who performed with Cliff in later years were Brenda Martine, Albie Harrop, Andy Baldwin, Graham Hepworth, Pete Bell, Ian Waller, Trevor Craven, Mark Hearn, Debbie Slingsby, John Pullan, Graham Turner, Pete Spencer, Don Maundril, Brian Abbot, Dave Freeman, Brian Chippendale, John Hawley, Tony Parking, Rod Owen and girl singers Trish Taylor and Helen Bufferey.

Cliff is now retired and lives with his partner Bettina and twin sons David and Julian in Germany, where he still plays his guitar and has a hand in the gardening.

Kenny Rhodes (b. 1941, Bradford) lead guitarist
Kenny attended St James's Infant School in Nelson Street, Carlton Primary and All Saints' School, Little Horton. Leaving school aged fifteen, he was employed by the railways as a trainee signalman. However, because of the incompatibility of shift work and membership of the newly formed Crusaders, he left the railways. Kenny was soon offered a position with Wilkinson's Furniture Company in Hall Road, Bradford – but he resigned in 1963 to go with The Crusaders on his only tour of Germany. On return he left the group to concentrate on a career with Magnate Joiners in Keighley, until his semi-retirement, aged sixty, in 2001. For a time he worked as a part-time van driver until final retirement in 2006.

Kenny has not forgotten his early years as a top lead guitarist and has maintained a love of the instrument and its music. He still plays his guitar for recreation as well as exercising every week on his bicycle. Kenny now lives in the Shelf area of Bradford with his wife Carole.

Norman Sutcliffe (b. 1940, Bradford) bass guitar
Norman was an original member of the Crusaders from 1960 until 1963. He still lives in the Bradford area.

Dennis (Duane) Oliver (b. 1944, Bradford) vocals
See Dal Stevens and the Four Dukes.

Keith Artist (b. 1941, Bradford) drums
See profile.

Trevor Calloway (b 1942, West Bowling, Bradford) guitar
Trevor was educated at Woodroyd Secondary Modern School. Leaving aged fifteen, he became an apprentice sheet metal worker for the local firm of C.H. Cooper. It was during his early teenage years that he became interested in rock 'n' roll, teaching himself to play the guitar and, like many others, was soon an accomplished musician. Such was his talent that in 1959 he was one of the original members of The Crusaders. His father impressed on him that his rock 'n' roll career should come second to his apprenticeship, however, so after a short while Trevor left the group. The Crusaders had lost a valued member, but his father's judgement paid off – as Trevor had much success with his own business. He retired in 2003, and now lives in Spain with his wife Denise.

Dave Arran (b. 1942, Bradford) vocals and bass
See The Dakotas.

Kenneth (Ken) Hickey (b. 1947, Bradford) drums
See profile.

Derek Nuttall (b. 1941, Halifax) bass guitar
Derek emigrated to Australia.

Laurie Baxter (1937–95?, Bradford)
Laurie was the manager and owner of the Ring Road Garage in Rooley Lane, East Bowling, and was one-time manager and driver for The Crusaders.

Allan Holdsworth (b. 1946, Bradford) lead guitarist
See profile.

John Verity (b. 1949, Bradford) lead guitar and vocals
See profile.

The Dakotas have a good night at the Craven Heifer, Manchester Road. Left to right: Terry Lee, Dave Cochrane, Dave Murgatroyd, Paul White.

Rehearsal time for The Dakotas at the YMCA, Little Horton. Left to right: Terry Lee, Dave Murgatroyd, Brian Smith, Paul White.

THE DAKOTAS

rock 'n' roll

The Dakotas were one of Bradford's premier groups from the early 1960s, with almost the same line-up until 1966. It was over thirty years later that the group re-formed, in 1994 with the same line-up, to play at charity venues – which has continued into the twenty-first century.

The band evolved from a skiffle group formed by Terry Lee in the late 1950s, but it was not long before tea chests and washboards were set aside in favour of the electric sound. There were one or two personnel changes at first, but the line-up and style became established in 1962 with Brian Smith, vocals, Paul White, lead guitar, Terry Lee, bass guitar, and Dave Murgatroyd, drums. For a short while Dave Cochrane, a rhythm guitarist, was a band member.

The group was well managed by Stephen Laverack, a non-playing member. The popular Dave Arran spent a few months with them in the early days before moving to The Crusaders. Throughout the early 1960s The Dakotas regularly performed at the main Bradford dance halls including the Locarno, Majestic, Kings and Queens, Gaiety and the Students Club. They also appeared at many of the working men's clubs in and around the area, where they competed against bingo, raffles, shellfish vendors and concert secretaries to get the artistic recognition they deserved.

It was great fun with great friends, but by 1966, when groupies had become wives, proper careers had been established and Billy J. Kramer had borrowed their name, it was decided to retire gracefully from the music scene. For the next ten years they kept in touch and met regularly, but then contact became less frequent, particularly when Stephen Laverack moved with his family to Cheshire.

In 1994 Terry, Paul, Brian and David agreed to re-form the group for a one off gig to celebrate Stephen's fiftieth birthday, and Stephen insisted that he should become a playing member on this occasion. The performance was well received and, more importantly, thoroughly enjoyed by everyone in the band. The rest is, as they say, history. They enjoyed it so much that they decided to keep rehearsing, and with an extended playlist they accepted their first formal engagement, a charity function at South Bradford Golf Club. Stephen is now the group's rhythm guitarist.

For a while they added an element of sweetness to their vocals with Paul's sister Josie (late of Jo White and the Bluenites), but following her retirement in 2008 the band is back to its original sound, playing in and around the Bradford area wherever they are invited to support a worthy charity.

The Dakotas have now raised several thousand pounds for such good causes as Macmillan Nurses, Cancer Relief, The Candlelighters and the Royal British Legion. It is great that five friends are still enjoying each others' friendship and continuing to play music from their youth. Although individual tastes now differ, they are finding many audiences for their simple brand of rock 'n' roll. Long may they reign!

Brian Smith (b. 1941, Halifax) vocals

Brian's family moved to Low Moor Bradford in 1944, where later he attended Grange Boys Grammar School. Leaving school at sixteen, he worked as a wages clerk at a local wire manufacturer. Brian had great talent and was a good rock 'n' roll vocalist in the early 1960s. After brief spells with The Rivals and The Matadors, he reached his pinnacle in the early 1960s when asked to join The Dakotas. He was a great asset to the up-and-coming group, and was still with them in 1966 when they disbanded.

In 1994 Brian was back with the lads, singing for good causes. In 1996, now a local government housing officer, he retired to pursue old and new hobbies, including angling, crown green bowls, golf and classical music. Married in 1974 to Jennifer, they both still live in the Bradford area.

Dave Murgatroyd (b. 1941, Bradford) drums

See Mick and the Tornadoes.

Paul White (b. 1941, Bradford) lead guitar

See Jo White and the Bluenites.

Terry Lee (b. 1942, Bradford) bass guitar

Terry attended Grange Grammar School. When he left, he became a textile designer. In the early 1960s he was a founder member of The Dakotas, and remained with them until they folded. In 1994 he was back with the re-formed group, and is still playing with them. Now retired, his hobbies and pastimes are DIY, gardening and working out at the gym. Terry still lives in the Eccleshill area of Bradford with his wife Maureen.

Stephen Laverack (b. 1944, Bradford) manager and rhythm guitar

Stephen attended St William's School in Ingleby Road and St Bede's Grammar School. Leaving school aged sixteen, he joined Post Office Telephones (now BT) in various positions, until taking early retirement in 1994. In the early 1960s he joined The Dakotas as manager until the group split up in 1966. When they re-formed he took up his old role as manager, as well as playing rhythm guitar.

Although now living in Poynton, Cheshire, with his wife Tricia, Stephen still visits Bradford regularly to rehearse with the group and to play for local charities. Any group managers in the early 1960s were never given the recognition they deserved, and professionals like Stephen spent many hours behind the scenes to make sure that everything ran smoothly.

Dave Cochrane (b. 1943, Bradford) rhythm guitar
Dave was only with The Dakotas for a short while, emigrating to Canada in 1963.

Dave Arran (b. 1942, Bradford) vocals and bass guitar
Dave attended Green Lane Infants School and Drummond Road Secondary School. Leaving school at fifteen, he was employed by Grattan Warehouse in Ingleby Road. He was born into a musical and theatrical family: his mother and father were both pianists and his sister appeared for three years as a Sunbeam at the Alhambra. Dave originally wanted to become a dancer and attended dance, ballet and tap classes. By the age of thirteen he was performing at the Gaumont ballroom in *Carousel* and *South Pacific*, where his dance talents and his vocal skills were noted. However, along came skiffle, guitars and rock 'n' roll, and he was hooked.

With a schoolfriend, Terry Lee, Dave eventually learned four chords on the guitar, enough at that time to sing any hit songs. With Terry on bass guitar and himself on rhythm guitar and vocals, with Paul White on lead guitar and Dave Murgatroyd on drums, this young group called itself Dave Arran and the Dakotas. After much rehearsal they were soon playing at local working men's clubs and even a free show for the YMCA. However, after a short time he met The Crusaders by chance in the Craven Heifer pub in Manchester Road, and discovered they were looking for a vocalist. After a short audition singing Cliff Richard's 'D in Love' and 'Move It', he was offered the job, and The Crusaders became Dave Arran and the Crusaders. This move brought Dave travel and success, with a three year contract in Germany.

Dave left the group scene after a few years to go solo, working from the late l970s in working men's clubs and nightclubs until 1991, having been almost forty years in the business. It had been a long time since as a fourteen-year-old guitar vocalist in 1956 he had sang at the Towers Hall cinema in Manchester Road under the name Danny Collins. The cinema advertisement outside said, 'Today, Danny Collins, Bradford's Tommy Steele'.

It wasn't so long ago that Dave was persuaded by his son and daughter to enter a 'senior star trail' while on holiday at Havens, Reighton site, backed by the resident trio Festival. He won the competition trophy singing the popular 'Unchained Melody'. Coincidentally with the trio was another Bradford icon of the early 1960s, Mick Kershaw of Mick and the Tornados.

Now retired, Dave still keeps his hand in by entertaining the Alzheimer's, Well Being Café in Bradford with melodies of Cliff Richard, Elvis and other stars of that era. As he says, once you have the bug...

Dave Arran still lives in the West Bowling area of Bradford with his wife Jeanne.

The author, seen here in 1959, never learnt to play the guitar – so he changed his name to Dal Stevens and passed himself off as a vocalist with his new group the Blue Jays.

One of the original Blue Jays, rhythm guitarist Dougie Lamb.

DAL STEVENS AND THE BLUE JAYS/THE FOUR DUKES

rock 'n' roll

The group was originally formed in 1959 with Derek Lister, aka Dal Stevens, vocals, Michael Farrell, bass guitar, Sam Flaherty, rhythm guitar Dougie Lamb, rhythm guitar, Alan (Keg) Grainger, drums, and Terry Moran, piano. Derek, as well as being the vocalist, became the group's manager. They decided to call themselves the Blue Jays because they decided to wear blue ties (Slim Jims), which gave them some kind of identity. Adverts of the time spell their name 'Jays' and 'Js'. The leader's first name came from his initials DAL, but Stevens was picked at random.

Through the kindness of Dougie Lamb's parents the group practised in their house in Alice Street, Lumb Lane; there was a piano for Terry. With practice they produced quite a repertoire, including some of the popular numbers of the time, such as 'Be-Bop-a-Lula', 'Blue Suede Shoes', 'Whole Lot of Shaking Going On' and 'Teenager in Love'. With these and other hits they were hopeful to take Bradford by storm, to be discovered, and to play at *Sunday Night at the London Palladium.*

Some of the venues played in 1959, and early '60s were Young Conservative dinners at the Connaught Rooms, Manningham Lane, the Majestic and Gaumont ballrooms and the Aim For Fame competition at the Alhambra, the Co-op Hall, a six week booking called the 2s Hop, the Students Club and many others. They played to audiences of all ages, mostly teenagers. Although they were not showing any profits, just covering expenses, they were becoming quite well known: they had made a record at Excel Records in Shipley, chased up bookings and spread further afield, when suddenly the group began to fold.

The Dingos had been making approaches for Terry to join them, so in early 1960 he parted company from the Blue Jays. This left the group in some disarray, as most of their numbers had been adapted to include a piano; therefore a complete re-appraisal was required. It was not to be, as within a week Dougie left for better things, Sam departed, and so did the drummer, Keg.

Within six days the only two left were Dal Stevens and Mike Farrell. Dal was now the manager of a totally defunct group. However, their luck turned, as within a week they had both a lead guitarist, Eric Holroyd, rhythm guitarist, John Lund, and a drummer, Keith Artist.

A new group name had to be found, and so Dal Stevens and the Four Dukes was born. Soon Mike Farrell had to leave, but a sixteen-year-old bass guitarist Dennis (Duane) Oliver stepped in to fill the gap. The new group practised at Storr Hill Baths in Wyke, the Unity Hall in Rawson Square and the Gaumont Theatre through the hospitality of the then manager Mr Wilcox. They were soon back on the same circuit, with the Gaumont and Majestic rock 'n' roll nights, the Students Club and a six week booking at a new venue teenage show, on Saturday mornings at the Gaumont Theatre.

Christie's at Selby was a good rock 'n' roll venue, and most of the local groups had bookings – as did the Four Dukes. Dewsbury Town Hall was remembered by the group because they were paid an extra 5 guineas for continuing to play while a violent fight took place among most of the 1,000 patrons. All was going well, and the group was becoming very popular, but after just a few months the group amicably split up.

Derek A.J. Lister aka Dal Stevens (b. 1938, Bradford) vocals

Derek attended St Patrick's Infants Boys School, Westgate. He left school aged fifteen and was employed at Brown, Muffs and Burton's in Westgate. From 1956 to 1959 he completed his National Service in Cyprus and Aden. From 1959 to 1960 he was manager and vocalist for Dal Stevens (his stage name) and the Blue Jays, and for Dal Stevens and the Four Dukes. As Dal Stevens he was a DJ from 1960 to 1961 at the Top Rank Gaumont ballroom and compère for their shows, introducing the Karl Denver Trio, Wee Willie Harris, The Spotnicks, Heinz, Dickie Pride, Ricky Valance, Screaming Lord Sutch, Vince Eager, Jess Conrad, Cliff Bennett and the Rebel Rousers, Marty Wilde, Sounds Incorporated and many others – including Gene Vincent, who over the years became a personal friend. Many of Bradford's local groups were also involved.

In January 1962 the Gaumont ballroom closed. Terry Moran had joined Dal a few months earlier, and they were known as Dal and Dadio. On that final night they played the last music to be ever heard at the Gaumont ballroom, Don Gibson singing *Sea of Heartbreak*.

From 1961 Dal was DJ at the Majestic and from 1962 he was joined again by Dadio, again appearing as Dal and Dadio. Some of the shows compèred were Emile Ford, Mike Sarne and Wendy Richard, singing their hit 'Come Outside' (he was invited out to supper with Wendy Richard after the show), Jet Harris and Tony Meehan, Gerry and the Pacemakers (Gerry was not pleased that his equipment had not turned up, resulting in a fracas with Dal), Brian Poole and the Tremoloes (Mr Poole was not pleased when he overheard Dadio saying 'he has a crap voice!'), Billy J. Kramer and the Dakotas, The Honeycombs, The Yardbirds, The Viscounts, The Flintstones, the Rocking Berries, The Foremost, Jimmy Crawford, Freddie Starr and the Midnighters, Nero and the Gladiators, Billie Davies of 'Tell Him' fame (as she was staying in town for two nights she accompanied Dal to the Ritz cinema on Broadway), Freddy and the Dreamers, The Allisons, Shane Fenton (later Alvin Stardust)

(far left) Terry Moran would soon leave the Blue Jays to join the Dingos.

(left) Terence 'Sam' Flaherty, an original member of the Blue Jays.

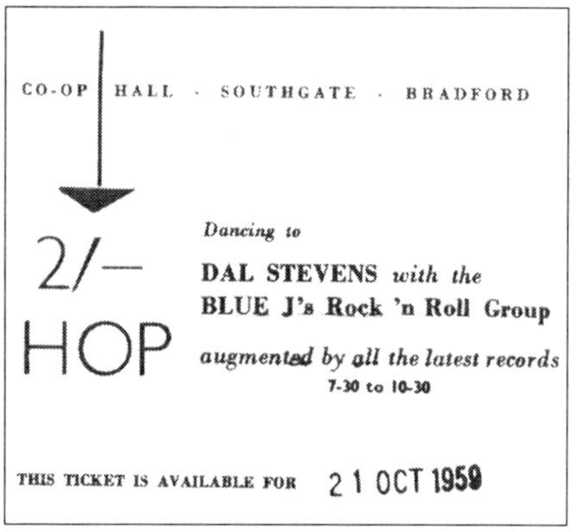

CO-OP HALL · SOUTHGATE · BRADFORD

2/– HOP

Dancing to

DAL STEVENS *with the* BLUE J's Rock 'n Roll Group

augmented by all the latest records

7-30 to 10-30

THIS TICKET IS AVAILABLE FOR 21 OCT 1959

An eight-week booking at the Co-op Hall in Bradford. Note 'J's' in place of 'Jays': such was life!

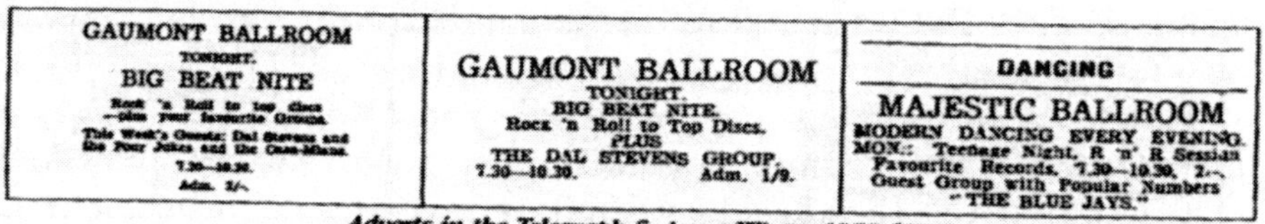

GAUMONT BALLROOM
TONIGHT.
BIG BEAT NITE
Rock 'n Roll to top discs —plus your favourite Groups.
This Week's Guests: Dal Stevens and the [illegible]
7.30—10.30.
Adm. 2/-.

GAUMONT BALLROOM
TONIGHT.
BIG BEAT NITE.
Rock 'n Roll to Top Discs.
PLUS
THE DAL STEVENS GROUP.
7.30—10.30. Adm. 1/9.

DANCING
MAJESTIC BALLROOM
MODERN DANCING EVERY EVENING.
MON.: Teenage Night, R 'n' R Session
Favourite Records, 7.30—10.30, 2/-.
Guest Group with Popular Numbers
"THE BLUE JAYS."

Adverts in the Telegraph & Argus Winter 1959-60

Drummer Alan ('Keg') Grainger, the youngest member of the Blue Jays.

CO-OP HALL — SOUTHGATE — BRADFORD

HEY! CATS! HEARD THE NEWS?

JIVE BE-BOP ROCK 'N ROLL

EVERY WEDNESDAY AT THE CO-OP HALL, SOUTHGATE

EVERYBODY'S WELCOME AT THE

2/- HOP

7-30 to 10-30

FEATURING

DAL STEVENS with the BLUE J's

AND ALL THE LATEST RECORDS

and the Fentones, Joe Brown and the Bruvvers, the Four Pennies, The Merseybeats, the Swinging Blue Jeans, Gene Vincent, Eden Kane, Del Shannon, and Millie of 'My Boy Lollipop' fame (the following day Dal accompanied Millie to Cartwright Hall in Lister Park; her mum came along too).

Among others whom he met while appearing at the Gaumont Theatre were Don and Phil Everly (the Everly Brothers) and Lulu, backed by her group The Luvvers. She was just beginning to make it with her number one hit 'Shout' – a rather small teenager without much personality, a beehive hairdo and a rather spotty face! Billy Fury was always amiable and chatty, while Bo Diddley had a superb rock 'n' roll group: he was a great guitarist and contributed much to the early days of rock 'n' roll. A real gentleman, he always called Dal 'DJ Dal' and gave him a hug on meeting and parting. Little Richard gave Dal his home address and asked him to look him up if he was ever looking for DJ work in the States. Dal met him again in 2006 and he asked Dal if he was still coming to the States, the offer after 40 years was still on!

In 1964 Terry (Dadio) called it a day at the Majestic and left Dal on his own. In early 1965 Dal also left the Majestic, which became bingo orientated. Soon afterwards it closed, reopening in May 1965 as a bingo hall. In 1965 Dal was a DJ for Peter Pugh Entertainments at the Victoria Hall in Keighley. The highlight of his time there was compèring the show with Screaming J. Hawkins. Dal was DJ for the Top Twenty Club in Idle and at summer fairs for Garth Cawood in 1966, and in 1967 he was DJ for guest spots at the Locarno Mecca. After this his showbusiness life ceased.

During his DJ days Dal was employed as a van driver for a cycle company and then as a representative for a well-known firm of insurance brokers. In the 1990s he did a few DJ and singing spots at the Pile Bar, Midland Hotel, as part of the Bradford rock 'n' roll reunions organised by Garth Cawood. In 1991 a Rock 'n' Roll Reunion CD (produced by Emile Ford) was made of eight of Bradford's original groups, on which Dal sang Cliff Richard's 'Move It'. In 1997 he recorded Johnny Kidd's 'Shaking All Over', which was produced by Richard Harding.

In 1998 Derek's wife Diana passed away. After four decades in sales he retired in 2003, after the full fifty years. Derek still lives in Bingley.

Terence Moran (1938–2004, Bradford) piano

Born in Listerhills, Terry attended St Patrick's RC School, Westgate. Leaving school in 1953, he was employed at Brown, Muffs. In 1956 he served his National Service and on leaving the army in 1958 he joined a local brewery as a maintenance engineer. It was during this time that thanks to his versatile piano playing he formed Dal Stevens and the Blue Jays with Derek Lister. After a few months Terry was approached by The Dingos and departed to join them. In 1960 Terry joined Dal, now the DJ at the Gaumont ballroom, using the stage name Dadio.

In 1961 Dadio had a burst ulcer, which caused the secondary effect of alopecia. Having lost all his hair, the effect on stage was that of father and son. With great courage he faced many teenagers for three months until his hair grew back, no mean feat and an indication of his professionalism and showmanship.

The author sings with his Four Dukes at a Grattan party in Clayton. Left to right: John Lund, Dal Stevens, Keith Artist.

Bass guitarist Michael Farrell, an original Blue Jay. He was the only member of the group to continue with the Four Dukes.

Eric Holroyd, one of Bradford's top lead guitarists, joined the Four Dukes and transformed the group during his time with them.

Mike Sarne and Wendy Richard of 'Come Outside' fame. After their show Wendy, Mike and Dal had a late supper at the Victoria Hotel.

Dennis 'Duane' Oliver gained good experience as a bass guitarist and vocalist with the group. Dennis went on to spend some time with the Crusaders and other local groups.

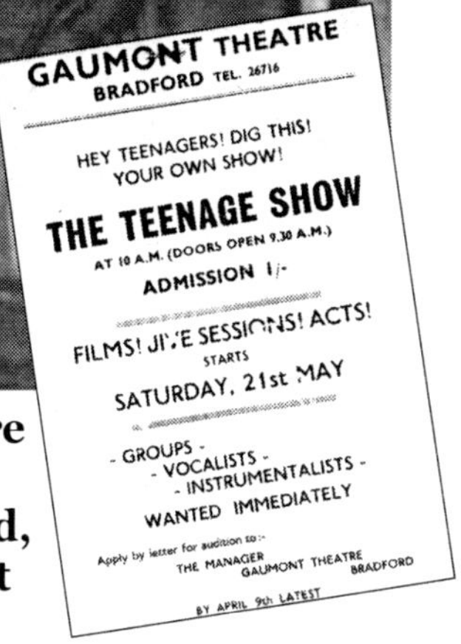
GAUMONT THEATRE
BRADFORD TEL. 26716

HEY TEENAGERS! DIG THIS!
YOUR OWN SHOW!

THE TEENAGE SHOW
AT 10 A.M. (DOORS OPEN 9.30 A.M.)
ADMISSION 1/-

FILMS! JIVE SESSIONS! ACTS!
STARTS
SATURDAY, 21st MAY

- GROUPS -
- VOCALISTS -
- INSTRUMENTALISTS -
WANTED IMMEDIATELY

Apply by letter for audition to:-
THE MANAGER GAUMONT THEATRE BRADFORD
BY APRIL 9th LATEST

Dal Stevens and the Four Dukes at the Gaumont Theatre Saturday morning teenage show. Left to right: Eric Holroyd, Keith Artist, Dennis 'Duane' Oliver, John Lund, Dal Stevens and the theatre manager Mr Philcox. What the group lacked in equipment was made up in style.

Billie Davies. The evening after her show at the Majestic, Dal took Billie Davies to the Ritz cinema.

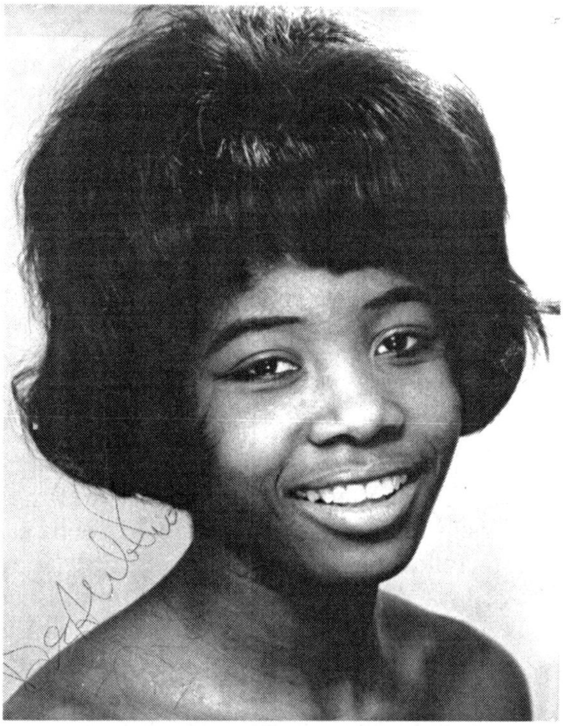

A date with Millie, holding hands in Lister Park – with her mother as a chaperone.

Dadio's style was not unlike that of the popular radio and TV DJ of the time Brian Matthew, both in voice and looks. It was in 1964 that he called it a day, to concentrate on his sales career with a brewery. During the following years many similar sales positions were taken, as well as running his own bar in the Canary Islands – until ill-health forced him to semi-retire in the 1990s. After a progressive illness it was in a Low Moor nursing home that Terry passed away in 2004, aged sixty-six.

Terry was a good friend and colleague from 1942, with a terrific sense of humour and infectious laugh. He was a brilliant pianist and will always be remembered as a true friend. He is sadly missed.

Terence (Sam) Flaherty (b. 1940, Bradford) rhythm guitar

The eldest of eleven children, Sam was educated at St William's RC School, Ingleby Road, then St Bede's Grammar School from 1952 to 1957. Leaving school, he was employed as an engineering apprentice at the English Electric Company in Thornbury. His introduction to the pop scene was as a young lad playing tea chest bass and a washboard with a local skiffle group, playing at working men's clubs and youth club dances. He soon moved on to the guitar when he met up with a young Dougie Lamb at the Nights of St Columba Youth Club on Bowland Street. They had soon learned a few chords and, meeting Derek Lister at a party, they were invited to help form a new group called the Blue Jays. Sam, like the other group members, played a very important role. He played at all the Blue Jays venues, from Aim for Fame at the Alhambra to the 2s Hop at the Co-op Hall.

After he left the Blue Jays Sam soon found other interests. He married Barbara in 1960 and made a good career for himself in computers and accountancy. In 1981 he married his second wife Dorothy, and he retired in 2005. His hobbies are gardening, reading and supporting the Bradford Bulls. Most of the rest of his leisure time is spent at Withernsea in a static caravan. He still lives in Bradford in the Fagley area near his many grandchildren and great-grandchildren; his wife Dorothy died in 2011. Sam has supported many charities over the years and has done the Windermere Row for St Gemma's six times and the Oxenhope Straw race for Manorlands three times. In 2004 all eleven of the Flaherty brothers and sisters entered the *Guinness Book of Records* when they completed the London Marathon, raising over £33,000 for Macmillan Nurses.

Alan (Keg) Grainger (b. 1942, Bradford) drums

Alan attended Daisy Hill Primary School and Belle Vue Grammar School. When he left school he worked at the English Electric on an apprenticeship. A self-taught drummer, he had been playing at Haworth Road Methodist Church Hall when he was approached by Dougie Lamb to join Dal Stevens and the Blue Jays. Although Alan was the first to admit that he was not a good drummer, it must be remembered that all group members were on a steep learning curve. Alan fitted in well for those few months – and also looked the part with his new set of Ajax Olympia drums. When the Blue Jays folded he helped out with other groups, including the Del Rio Four, and for a while turned semi-professional as a stand-up comedian. After a lifetime in engineering he is now retired, and lives with his wife Joyce in Greengates.

Michael Farrell (b. 1939, Bradford) piano and bass guitar
Born in Handel Street, Mike attended St Patrick's RC School Westgate and later St Bede's Grammar School. Leaving school in 1954, he was an apprentice moulder with Haworth and Walter Limited Foundry, which had premises a few yards from his home. He served his National Service from 1957 to 1959 as a medical orderly RAMC on troop ships to and from Hong Kong and Aden. On demob in 1959 he returned to the foundry.

It was at this time that Mike, an accomplished pianist and a good bass guitarist, joined the Blue Jays. A few months later, after the group had folded, it was re-formed as Dal Stevens and the Four Dukes thanks in part to Mike's help and loyalty. Some time later Mike left to join the police force in Morley, where he spent most of his career and where he, his wife Adie and family still live.

Another good friend from my school days, Mike's cheeky grin and humour are always remembered, as well as his special friendship when he helped me form a new group.

Douglas (Dougie) Lamb (b. 1942, Bradford) rhythm guitar and bass guitar
Dougie was born in and lived on Alice Street off Lumb Lane and attended Drummond Road School. Leaving school aged fifteen, he was employed at Listers Mill in Manningham. A self-taught rhythm guitarist from the age of fourteen, he played skiffle in the early days until he had developed his own style with the bass guitar. In 1959 aged seventeen, he joined Dal Stevens and the Blue Jays as a rhythm guitarist. The group practised at his mother's house. When the group broke up in early 1960, now a bass guitarist, Dougie joined Spike O' Brien in forming The Intruders. (Spike's comment was that they intruded on all other groups!) In 1961 until they folded in 1962 he was with The Dingos. From 1962 until 1965 he played with the Billy Thompson Trio, Billy Walker on vocals, Joe Marshall on drums and Doug on bass guitar, performing at pubs and clubs in the area. From 1965 until 1982 Dougie was resident bass player with a group called The Waysiders at the Listers Arms in Manchester Road (the pub landlord named them). Seventeen years, more or less, at the same venue must surely be a local record. From 1982 he played with many local musicians, among whom were the reunited Dingos, The Elderberries, The Cresters, the Mel Clarke Four and the Dave Lee Sound.

Dougie is known throughout the north as one of the most reliable bass guitarists. He backed P.J. Proby, Marty Wilde, Jess Conrad, Vince Eager, Eden Kane, Gene Vincent during the rock 'n' roll years. Bass guitarists are generally overlooked when accolades are handed out, but for over fifty years Dougie has excelled with his unstinting backing throughout the UK. He is now retired, and still living in his home town of Bradford, but his talent is still required at many rock 'n' roll venues.

Dennis (Duane) Oliver (b 1944, Bradford) bass guitar
Dennis lived on Lincoln Terrace, Manningham, and attended St William's RC School. On leaving school aged fifteen he was employed at Grattan Warehouse in Ingleby Road. From the age of fourteen he taught himself to play the bass guitar, and became proficient enough in 1960 to join Dal Stevens and the Four Dukes when Mike Farrell moved on. He was also an excellent vocalist, not unlike Cliff Richard, so he made quite an addition to the group. In the beginning he was very shy, but soon became a very polished and professional artist. When Dal Stevens's group broke up he was quickly picked up by The Crusaders, becoming their vocal front man.

From 1963 until 1965 Dennis played with a newly formed group called the Four Musketeers, and in 1966 performed with Dave Lee for a while. In the 1980s he teamed up again with Keith Artist and re-formed the Four Musketeers, later renamed Resurrection. In 2003–4 Resurrection was again re-formed, albeit only for a short while.

During his rock 'n' roll years Dennis was employed by Baird Television in Bradford and British Telecom. Now retired, he still plays and sings with his friend of many years Keith Artist, and now lives in Epworth, Doncaster, with his wife Noreen and family.

John Lund (b 1940, Bradford) rhythm guitar
John was born in and lived on New Hey Road in West Bowling and worked at Grattan Warehouse in Ingleby Road. He was a quiet artistic youth who was quite an accomplished rhythm guitarist. He was a member of Dal Stevens and the Four Dukes until the group folded in 1960. It is not known if he participated in any other groups later.

Eric Holroyd (b 1938, Bradford) guitar
Eric attended Heckmondwyke Grammar School. Leaving school, he was employed at Illingworth Morris Mills, Thornton Road.

A multi-instrumentalist, Eric's main instrument is trumpet (or cornet), although his musical training began with classical piano at the age of six. In his early teens he learned cornet, trombone and tuba, later switching to electric guitar to play in rock 'n' roll bands. Eric took his first professional music job aged sixteen at the Textile Hall, Westgate. With this sixteen-piece dance orchestra, complete with three vocalists, Eric's love of jazz blossomed. He later became the trumpeter in the band's seven piece jazz group, which played Harry Gold 'Pieces of Eight' Dixieland orchestrations and improvised jazz.

In his early twenties Eric joined Dal Stevens and the Four Dukes, re-formed from the Blue Jays, and he transformed it into a very professional rock 'n' roll group. It was Eric's lead guitar performances that gave them some success for a short time.

It was at the Textile Hall that Eric had met his future wife Jean, and they were soon married. When they were both aged twenty-three in July 1966, they and their two daughters left the UK for a new life in Australia. Eric is now a very famous jazz musician both in Australia and throughout the world. He is a regular at Australia's annual jazz conventions, and features regularly at jazz festivals around Australia both as a soloist and with various bands. He has toured in California several times with Melbourne's Creole Bells, playing the Sacramento Jazz Jubilee, Santa Rosa Jazz Festival, the Los Angeles Sweet and Hot Festival and a short season in Las Vegas.

A foundation member of Tom Baker's mid-1970s San Francisco Jazz Band, Eric has played trumpet with other popular jazz groups such as the Abbey Jazz Band, Ocean City Jazz Band, Southern Jazzmen, as well as featuring regularly with Graeme Bell's All Stars. Eric's own band has several times played as support to Britain's Kenny Ball and his Jazzmen on their tours to Australia. From a superb rock 'n' roll lead guitarist to a world renowned jazz musician, Eric was married for just over fifty years. Sadly his wife Jean passed away in January 2007.

Keith Artist (b. 1941, Bradford) drums
See profile.

Aged fifteen, Dave was an accomplished cornet player with the Salvation Army.

Early days for Dave Lee at the Blue Moon pub in Stanningley. With Dave are Mick Craven on drums and bass guitarist Brian Haw.

DAVE LEE SOUND

rock 'n' roll

David Harper aka Dave Lee (1940–2004) was born in Bradford and attended Buttershaw School. As a twelve year old in 1952 he joined the local Salvation Army band, learning to play the cornet. During his time with the band he taught himself to play the piano, and by the age of sixteen had become quite proficient. The 1950s found him playing rock 'n' roll music in many pubs and clubs in and around Bradford.

Dave's full-time employment during this time was in the warehouse of Ringtons Tea in Ashton Street, Bradford. However, by 1958 and now married, he was looking for more security, and he joined William Bussey, wool merchants in Bradford.

In the 1960s Dave's authentic rock 'n' roll style was beginning to be noticed and admired by the listening public. He was now sounding like his idol Jerry Lee Lewis and also looking like him. In 1968 he turned professional and formed the Dave Lee Sound with Dave de Courcy, bass, and Andy Greaves, drums. In 1968 Andy left and his place was taken by Malcolm (Mal) Crossley, before a season at Butlin's.

In 1970, with a new line up the group came second on Hughie Green's *Opportunity Knocks*, but the highlight of Dave's career was undoubtedly meeting Jerry Lee Lewis in Manchester in 1971, when he joined him on stage as well as having a drink with him back stage after the show. In the 1970s the band was based in Bingley and had its own record label called Throstle's Nest, which released three LPs and two EPs. In 1993 Dave picked up the role of Jerry Lee Lewis in the musical *Lipstick on Your Collar* before moving to Benidorm, where he performed solo at a number of clubs in the resort.

It was Dave Lee who virtually single-handedly kept the authentic 1950s rock 'n' roll revival scene alive, not only in Bradford but throughout the country and abroad, for over four decades. Sadly, Dave passed away in Bradford's Royal Infirmary in 2004. He was a brilliant showman and musician, who will always be remembered and missed by his many friends and fans.

Throughout his years in rock 'n' roll many local musicians formed part of the Dave Lee Sound, among whom were Dave de Courcy, bass, Andy Greaves,

Dave Lee epitomises the style of his hero Jerry Lee Lewis.

drums, Mick Craven, drums, Malcolm (Mally) Crossley, drums, Brian Haw, bass, Johnnie Rickman, bass, Eric Saunders, bass, Kim Jacques, bass, Charlie Chuck, drums, and many others. Some other musicians named in this book did session work with the Dave Lee Sound.

Dave's daughter Susan Trudgill, aka Swinging Sue, was born in Bradford in the 1950s and grew up with rock 'n' roll music all around her. Inspired by her late father's music she danced from the age of six, but it was not until the late 1990s that she attended rock 'n' roll classes, then achieving considerable success in competitions. In 2001 she undertook further training, so that she could teach rock 'n' roll to men and women alike. Like her father, who gave her the name 'Swinging Sue', she has brought the rock 'n' roll revival to a new generation.

The Dave Lee Trio performs at the popular Law Moor Working Men's Club, 1966.

Ray Kennan reaches new heights with the Del Rio Four. Left to right: Martin Kershaw, Kenny Gough, Ray Kennan and Malcolm Ives.

An almost completely new line-up for the Del Rio Four. Left to right: Malcolm Ives, Mick Kershaw, Malcolm Crossley, Ian Atkinson.

THE DEL RIO FOUR

rock 'n' roll

A notable group of the early 1960s was the Del Rio Four, which made the rounds of the dance halls and clubs in Yorkshire. In 1960 the very talented line up consisted of the popular vocalist Ray Kennan (the group's mainstay), Malcolm Ives, lead guitar, Martin Kershaw, bass guitar, and the well-known Kenny Gough, drums.

For three years the Del Rio Four were at the forefront of their profession, with regular bookings at the Bradford Majestic and the Students Club, and their name was on many billboards, either topping the bill or backing some of the time's pop idols.

By 1963 Ray Kennan had moved on, as had Kenny Gough, and they were followed by Martin Kershaw. New members were appointed: Cleckheaton lad Malcolm Crossley on drums, another Kershaw, Mick Kershaw from Bradford, playing rhythm guitar and singing lead vocals, Ian Atkinson from Halifax on lead guitar and, from the original group, Malcolm Ives – who switched from lead guitar to bass guitar. The group continued where it had left off, and within a few weeks had been booked for a season at Butlin's Holiday Camp in Clacton, performing in the Pig and Whistle bar. Next door in the Shellfish Bar, Dave Dee, Dozy, Beaky, Mick and Tich were performing!

At this time the group was managed by John Helm (later a well-known journalist and TV broadcaster) and group member Malcolm Ives. The Del Rio Four now wrote many of their own numbers, and made demo discs with Excel recording studios in Shipley. One of their numbers recorded there was 'I'll Come Back to You', which was quite a hit with their many fans.

The group began to change its members regularly, resulting in 1965 with a change of name to The Chapters. They had some success after gaining a recording contract with Pye records, which led to the release in May 1965 of 'Can't Stop Thinking About Her' and 'Dance Little Lady'. A little later the group disbanded.

Ray Kennan (b. 1942, Bingley) vocals

Ray lived on Kent Road close to the Oval housing estate, Bingley. He was a supreme showman, whose rock 'n' roll career demands to be recorded. His on-stage exhibitions pervaded every aspect of his musical career. Recently he revealed that in his capacity as group newsmaker, many of his outrageous tales were greatly exaggerated for publicity's sake, while others were pure fabrication.

After attending Bingley Grammar School Ray was employed for a short while by Harvey Smith (the show-jumper), who lived in High Eldwick on the outskirts of Bingley. However, he found that he had quite a good singing voice, the type that local rock 'n' roll groups were looking out for. His first group was The Belvardos, and he followed this with The Deepbeats – having left his employment with Harvey Smith. To supplement the small income from his singing, he worked for a joiner in Bingley and as a petrol pump attendant. Things got better when he joined the Del Rio Four as vocalist and compère, playing a season with them at Butlin's.

Tales about Ray soon became legion. Examples include the time he set fire to the piano during a performance. He drove a van through double locked doors at Bradford's Lyceum ballroom and onto the stage, then got out and calmly took a bow. On another occasion he turned a fire hose on a compère. Though his antics gained him extreme sanctions from the group he was with, his talents were considered far greater than his liabilities, a judgement that was borne out later when he went on to perform with many international artists.

Ray later formed the Ray Kennan Combo, which was considered to be one of the most professional groups in Yorkshire. Being the consummate showman, he kitted out the band in smart dark suits, white shirts and fashionable Slim Jim ties. After he disbanded the Combo he joined The Toledos, followed by the Quiet Three and then a ten-piece rock 'n' roll band called The Governors. Then Ray decided to go it alone and overnight became a single vocalist compère, which brought him instant success.

Now firmly established, he went on tour with Lulu, the Rolling Stones, Manfred Mann and Screaming Lord Sutch. Shows followed at famous Eden Saloon in Berlin, with Sammy Davis Junior, Jerry Lee Lewis and Johnny Cash. Tom Jones, an unknown quantity in the early 1960s, spent some time working with Ray. It is hard to imagine today: Ray Kennan and Tom Jones in the phone box on Cornwall Road in Bingley chasing bookings! Ray generally used that phone box as his office.

He went on to compère shows. At one of his last he took Blackpool by storm. P.J. Proby failed to turn up to perform at the North Pier and Ray was asked to take over. His stage presence, experience and easy singing style more than compensated the disappointed Proby fans.

With the world seemingly his oyster, with his usual unpredictability Ray coolly packed his tent and slowly stole away. He had had enough. He later said that 'Bradford had a lot of talent, but perhaps we were a bit lazy. There was so much going on locally that many of us did not bother to seek our fortunes in London, where the real money was being made. Besides, some of the clapped-out vans we drove probably wouldn't have got us there. With respect, some of

The consummate showman Ray Kennan.

the groups were managed by men who had been greengrocers or butchers. They were successful local tradesmen but they weren't Brian Epsteins.'

Later Ray became a successful property developer. He is truly a man of many talents.

Martin Kershaw (b. 1942, Bradford) bass guitar
Martin later moved to London and became a session musician.

Malcolm Ives aka Mark Jordan (b. 1940, Shipley) lead guitar
Malcolm lived in Shipley. After the Del Rio Four had folded, Malcolm continued in showbusiness and became a well-known and respected theatrical agent, under the name of Mark Jordan.

Kenny Gough (b. 1941, Bradford) drums
See Mick Sagar and the Cresters.

Malcolm (Mally) Crossley (b. 1939, Cleckheaton) drums
Formerly of the Del Rio Four, Mally joined the group, now called The Chapters, in 1965 and remained with them until they disbanded in 1966. In 1968 he joined up with his good friend bass player Dave de Courcy, who was playing with the rock 'n' roll pianist Dave Lee as part of the Dave Lee Trio. The drummer had just left and they were due to appear at Butlin's, Pwllheli, so Mally filled the position. He had previously done a summer season there with the Del Rio Four. The season ended in September, and after returning home they made a short tour of the northern clubs.

It was now late 1968 and Dave and Mally both decided to leave and form a new band. This never materialised, however, as Mally, his wife Ann and two children, Andrew and Joanne, emigrated to Australia at the beginning of 1969. He continued to play with bands there, and his son also became a drummer for a few years. Sadly Ann died, but Mally and his family still live out there.

Mick Kershaw (b. 1942, Bradford) rhythm guitar and vocals
See Sansovenos.

Ian (Junior) Atkinson (b. 1943, Hebden Bridge) lead guitar
Ian attended St Thomas More Secondary School. He was with the Del Rio Four for only a short time but made his mark. Leaving them to join Hedgehoppers Anonymous, who had already had a hit with 'Good News Week', Ian later joined the popular Morton Frazer Harmonica Gang, who played in many clubs in and around Yorkshire in the 1960s and '70s. He now lives in America, where he has acquired fame as a full-time blues harmonica player – appearing many times in Las Vegas.

THE DEL-FI'S

rock 'n' roll

The Del-Fi's were, like many of the groups of that time, good musicians. They played between 1960 and 1963 and, as their publicity photograph shows, they were also very well dressed, no mean achievement when wages in the early 1960s were just a few pounds a week. The group line-up was Chris Young, lead guitarist, Harry Unsworth, bass guitar, John Whalley, rhythm guitar, and a fresh faced young lad, drummer Barry Young. They became very popular, playing many times at the Craven Heifer in Manchester Road, the Students Club, the Gaumont and Majestic ballrooms and many of the Conservative, Liberal, and Labour social clubs in a radius of 40 miles. After three years they parted company. However, they had made their mark and are still remembered as part of 'the scene'.

Chris Young (1945–2000, Bradford) lead guitar

Harry Unsworth (b. 1938, Bishop Auckland, County Durham) bass guitar

Harry attended Green Lane Junior School and then Drummond Road Secondary Modern School in Bradford. Leaving school aged fifteen, his first job was for Grattan Warehouse on Ingleby Road. Later he joined Modern Paviors in Saltaire Road, Shipley, in their market garden for three years.

It was during this period that he learned to play bass guitar (Fender bass), and he joined the newly formed Del-Fi's in 1960. When the group broke up in late 1962 he joined Alan Knight and the Chessmen, and was one of the group members who played at the world famous 2i's Coffee Bar in Old Crompton Street, Soho. This was a rare achievement in itself and worthy of inclusion in any rock 'n' roll CV.

After leaving The Chessmen in 1965 Harry wanted a 'proper job', and after various positions he became self employed, cleaning windows, painting houses and sandblasting and restoring houses and the 'dark satanic mills' of Bradford, culminating in the cleaning of the British Museum in London.

The polished and well groomed Del-Fi's, 1960–3. Left to right: Chris Young, Harry Hunsworth, John Whalley, Barry Young.

Other businesses followed, including Bradford Kart Racing, situated at the bottom of Manchester Road, Direct Dial Chauffeur, based at his home in Baildon, and Advanced Driver Training Services. His hobbies and pastimes are hang gliding and flying microlights, which he has done for eighteen years. He has been married to Dorothy for fifty-two years, and is still going strong.

John Whalley (b. 1942, Bradford) rhythm guitar
In late 1962 John joined Alan Knight and the Chessmen.

Barry Young (1947–2008, Bradford) drums
Barry was later a professional drummer and teacher. For a time he also had two shops that sold drums and other percussion, Koda up Church Bank and Buddies on Manningham Lane.

The Dingos at the Majestic, 1959. Left to right: Irvine 'Smudge' Smith, Garth Cawood, Kenny Fowler, Malcolm Clark, Ian Bannister.

1960. A pianist joins the group: Terry Moran, later to be known as Dadio. Back row, left to right: Garth Cawood, Terry Moran. Middle row: Malcolm Clark, Irvine 'Smudge' Smith. Front row: Kenny Fowler, Ian Bannister.

THE DINGOS

rock 'n' roll

Between 1956 and 1962 probably one of the best of Bradford's rock 'n' roll groups was The Dingos. Originally formed as a skiffle group, it was a young DJ entrepreneur named Garth Cawood who saw the group's potential. In a short time he made them into one of the most professional and entertaining groups in Yorkshire and beyond. As their front man he used his charisma to full effect as compère, and from time to time accompanied the group with vocals, or playing the tambourine or maracas – which was a sight to behold.

The founder members of The Dingos skiffle group were Kenny Fowler, lead guitar, brothers Irvine Mcveagh and Maurice Mcveagh, both rhythm guitar, Irvin (Smudge) Smith, washboard and thimbles, and Brian Lawrence, tea chest bass (painted by Smudge with the group's name). They were part of the Bradford Police Bugle and Drum Band, a marching band based at the former Feversham Street School in Leeds Road, Bradford. One night in 1956 Kenny Fowler arrived at band practice with a guitar and before practice began, improvised a jam session with Billie Gillespie, one of the drummers in the police band. On hearing them Irvin Mcveagh suggested they should start a skiffle group! Lonnie Donegan's 'Rock Island Line' was number eight in the hit parade at this time. Kenny's dad came up with the name The Dingos.

Their first paid booking was at Tyersal Working Men's Club and they also entered the skiffle group competition at the New Victoria, hosted by Jim Dale, coming second to The Sidewinders, a group from Bradford University. After a couple of years skiffle was on the decline and rock 'n' roll numbers were in the group's repertoire. With the intervention of Garth in 1958 the group was transformed.

Brian Lawrence left at this time, as did Maurice and Irvine, because of career moves. The new line-up was Garth Cawood, manager, vocals and compère, Kenny Fowler, lead guitar and vocals, the irrepressible Malcolm Clark, rhythm guitar and vocals, Ian Bannister, bass guitar, and Smudge Smith, drums.

The Dingos' repertoire for the next four years was of top quality, and was played by top musicians at most venues in Yorkshire. The line-up changed

The Dingos play at the Majestic, 1960. Left to right: Terry 'Dadio' Moran, Garth Cawood, Malcolm Clark, Ian Bannister, Kenny Fowler, Irvin 'Smudge' Smith.

A duet from two of Bradford's most talented musicians. Malcolm Clarke (left) and Kenny Fowler.

Brothers Irvine and Morris McVeagh, two of the original Dingos.

Spike O'Brien and Sammy King both joined The Dingos in early 1960. Garth Cawood looks on with approval. Left to right: Spike O'Brien, Sammy King, Garth Cawood.

Bass guitarist Dave Butterfield left The Cresters to join The Dingos, becoming a great asset to the group.

Keith Sivyer was a vocalist for The Dingos in 1961 and 1962. He went on to be a top comedian for over twenty-five years, known as Bobby Kimble.

many times, with most members going on to play with other popular groups. Later members were Terry (Dadio) Moran, piano and vocals, Sammy King, guitar and vocals, Keith Sivyer, vocals, Stuart Sutcliffe, bass guitar, Dougie Lamb, bass guitar, Dave Butterfield, bass guitar, Brian (Spike) O'Brien, piano, and for a short time three girl singers, the Three Ds, as well as Helen McCaffery, later of The Tomboys.

Some of the original members still get together, especially for the very successful Bradford rock 'n' roll reunions held each year.

Kenny Fowler (b. 1940, Bradford) lead guitar and vocals

Kenny attended Bradford Moor Junior School. Later, being a gifted artist, he was given a place at Carlton Junior Art College, which as well as teaching general education gave young artists like Ken an early opportunity to develop their artistic flair. Then he became a student at Bradford Art College.

It was during these early years that Kenny taught himself to play the guitar, becoming one of the most brilliant lead guitarists and vocalists in the area. He was with The Dingos for over seven years, until the group disbanded in 1962. Who can forget his rendering of the Elvis Presley hit 'Honey Don't'? It was one of his best.

After leaving art college Kenny joined the advertising firm of Downey Parker, the first rung of the ladder in his career as an illustrator. He later moved to Leeds with another advertising company.

When The Dingos disbanded Kenny played for some time with Cliff and Brenda with the Dominators, after which he called it a day to concentrate on his career. Over the years his work as an architectural illustrator has been much respected in the building industry. From 1990 he has sometimes returned to the world of rock 'n' roll, especially at the Bradford rock 'n' roll reunions. Kenny, now semi-retired, still lives in the Bradford area with his wife Jenny and family

Irvin (Smudge) Smith (b. 1942, Bradford) washboard and drums

Smudge worked in the ticket office (designing price cards, etc. for display) at Busby's on Manningham Lane. He was not only a very proficient drummer but one of the few who always seemed to have a smile on his face. After The Dingos, he went on to play with other groups, including The Tuxedos. In the mid 1960s Smudge got married and went to live in Australia, where his sister was living. He now lives in California with his wife and family, and he still plays the drums from time to time.

Irvine Mcveagh (b. 1939, Bradford) rhythm guitar

On leaving school Irvine became an apprentice wool grader at Scottish Wool Growers in Church Bank. As well as playing rhythm guitar he managed The Dingos during their skiffle days. He later moved to Hexham. Now retired and living in Scotland with his wife Maggie, Irvine spends most of his time doing voluntary charity work, and is an inspector of elderly people's homes. From time to time he enjoys folk signing.

Brian Lawrence (b. 1942, Bradford) tea chest bass
While still at Lapage Street Secondary Modern School, aged fourteen he joined The Dingos skiffle group, playing the tea-chest bass until 1958. He later worked as a wool sorter at Dawson's Mill, Leeds Road.

Maurice Mcveagh (b. 1940, Bradford) rhythm guitar
Maurice played rhythm guitar and shared vocals in The Dingos skiffle group. When he left school he worked at Brown, Muffs as a junior salesman in the radio and TV department. He later moved to Super Radio Company on Bank Street. Now retired, Maurice lives in the Shipley area with his wife Sandra; they are both prominent line-dancers. Maurice has also been connected for over thirty years with semi-professional football club Eccleshill United, and is now an ambassador for them.

Malcolm Clark (1943–68, Bradford) rhythm guitar and vocals
Malcolm lived on the Thorpe Edge estate and attended Belle Vue Grammar School. Leaving school at sixteen, he worked in a tailor's shop on Thornton Road. When he left The Dingos he joined The Cresters and turned professional. Malcolm's rendition of Roy Orbison's 'Crying' was magical, and almost identical to the original. Malcolm sadly passed away in his twenties, a sad loss to his many friends and admirers, leaving an underlying regret of what might have been.

Ian Bannister (b. 1942, Bradford) bass guitar
Ian attended Swain House First School and Eccleshill Secondary Modern School, leaving in 1957. Aged fifteen, he started work at English Electric as an armature winder. He was only there for six months before he left for what he said was 'the best job in the world', at Kay Thornham Wholesale Hardware in Bradford.

He had taught himself to play bass guitar, and in 1958 was proficient enough to join The Dingos. He would later say how lucky he was to join such a group where he could learn so much from the other members. In 1959 Ian heard that The Cresters were looking for a bass player, so he rang Richard Harding and asked for an audition, and was amazed when he said yes. The audition was a success, and he was asked to join them. Though very sorry to leave the Dingos, he felt privileged to join such a high-profile group as The Cresters.

After his musical life came to an end in 1963, Ian started work in the building industry, and in about 1965 he formed his own building business. In 1974 he left the UK to live in Australia, and is now retired with his wife Chiz (short for Chizuru); they live on the Gold Coast, Queensland, and spend their time travelling and generally relaxing .He says he still dreams about his wonderful rock 'n' roll days.

Terry (Dadio) Moran (1938–2001, Bradford) piano
See Dal Stevens and the Blue Jays.

Sammy King (b. 1941, Dewsbury) guitar-and vocals
See profile.

Stuart Sutcliffe (b. 1944, Bradford) bass guitar
Stuart lived in the Manchester Road area. He took over from Ian Bannister after his move to The Cresters. Stuart was quite an accomplished bass player and was with The Dingos until they disbanded. His father Wilf, who had a fruit and vegetable shop in Bankfoot, sometimes used his van to drive the group around.

Dougie Lamb (b. 1942, Bradford) bass guitar
See Dal Stevens and The Blue Jays.

Dave Butterfield (b. 1940, Bradford) bass guitar
See Mike Sagar and the Cresters.

Keith Sivyer (b. 1936, Birkenshaw) vocals
Keith attended Waterloo Junior School and Pudsey Grammar School. Leaving school in 1951, he worked for Bastow and Ryder (posters and showcards) in Bradford, and later spent three years at Busby's (ticket writing and show cards) until 1957, when he served his National Service with the Duke of Wellington's Regiment. Afterwards he returned to Busby's.

In the winter of 1961–2, now married to Frances and with two children, he found that he had quite a flair for rock 'n' roll vocals. Keith answered an advert in the *Telegraph and Argus* that invited singers to audition to join The Dingos, advertised as a 'rock, rhythm and blues group'. He attended the audition at the Tudor ballroom in Dudley Hill, and discovered that his former workmate at Busby's Irvin (Smudge) Smith was already well established as the group's drummer.

Many hopeful lads applied, and when Keith's turn came he sang Elvis's 'Surrender' and Gene Vincent's arrangement of 'Over the Rainbow', and got the job. His first appearance was at Croft's Annual Dance at the Kings Hall and Queens Hall, for which he had only a couple of nights' practice, being replacement vocalist for the great Sammy King. He sang four songs that Sammy had performed – an up-tempo 'Mona Lisa', 'You Must Have Been a Beautiful Baby', the up-tempo 'Lonesome Road' and a slow rock version of 'My Mother's Eyes'. These were numbers that the group was comfortable with, and Keith knew the words!. They went down well.

As the weeks progressed Keith was still confined to his four standard performances, and after a Saturday night at the Kings Hall Garth took him to one side and said that he was going to have to let him go – so his dream ended. Keith had never in his heart of hearts looked upon himself as a rock 'n' roll singer, but at the time had needed the money – so needs must! To compensate, Garth had fixed up an audition for him with Billy Hey's Dance Band at the Majestic ballroom. A singing group, the Clive Carnazzo Trio, appeared between the band sets, and when they heard him sing 'Autumn Leaves' and 'Blue Moon' (performed without any rehearsal) they asked if he would be interested in joining them for a summer season in Bournemouth. Keith's home life did not allow this, so he had to decline what might have been a promising offer.

Once again Garth Cawood did him a favour by pointing him down another path, a path that let him sing and make people laugh. Keith went on to perform for over twenty-five years as Bobby Kimble, one of the North's top comedy entertainers, until finally retiring in 2001. Keith is also a well-known cartoonist, especially for his beloved Bradford City fanzine cartoon 'The City Gent'. Keith still lives in the Allerton area of Bradford with his wife and family, and still looks back on his few months with The Dingos with great affection.

Brian (Spike) O Brien (1940–2000, Bradford) piano
See profile.

The Three Ds vocal trio
See profile.

Ellen (aka Helen) McCaffery (b. 1946, Bradford)
See the Tomboys with Helen.

The original Evergreens, looking very smart. Left to right: Dave de Courcy, Derek Rotheray, Tony Bentley, Paul Bentley.

The Evergreens among the evergreens! Left to right: new drummer Alan Jones, Dave de Courcy, Tony Bently, Paul Bentley.

THE EVERGREENS/THE CHARRINGTONS/ THE CHAPTERS

rock 'n' roll

The Evergreens sprung into life in 1962 when Dave de Courcy, with YMCA football colleagues Tony Bentley and brother Paul, all keen to play the guitar, decided to have some lessons from a local banjo and guitar teacher, Ernie Foster. As soon as they knew a few chords they decided to form their first group, The Evergreens. The line-up was Tony, lead guitar and vocals, Paul, rhythm guitar and vocals, and Dave, bass guitar and vocals, with the addition of a drummer, a West Bowling lad named Derek Rotheray. With practice and endeavour their talent showed through, and soon they were playing at many local venues including the East Bowling Unity Club, the Mecca and Majestic ballrooms, the Star and Garter at Kirkstall, where they secured a weekly booking, and still in Leeds the Boulevard Beat Club and the Wild Man on the Leeds to York ring road, both favourite venues with the group.

Later in 1962, while playing at the famous 2i's Coffee Bar in London (where such stars as Tommy Steele, Cliff Richard and Wee Willie Harris were discovered), a London agent offered them a contract to play in Germany on the Hamburg circuit, but owing to other commitments and the short notice given they had to decline the offer. Around this time drummer Derek Rotheray decided to move on, and his place was taken by Alan Jones who lived at The Napoleon pub in Wakefield Road. Alan was not only a very good drummer but also an equally good vocalist.

The group now had four vocalists, which allowed them to increase their repertoire to include hit songs of the time by Cliff Richard, Shadows instrumentals and later The Hollies, The Searchers, The Beatles and many more. Unfortunately, after a sudden exodus of members the group disbanded, leaving just Alan Jones and bass player Dave de Courcy. Not giving up, they decided to advertise for two new members, and after the first audition at The Napoleon they were joined by rhythm guitarist Dave Clegg from Frizinghall and Alan (Ed) Thornton from Girlington on lead guitar, both of whom were also good vocalists. At this time they changed their name to The Charringtons (taken from the brewery that owned The Napoleon), and Alan's father started to manage them. The style of music they performed also changed, and they began to be more rock 'n' roll and blues orientated, mainly thanks to Ed Thornton, who was a great lead guitarist.

Sadly the Charringtons did not reign very long and in 1964, owing to disagreements, a new drummer was required again. The position was taken by an ex-member of the Del Rio Four, the popular Mally Crossley. In early 1965 the group's name was changed to The Chapters, after a group that Mal Crossley had previously been with but no longer played. It was now a really good line-up that played exciting rock 'n' roll and great blues numbers (Chuck Berry, John Lee Hooker, etc.) but was also still able to cover The Beatles, The Hollies, The Searchers and The Kinks. It was an exciting time, particularly around the vibrant pub scene of Leeds like Haddon Hall, the Yorkshire Hussars at the end of The Headrow and up York Road, The Broadway, the White Horse, The Prospect and their earlier favourite in Kirkstall, the Star and Garter. They played all of these venues many times to packed houses.

Then in mid-1966 Ed Thornton left the band to emigrate to Canada and the group disbanded, as it was said they could not replace such a brilliant guitarist.

Dave (The Baron) de Courcy (b. 1944, Bradford) bass guitar and vocals

Dave lived in the Manchester Road area and attended All Saints' School in Little Horton. Aged fifteen and with an interest in skiffle, in his last year at school he made a Spanish guitar with the help of his teacher. Unfortunately at that time he did not know how to play it! His first job on leaving school was 'int mill' like many other fifteen year olds of the time, and he took a six year apprenticeship as a woolcomb hackle and gill maker (pinsetter). As rock 'n' roll came into his life he soon became a talented bass player, and spent his early years with The Evergreens, The Charringtons and The Chapters, leaving them in 1966.

A few months after The Chapters had disbanded Dave was at the East Bowling Unity Club with his girlfriend Carole, and he saw the Dave Lee Trio performing the pure rock 'n' roll of Jerry Lee Lewis. He was impressed, and happened to mention to a guy sitting close to them that he would not mind playing in a band like that. He replied that he was Dave Lee's cousin and that Dave was looking for a bass player. Dave introduced himself, and arranged to meet the group the next day at a venue in Leeds. He got the job, and started almost straight away, with Dave Lee on piano and lead vocals, Mick Craven on drums and himself on bass guitar.

They had many resident weekly bookings, for example The Castle and The Talbot in Bradford. They also played many clubs, mainly around Yorkshire. It was in 1968 that they accepted a summer season at Butlin's Holiday Camp, Pwllheli. Unfortunately Mick Craven could not go, so Dave brought in his good friend and drummer Malcolm (Mally) Crossley. They were now working professionally, and had given up their jobs. The summer season was hard work, playing every lunchime and night, with one day off per week, but it was worth it. Sometimes they worked with the likes of Ken Dodd, Bob Monkhouse, Kenny

Dave (The Baron) de Courcy, an excellent bass guitarist and founder member of The Evergreens.

Ball and resident camp comic Frank Carson. Their residency at the camp was the Regency Bar, a huge building that held around 2,000 people. When word got around that they were rock 'n' rollers, they broke all records for bar-takings and attendances.

The season ended in September, and after a short tour of the northern clubs Dave and Malcolm left. In 1969 Dave married his girlfriend Carole; he took a job with a local builder and settled down to married life. He did not play again until 1972, when he joined a vocal harmony group called Jan, Dil and Joe, and he stayed with them until they disbanded in 1976. Later Dave joined a new band called Hi-fly, and stayed with them until 1979 when he stopped playing. By this time two daughters had been born, Sarah and Leanne, and he had formed his own building business – which still exists.

Now married for over forty years, Dave lives with his wife Carole and family in Gomersal and has still not retired. He still gets the old bass guitar out for the rock 'n' roll reunions: as he says, 'Old habits die hard'.

Paul Bentley (b 1942, Bradford) rhythm guitar and vocals
Paul lived in Bierley. Some time after the group disbanded he left England to seek pastures new in San Francisco.

Tony Bentley (b. 1944, Bradford) lead guitar and vocals
Tony was Paul's younger brother and also lived in Bierley. When the group disbanded he went on to concentrate on his own butcher's business, and never resumed his musical career.

Derek Rotheray (b. 1942, Bradford) drums
Derek left the group in 1962 and finished his drumming career. Later he went to live in London.

Alan Jones (b. 1949, Bradford) drums
Alan lived in Wakefield Road at his father's pub, The Napoleon. An excellent drummer and vocalist, Alan was with The Evergreens for only a short time, through its transition to the Charringtons. In 1964 he and his father moved on, and he later became an accomplished solo artist.

Alan (Ed) Thornton (b. 1945, Bradford) lead guitar and vocals
Alan lived in Girlington and was a rock 'n' roll guitarist and blues player. He left the group in 1966 to emigrate to Canada. He was irreplaceable, being a brilliant guitarist and way ahead of his time.

Dave Clegg (b. 1945, Bradford) rhythm guitar and vocals
Dave lived in Frizinghall. He joined Charringtons and continued with The Chapters until 1966 when the group disbanded. During 1968–9 he went on to play on the cruise ship *Carmania*, then based in Miami and touring the Bahamas. He met his future wife Virginia on board and then went to live in Melbourne, Australia, where they married and had two daughters. In Australia he played with bands called F Troop and The Rockafellas up until 1989, and

even met up with former group member Mally Crossley to play at the odd venue.

Malcolm (Mally) Crossley (b. 1939, Cleckheaton) drums
See the Del Rio Four.

Glyn Whiteoak in the teenage pose of the 1950s.

THE FLAMINGOS

rock 'n' roll

Between 1960 and 1962 another group of lads who were born and lived in the Keighley area got together to form The Flamingos. The group line-up was fourteen-year-old Jeff Birtley, rhythm guitar, Glyn Whiteoak, lead guitar, Maurice Atkinson, bass guitar and his brother Ray, drums. Unusually the group had no vocalist, so for the first few months their small repertoire was that of the popular Shadows and The Ventures, which left their audience more than a little perplexed and frustrated. The time came when a change was required, and it was the drummer Ray Atkinson who took on the role of vocalist, while Jeff tried his hand as a drummer.

This worked quite well, and what the lads lacked musically they compensated for with enthusiasm, which resulted in them obtaining many local bookings. Haworth Cycling Club and the RAOB Skipton, Crosshills Working Men's Club, Glusburn Gala and St Thomas's Hall, Sutton, were among the popular venues, and they also had a regular weekly booking at the South Craven School Youth Club. As the group were short of transport and the school was only 100yds from where they practised, they were able to transport their equipment in a wheelbarrow! Similarly, when they were playing for a private function at the Coronation Hotel in Gisburn, they were able to send their equipment on the bus that was taking the guests. The trials and tribulations of new groups at that time were daunting.

Like other groups trying to get on the ladder of success it did not work out for The Flamingos, and in mid-1962 the lads went their own way.

Jeff Birtley aka Jeff Daniels (b. 1946, Keighley) rhythm guitar and drums

Although born in Keighley, Jeff later moved to Crosshills, where he attended schools in Sutton. Aged fourteen in 1960, after learning to play the rhythm guitar, he joined The Flamingos. Leaving school aged fifteen, Jeff was employed for the next three years at the Crosshills Co-op. During his time with The Flamingos he was not satisfied by playing rhythm guitar, and after much practice he became a proficient lead guitarist. In 1962 he left The Flamingos to

The Flamingos from Craven practise in Silsden Hall. Left to right: Glyn Whiteoak, Jeff Birtley, Maurice Atkinson, Ray Atkinson.

join a Settle based group called The Dalesmen as lead guitarist. Work was plentiful as the group could also play for ballroom dances, because they had a clavioline player. Venues stretched from clubs in Settle to the Floral Hall in Morecambe, and the group played regularly at the Imperial ballroom in Nelson, which was quite a hot spot in the 1960s. Some of the acts they supported were P.J. Proby, Johnny Kidd and the Pirates and Manfred Mann. However, the group started getting complaints from the management about their vocalist and were threatened with no more bookings unless he was replaced. This was the start of Jeff's singing career, as he took over as lead vocalist and they continued to be booked at the Imperial.

In 1964, with four years' experience behind him, Jeff left The Dalesmen to form a new group called Sandra and the Montanas. This was the same year that he left the Co-op to work for C.H. Fletchers in Silsden, where he would spend the next nineteen years. In 1966 he married Elizabeth.

The Montanas changed their name to the Mark Russell Four, and Jeff continued with them until well into the 1970s. Later he purchased a keyboard, and after tuition he became so proficient that he decided to go solo, playing the circuit of working men's clubs – and at the same time (for Equity reasons) changing his name to Jeff Daniels. He went on to play at many popular local venues, including the Furnace Inn in Bradford, where following artistes like Roy Bould and Dave Lee could be quite a challenge.

In 1983 Jeff was made redundant and decided to play the clubs professionally as a guitarist/vocalist. During his spare time he had been creating backing tracks, and having developed this line of work into quite a successful business he retired from his solo work in about 1990, and he is still concentrating on backing tracks.

During the 1990s an old friend of his, Brian Tordoff (of Brian T. and the Strollers), asked him to join his group, which had re-formed earlier for an anniversary bash. This was a fabulous trip down memory lane for Jeff, back to the music he grew up with.

In 1995 Jeff moved to Silsden, and he still lives there with his second wife Jean and daughter Sarah.

Glyn Whiteoak (1941–86, Sutton) lead guitar
Glyn lived in Wighill Street. He attended Sutton Primary school and Keighley Boys Grammar School. A very accomplished and well-respected self-taught guitarist, after his time with the Flamingos he only played for his own amusement. Sadly, Glyn passed away aged forty five.

Maurice Atkinson (b. 1940, Crosshills) bass guitar
Maurice was the eldest member of the group. He attended Sutton Primary School and Keighley Grammar School. A self-taught guitarist, he purchased the cheapest on the market, a Rossetti 7. After The Flamingos he never bothered playing again.

Ray Atkinson (b. 1943, Crosshills) drums and vocals
Ray was younger brother of Maurice Atkinson, and he took over as compère and vocalist. After the Flamingos broke up Ray went on to front local group Cheap 'n' Nasty on the keyboards. This group had a cult following in the Keighley area for a few years.

ROCK • POPS • BALLADS • RHYTHM'N BLUES
CLUBS • PUBS • PARTIES • CABARET Etc:
THE
FOUR
MUSKETEERS
Rock'n Rhythm Combo'
Write:
Mr.K.S.ARTIST.
25,RAYMOND DRIVE,
BRADFORD. 5.

THE FOUR MUSKETEERS

rock 'n' roll

When drummer Keith Artist left The Crusaders in 1963 he decided to form his own group, something he had wanted to do for a while. The first to join him was his good friend Dennis (Duane) Oliver, also late of The Crusaders. Dennis, as well as being a good bass guitarist, was also a first-rate vocalist in the style of Cliff Richard. The important position of lead guitarist was soon taken by the very competent Paul Flintoft, who was matched by the excellent rhythm guitarist Dave Biven, and of course the group leader Keith. So the Four Musketeers were born.

As all members had experience of some kind, it was not long before they had quite a repertoire of rock numbers, including Beatles, Rolling Stones and Chuck Berry covers, and especially Cliff Richard numbers for Duane to emulate. Soon they had quite a following at many of the dance halls that were still open, and also performed at working men's clubs, which paid top groups well.

It has to be said that most, if not all groups, had times when things did not go well, and The Four Musketeers had theirs – a memorable occasion at The Railway pub in Dewsbury. It was mid-winter with heavy snow falling, and The Four Musketeers had a mid-week booking. They arrived at approximately 7.30pm and went to the music room to set up, with not a soul in sight. The landlord said, 'Well, seeing as you've turned up I'd better pay you, but if I do you'll have to play.' This was fair enough. By the time they were ready to play an old man had come into the room with his dog, and had sat down at the back smoking his pipe and drinking his pint. The Musketeers did their first spot to this lonely figure in the room, with a resounding silence after each number. Just before the second spot the old man went to the gents, leaving his dog waiting for his return. For the first two numbers they played to the dog. Fortunately a few more people arrived as the night went on, so it wasn't a total disaster.

Similar situations were put down as just one of the many tribulations on the way to stardom, but in 1965, after two years of some success, the group decided to pack in, the main reason being career commitments.

However, this was not the end of the Four Musketeers. In 1981, after sixteen years, they were back again with the original line-up, the only change being that they now called themselves Resurrection, and had reinvented themselves as a comedy show group. For the next five years until 1986 Keith, Dennis, Paul and Dave played on the working men's club circuit in the north of England. In 2003–4 they were back again, playing charity gigs for Take Heart, and at private functions and birthday bashes. Over the years there are not many groups of four members who have got together to entertain over a forty year period with the same line-up, albeit with a different name.

Keith Artist (b. 1941, Bradford) drums
See profile.

Paul Flintoft (b. 1946, Bradford) lead guitar and vocals
Paul attended Wibsey Secondary School. Leaving school aged fifteen, he served an apprenticeship as a gas fitter for the Halifax gas board. Later he moved to Dewsbury as a gas inspector. In 1981-86 he rejoined the Four Musketeers under its new name of Resurrection, and again in 2003–4. Paul, a widower, now lives in Middlesbrough.

Dave Biven (b. 1943, Bradford) rhythm guitar
Dave went to Priestmans Secondary School and was later employed as a joiner at Wilkinson's in Hall Lane. In 1981 he rejoined the Four Musketeers, when the group re-formed as Resurrection, and was back with them again in 2003–4. Later Dave moved to St Anne's on Sea, where he now lives with his wife Pat.

Dennis (Duane) Oliver (b. 1944, Bradford) bass guitar
See Dal Stevens and the Four Dukes.

GARTH CAWOOD
rock 'n' roll DJ and showbusiness entrepreneur

The name of Garth Cawood is synonymous with Bradford rock 'n' roll. He was born in Idle in 1940, and attended Greengates Primary School and St Barnabas's School in Heaton, when the family moved to Victor Road. Later, when his parents took over the Tudor ballroom, he attended Buttershaw School, and after numerous moves the family finally made their home in Undercliffe.

Garth was probably one of the earliest ballroom DJs in the UK. He began his career at the Tudor ballroom, Dudley Hill, in the mid-1950s, where he used a modern radiogram that held eight 78rpm records. While the machine was making the automatic change between discs Garth gave some form of introduction. It was primitive but it worked, and he became the forerunner of the modern disco DJ.

Garth left school at fifteen and joined the *Telegraph & Argus* as a trainee press photographer. After four years he moved to well-known Bradford photographer Eric's, situated in the Mechanics' Institute opposite the Town Hall. In the late 1950s he joined The Dingos. Garth had seen them many times at his parents' ballroom, and while they were clearly quite talented he quickly recognised that their organisation and professionalism were not so hot. At the end of each number played, for example, there was no thank you or an introduction to the next song. Garth's arrival turned The Dingos into one of the most professional and entertaining rock 'n' roll groups in Yorkshire.

After a few years it was time to move on, and with his talent as a compère Garth was soon in demand from the many package shows performing at cinemas and other venues around the UK. He soon became a top compère and a friend of The Beatles, the Rolling Stones, The Searchers and many others. He also had DJ spots in the late 1950s at the Gaumont and the Majestic in Bradford, and was the first DJ at the new Mecca on Manningham Lane.

After all this, in the mid-1960s Garth spent five years at Brigitte Bardot's club Esquade in St Tropez, entertaining the wealthy. In 1970 he was back in the UK in his capacity as compère, notably at the Savoy Club, Wakefield, Batley Variety Club and Keighley Variety Club, all top cabaret venues. During this

Garth Cawood was one of Bradford's original DJs.

While with the Dingos, Garth sang a repertoire of pop numbers, enhancing the group's versatility.

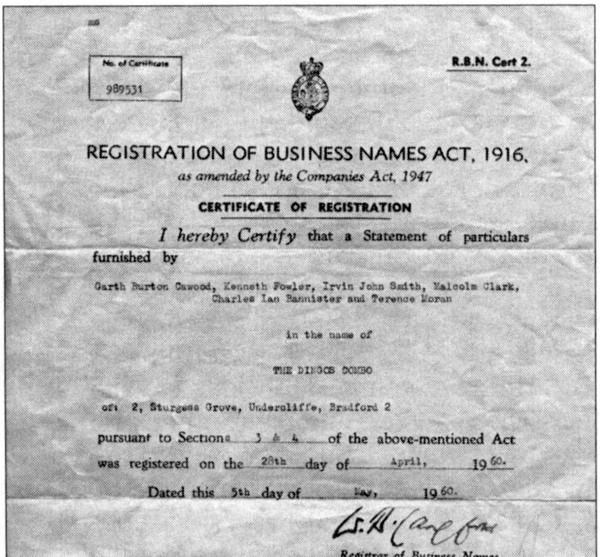

No. of Certificate 989531

R.B.N. Cert 2.

REGISTRATION OF BUSINESS NAMES ACT, 1916,
as amended by the Companies Act, 1947

CERTIFICATE OF REGISTRATION

I hereby Certify that a Statement of particulars furnished by

Garth Burton Cawood, Kenneth Fowler, Irvin John Smith, Malcolm Clark, Charles Ian Bannister and Terence Moran

in the name of

THE DINGOS COMBO

of: 2, Sturgess Grove, Undercliffe, Bradford 2

pursuant to Sections 3 & 4 of the above-mentioned Act was registered on the 28th day of April, 1960.

Dated this 5th day of May, 1960.

Registrar of Business Names.

This document shows the registration of The Dingos' name as a company.

Always the showman: Garth in serious mood.

period he lived at his parents' home at Sturgess Grove, which became a travel stop for many artists of the time, including Tom Jones, Gene Vincent, Jess Conrad and Carl Denver. Garth was now working with his house band, the Mike Stuart Sound, and for a few months he had a permanent position working six days a week at the Lyceum (Talk of Yorkshire). From there he and the band moved to four days a week at the Keighley Variety Club. During this time they brought a 'theatrical illusion' act to the concerts, what was described as a 'showground experience with music'.

Building on their success, Garth and his business partner Stuart Reynolds purchased Keighley Variety Club, changing its name to the Funhouse Bar. Then they acquired the Flying Dutchman Club in Leeds Road, Bradford, and changed its name to Funny's, creating a fun club with continental overtones. The constant stream of guest stars included Garth's good friend Diana Dors and many of the cast of *Coronation Street*. In 1984 they sold both businesses, and Garth went on tour with the house band under the new name Garth Cawood's Fun House. It was in the late 1980s that he and Stuart formed Funhouse Productions, which now represents a formidable list of TV and theatre personalities. Garth still organises the very popular Bradford rock 'n' roll reunions, and fifty years on he still performs his rendition of Johnny Preston's 'Running Bear'. He lives in the Calverley area with his wife Sandra, and to date has no thoughts of retirement.

An event at a working men's club, 1964. Left to right: Dave Wiltshire, Gary Tottle (Gary Lane), Warwick Moore, Ian Brogden and Derek Searle.

Tune-up time at the Oddfellows Hall, with an older generation looking on: the one on the left is holding the microphone! Left to right: Dave Wiltshire, Gary Tottle, Derek Searle.

THE TRAVELLERS/GARY LAYNE AND THE ROCKETS

rock 'n' roll

This group started as The Travellers in the late 1950s, when a group of friends at Bolton Villas Youth Club got together. One had just got a guitar for Christmas, another made a bass out of a tea chest and somebody got a washboard – and The Travellers were born, a skiffle group playing for their own pleasure. Soon another guitar was added, then a drum, and a home-made bass replaced the tea chest: it was now a rock 'n' roll group. The line up was Gary (Lynn) Tottle (Gary Layne), vocals, Ian McCallum, lead guitar, Robert Riley, bass guitar and manager, Malcolm Egginton, rhythm guitar, and Ian Brogden, drums. In the early days, as the band moved from skiffle to rock 'n' roll, two other friends from the youth club played major roles for a short time: David Carling, bass, in 1958, and Ronnie Taylor, lead guitar, in 1958–9. Without their participation the group would never have formed. They both later moved out of the area.

As the group played their friends started dancing to their music, and soon they began playing at dances at their own and neighbouring youth clubs in Wrose and Bolton Lane. As the venues grew in size and the number of engagements increased, equipment was slowly upgraded, and practising became a routine – usually in each others' homes, to the dismay of the neighbours. Weekend performances became the norm, relying on parents to provide transport as the band members were too young to drive. Thus venues were restricted to the greater Bradford area.

Soon semi-professional, they rented a practice room at the New Inn at the top of the High Street, Idle, further upgraded their equipment, chose stage attire – red suits – and developed choreographed stage movements-of the kind that were much in vogue at that time. As the band developed and its members matured they moved on from venues like the Gaumont ballroom in Bradford and Lakean in Shipley to the Mecca ballrooms in Bradford (Locarno), Burnley, Wakefield and Leeds, and Top Rank ballrooms in Rochdale, Huddersfield, Leeds and Bradford (Majestic). These developments brought with them the necessity to have a unique name, and The Travellers wasn't seen as distinctive enough. Common practice was to use the vocalist's name, usually modified, and a group name with some sort of theme. They chose Gary Layne (from Gary Lynn) and the Rockets (since it was the era of the space race).

By 1961 they were providing their own transport, so the range of venues increased to South Yorkshire, and they played at dances throughout the mining areas around Barnsley and Doncaster and the steel areas of Rotherham and Sheffield. This included the major dance halls and also the many dances put on in local halls, and miners welfares and similar places in Wombwell, Mexborough, Upton, Maltby, South Emsall, South Kirby, Royston and Wath on Dearne. They also played at the US base at Menwith Hill, miles from anywhere. They wanted an all-night dance, but there were no girls! This minor detail was solved by sending coaches to Harrogate, Leeds and Bradford for the missing ingredient.

From 1962 the group was fully booked for more than a year in the whole of the West Riding of Yorkshire and East Lancashire, from the Imperial in Nelson to Burnley, the Co-op Hall in Darwen, Rochdale, Palins and the YMCA in Halifax, the Regent in Huddersfield, South Yorkshire, the Empire in York, venues in Harrogate, Ripon and Skipton, numerous town and village halls, including Cleckheaton, Dewsbury and Yeadon, as well as major venues in Leeds and Bradford, of which the Bradford Mecca, the Locarno ballroom, with its famous revolving stage, was the jewel in the crown.

The group was now stretched to its geographical limit. Further development would have meant going on the UK tour circuits operated by various promoters, which the Yorkshire area was sadly lacking. To do this would have meant going full time, and no doubt moving out of the area. Even so, occasional performances were made on some of the national circuits, notably at the North Pier, Blackpool.

While the group was primarily a dance band, on nights when there were no dances they continued to perform at clubs in the area, such as Laisterdyke, Lilycroft, Great Horton, Princeville, Clayton and Cottingley working men's clubs, and further afield in Morley, Kippax, Hanging Heaton, Garforth and Batley, and the Corner Pin in Barnsley – where they were greeted with words to the effect that if you were all right you might get out in one piece! They survived to play another day.

The club scene increased to compensate for the reduction in dance hall venues, with such places as the City Band Club (Bradford), Bramley Band Club and the Railway Club (Bradford), political clubs such as Idle and Shipley Conservatives, East Ward Labour and East Bowling Unity Clubs (Bradford) and the Irish Democratic Club in Batley. Sporting clubs such as Laisterdyke, Windhill and Idle cricket clubs, Sandal RUFC (Wakefield), the Old Thornesians RUFC (Thorn, Doncaster and the University of Bradford Students Union. A notable new dance hall was the Mecca in Leeds, and the group also performed at the ice skating rinks in Leeds and Bradford.

Gary Layne and the Rockets were a stand-alone group that rarely performed with other acts. There were a few exceptions, however, when they performed with notable acts such as the Four Pennies in Blackpool, and Rod

Stewart and Long John Baldry at Bradford University. In Ilkley they even shared equipment with the Nashville Teens.

The five-piece group had a stable line-up during the heyday of Bradford's rock 'n' roll scene (1959–66), but as the scene began to fade in the mid-1960s most band members moved on to pastures new. They were replaced by others including, on vocals; Kevin Woodward and Richard Jennings, Warwick (Ricky) Moore on bass guitar, and David Wiltshire on rhythm guitar. Some dates were played in 1970, but as members left it became more difficult to replace them. From a five-piece the group changed to a four-piece and then just three, until in 1970 it was no more and faded away into memory – but what a memory!

Gary (Lynn) Tottle (Gary Layne) (1944–97, Bradford) vocals

Gary lived in the Plumpton area off Wrose Road. Like the other original band members he went to Bolton Villas Congregational Church, where he was in the Boy Scouts and the youth club. Gary attended Swain House Junior School and Hutton Secondary Modern School, and later Fulneck, a private school in Pudsey for senior boys. Gary was easily identifiable in any crowd thanks to his mop of ginger hair, and answered to the name Lynn.

He worked in sales for Wilkinson and Warburton Ltd, a long-established Pudsey company engaged in the manufacture, distribution and marketing of ladies, gents' and children's wear and domestic furnishings. In 1975 he married, and for a time lived in the Northallerton, North Yorkshire, and Darlington, County Durham, areas. Later, now divorced, he moved back to Bradford, where in 1995 he married Susan Elizabeth Gooding. They lived in the Heaton area near Emm Lane.

In November 1997 Gary suffered a heart attack while playing golf, and sadly passed away.

Malcolm Egginton (b. 1943, Bradford) rhythm guitar

Malcolm attended Swain House Junior School and Thorpe Secondary Modern Schools; like the others he lived in the Plumpton area of Wrose and attended Bolton Villas Congregational Church, where he was in the Boy Scouts and a member of the youth club.

After leaving school he went to work for C&A and then Dolcis, before becoming a delivery driver for Bishops Wholesale Sweet Merchants in Bradford. In 1969 Malcolm found his true vocation when he joined the West Yorkshire Ambulance Service, whom he served in various capacities until ill health caused his premature retirement in 1995. He continued in a voluntary capacity with the service until 2007 – a highly commendable thirty-eight years of public service.

In 2005 Malcolm suffered a heart attack and in 2009 underwent a heart valve replacement procedure, after which his health improved dramatically. He has not looked back since. Malcolm first married in 1963; this ended in divorce. In 1983 he married a Bradford girl, Elizabeth Booth, and they still live in the Bradford area. They have one daughter, Lindsey, of whom they are very proud, and she is a teacher in the London area.

Ian W. Brogden (b. 1944, Bradford) drums
Also from the Plumpton area, Ian attended Swain House Junior School and Thorpe Secondary Modern School. He was a patrol leader in the Boy Scouts and a member of the youth club at Bolton Villas Congregational Church.

Following the completion of his full-time education Ian was employed by the North Eastern Gas Board. He started in 1959 as an apprentice gas fitter, and following a five year apprenticeship he completed his mandatory training and became a qualified gas engineer. He moved up into management, and during his thirty-seven year career with British Gas he held several managerial positions, his final post being as a national project manager working in Staines, Middlesex, but covering the whole of the country. He took early retirement in 1996.

In 1966 Ian married Vickie Ellam of Bradford, and they have two sons. As these children grew up Ian was heavily involved from 1977 to 1983 with their junior football club, Bradford Villa. The club was formed and managed by parents and involved youths from all over the city. They were fortunate to receive playing and training facilities at Buttershaw and Priestman Schools from the local authority. The club had four teams of different age groups playing in the Bradford and Heavy Woollen youth football leagues.

Since his retirement Ian has been greatly involved with amateur golf in the Bradford area. From 1999 until 2006 he was employed as secretary/manager of the now defunct West Bowling Golf Club, and in 2007 he was president of the Bradford and District Union of Golf Clubs.

Ian and his wife Vicky still reside in Bradford, and Ian can often be seen on many of the area's golf courses. He was a founder member of the Rockets, and the only one to remain with the group throughout its lifetime.

Ian McCallum (b. Bradford) lead guitar
Brought up in Glasgow, Ian returned to Bradford at the age of ten. He was a member of the brass section of the Hanson School Orchestra, and his musical interests included guitar, trumpet, piano and church organ. Much to his personal regret he never succeeded with the bagpipes! Ian was equally at home with classical, folk, jazz, blues and rock. He performed with The Rockets during their formative years. Leaving the group in 1963, his place was taken by Derek Searle.

After leaving full-time education, Ian initially worked in Leeds, but left the UK for Austria and Switzerland. Since his return he has lived and worked in the Leeds/Bradford area. Ian is married with a son, three daughters and a labrador.

Derek Searle (b. 1946, Bradford) lead guitar
Derek attended Drummond Road Secondary School until 1962. He worked in Bradford for Woolcombers and later for Carter Gears. He joined the Rockets when aged only seventeen, but was more than competent to take over from the experienced Ian McCallum. Derek continued with the group until it folded in 1970.

After Carter Gears Derek worked for the Kirkstall Forge Company and later for many years at Optare in Leeds. He has one daughter. Derek now lives

Drummer Ian Brogden was a founder member of The Rockets and the only one to be still with them at the end.

near Scunthorpe and travels extensively for work in the UK. He is looking forward to his retirement.

Robert (Ian) Riley (b. 1944, Bradford) bass guitar and manager

Robert initially lived in the Leaventhorpe (Thornton Road) area before his family moved across town to the Plumpton area, off Wrose Road. He was educated at Fairweather Green Junior School and Swain House Junior School. From there he went to Belle Vue Boys Grammar School. He was troop leader in the Boy Scouts at Bolton Villas Congregational Church, and was active in the youth club there, frequently organising their dances. This led to him becoming manager of the group. When a new bass guitarist was needed he was the only spare body around, so the others said to him, 'Here's a guitar, we're going to make you a star!'

After leaving the group Robert went on to the University of Bradford for seven years as an undergraduate and post-graduate student in the School of Textile Technology. He worked in the textile industry at James Drummond and Sons Ltd in Bradford, Thomas Burnley and Sons Ltd, Gomersal, and the Riding Hall Carpet group of Homfray Ltd at the former Velmar Carpet (later Whitworth Hall) plant in Batley. He was the first graduate of the University of Bradford to become a member of its staff, when he became a lecturer in textile technology. He was also appointed as external examiner for the textile degree courses at Leicester Polytechnic.

When Robert moved to Hebden Bridge he became a councillor on the Hebden Royd Town Council. When the government forced the closure of the School of Textiles he was recruited by the US, and became a professor of textiles at North Carolina State University in Raleigh. He is now a US citizen.

Robert married Lesley Bowler, a student nurse from Halifax, in 1965, and now retired they still live near Raleigh, North Carolina. They have three children (all born in Bradford) and four grandchildren (all born in America). He still supports Bradford Bulls, and was a season ticket holder at Bradford Northern before he emigrated.

David Wiltshire (b. 1945, Bradford) rhythm guitar

David attended Allerton Primary School, Daisy Hill School and Belle Vue Grammar School. In 1961, having learnt a few chords on the guitar, he tried to start a group called Lee Grant and the Toreadors at a youth club, but it never got off the ground. Leaving school in 1962, he joined the Ministry of Pensions and National Insurance in Bradford as a clerical assistant.

Having become quite a good rhythm guitarist by 1963, he was invited to join the Rockets to take the place of Malcolm Egginton, who was leaving to get married. In late 1964 David left The Rockets and moved to Nottingham, where in 1965 he joined a group called The Incrowd. In 1968 he gave up the music scene and settled down with his career in the Civil Service and took voluntary early retirement in 1995. He still does a couple of days a week for the NHS managing a large IT department in a primary care trust.

David now lives in Broadstairs in Kent with his wife Josephine, whom he married in 1973; they had two children, Rachel and Simon. Rachel now lives in Christchurch, New Zealand, and in 2009 her son Joshua was born.

Warwick (Ricky) Moore (b. 1942, Bradford) bass guitar and backing vocals

Warwick lived at Cumberland Road, Lidget Green. In the late 1950s he played double bass at Bradford's Students Club, in the same line-up as his brother, on their jazz nights. Having taken up the bass guitar, he joined The Rockets in 1963, but later left to play with the resident dance band at the Leeds Majestic. It was not long before he discovered it was not his forte, and he was soon back in the world of rock 'n' roll – and he played with The Rockets until the end in 1970.

Five handsome young men pose for a publicity photograph with their lovely female manager.

GEOFF AND THE FAIRLAINES
rock 'n' roll

Early in 1961 Geoff and the Fairlaines set off on that elusive road to stardom. The lads, all from the Bradford area, were Geoff Cowler, vocals, Paul Wilkinson, bass guitar, Ronan Baker, rhythm guitar, John Ramsden on lead guitar and the drummer, remembered only as Malcolm. This new group was managed by the young and attractive Anne Mason.

After much practice (their favourites were Shadows numbers), the group set out to establish themselves musically, and also to develop a distinctive dress: they wore matching light blue jackets with silver shoal collars, finished off with the dependable Slim Jim ties. Within a short time they were performing in an assortment of popular local venues, including working men's clubs, local town hall rock 'n' roll events, St Georges Hall, dance halls and theatres, as well as garden fetes that were now including rock 'n' roll groups in their entertainment. Like many of their compatriots they also played a few times at the US airbase at Menwith Hill.

It was Geoff and the Fairlaines and Terry Sexton's group The Shakes who helped Gerry and the Pacemakers out at the Majestic dance hall, loaning them instruments and equipment after The Pacemakers' transport (carrying their equipment to the venue) had broken down in Manchester.

For the next two years, under the talented managerial skills of Anne Mason, they were one of the top ten groups in the area. In 1963 the group disbanded.

Geoff Cowler (b. 1943, Bradford) vocals
Geoff lived in the Fairweather Green area, later attending Fairweather Green and Thornton West schools. As a child he went to Sunday School at Allerton Methodist Church, and later he was a choirboy at St Saviour's Church at Fairweather Green. During his latter school days he tried to master the guitar, purchased from one of the many mail order outlets of the time. He found this was not his forte, however, but he had a good singing voice, especially for rock 'n' roll numbers.

In 1961, aged eighteen, Geoff helped to form Geoff and the Fairlanes. After the group disbanded, later in 1963 he became vocalist with Geoff and the Prosecutors. His daytime career was the joinery business, and he spent most of his working life with an assortment of shopfitters, such as Sharp and Law, Wadsworth's of Brighouse and Taylor's of Denholme. Still a semi-professional vocalist in 1975, Geoff spent the next twelve months with the local group Denim, playing at local clubs on the club circuit. This was followed by a two year stint with Stormy Affair, again on vocals, starting in 1976. Afterwards Geoff began to concentrate more fully on his career.

Now retired, Geoff lives in Low Moor with his wife Tricia. His hobbies are dog walking, fishing and DIY. He believes that those rock 'n' roll days of the 1960s were some of the best years of his life.

Paul Wilkinson (1943–64) bass guitar
Paul lived in Baildon. Sadly he died very young in a motor vehicle accident.

Ronan Baker (b. 1943, Baildon) rhythm guitar
Ronan lived in Baildon.

John Ramsden (b. 1943, Baildon) lead guitar
John lived in Baildon, and later attended Sheffield University.

Malcolm ? (b. 1943, Fagley) drummer
Malcolm's surname has been forgotten. He lived in Fagley, and was employed at Grattan Warehouse.

Anne Mason (b. 1944, Baildon) manager
Anne lived in Baildon, and later worked in a solicitor's office on Manningham Lane. Managing a rock 'n' roll group in the early 1960s was quite an achievement for a young woman. By all accounts, she was very proficient.

Pop group had no instruments

TOP pop group Gerry and the Pacemakers came to Bradford last night and nearly found themselves in the middle of a riot. For Gerry was there, the Pacemakers were there—but no instruments were there.

And Mr. Harry Radley, manager of the Majestic Ballroom, where Gerry and his boys were billed as the top attraction at a teenage dance, peeped cautiously out of his office at 1,100 milling youngsters, and shuddered.

The driver of the van bringing the Pacemakers' instruments from Torquay had just rung to say that he had broken down outside Manchester and couldn't get to Bradford in time.

"I had the makings of a full scale riot on my hands," said Mr. Radley today. "The group wouldn't have been able to perform and the kids would have torn the place apart."

The night was saved by two local groups—Geoff and the Fairlanes, from Shipley, and Terry Sexton and the Telecasters, of Bradford. Mr. Radley rang each of them. They came round and lent the Pacemakers their own instruments—two guitars, a bass guitar and a set of drums, plus amplifying equipment.

Gerry and the Pacemakers, the lads from Liverpool who top the hit parade—or thereabouts—were able to perform their latest hits to delighted squeals from the teenagers.

Geoff and the Fairlanes were 'instrumental' in lending equipment to Gerry and the Pacemakers in time to stop a riot.

Four smart lads at a working men's club evening. Vocalist Geoff misses out on the photo – gone for the drinks! Left to right John Waite, Ian Greenwood, Mick Duffy, Paul Young.

GEOFF AND THE PROSECUTORS
rock 'n' roll

In 1963 a rock 'n' roll group was formed by local lads who had seen most of the top rock 'n' roll artists at the Gaumont Theatre and decided this was the life for them! Two school friends, Mick Duffy and Paul Young, bought themselves guitars and practised at each others' houses. After learning a small repertoire they did a spot at the John Dillon Club in Little Horton Lane – like a modern karaoke where people got up on stage and sang, accompanied by a resident pianist. They enjoyed this and had some acclaim, which gave them a little more confidence and resulted in their decision to form a group, with Paul on lead and Mick on rhythm guitar. They advertised in the *Telegraph and Argus* for a drummer and bass guitarist, and along came bass guitarist John Waite and drummer Ian Greenwood.

A name was required for the group, and it was Paul's sister who came up with the unusual name The Prosecutors. The lads seemed to gel from the outset, and with constant practice they soon had a good assortment of rock 'n' roll numbers under their belt. As there was no regular vocalist John Waite sang most of the pop numbers, with Mick and Paul covering with backing vocals. They were soon playing on the local pubs and working men's clubs circuits, including the Old Vic on Holme Top Street, Belle Vue, Manningham Lane and the Listers Arms on Manchester Road, They even ventured into the Leeds area, appearing at the Star and Garter in Kirkstall.

The Prosecutors were now doing well, but were beginning to feel that a good vocalist was required, so they placed another advert in the local paper. This paid off when the very talented Geoff Cowler (late of Geoff and the Fairlanes) joined them. Their name was changed to Geoff and the Prosecutors to reflect this. Geoff, being somewhat older than the others, soon brought his experience to bear, and they were soon noticed as no mediocre group – gaining better bookings at the local dance halls, and larger venues such as Bradford University's annual dance, where they supported Wayne Fontana, The Kinks and Long John Baldry at the Queens in Morley Street.

Geoff and the Prosecutors' popularity brought them to the notice of Garth Cawood's popular Top Twenty Club in Idle, where they appeared many times.

Soul music and r&b were now part of the music scene, but Geoff and the Prosecutors kept with rock 'n' roll, which was still thriving.

For nearly two years the group were at the forefront, until they parted company in 1965, mostly because of their careers.

Paul Young (b. 1948, Bradford) lead guitar
Paul lived in West Bowling. He attended St Joseph's RC Infants and Junior schools, before moving on to St Blaise School on Tong Street. Leaving education at fifteen, Paul became an apprentice overlooker at Hutchinson's Textiles in Greengates.

After his time with the Prosecutors, Paul went on to be part of the successful Hornets and Carolanne for three years, until 1968. He later married Frances Ann Robertshaw (Carolanne), and in 1970 they went to live in the USA, first in Philadelphia and later in New England.

Mick Duffy (b. 1948, Bradford) rhythm guitar
Mick lived in Marshall Street off Manchester Road. Like his pal Paul he attended St Joseph's schools, and later St Blaise School. Leaving school aged fifteen in 1963, Mick went into the glass trade as an apprentice glass beveler.

When The Prosecutors disbanded Mick, again like Paul, joined the Hornets and Carolanne on rhythm guitar, until the group broke up in 1968. He continued his career in the glass industry for forty-five years, until his retirement. Living in East Bowling with his wife Beverley, he now spends most of his time with his family and grandchildren. Mick now looks back with nostalgia to those distant days of rock 'n' roll, and his time in the limelight.

John Waite (b. 1946, Bradford) bass guitar
John lived in Allerton.

Ian Greenwood (b. 1948, Bradford) drums
Ian lived in West Bowling.

Geoff Cowler (b. 1944, Bradford) vocals
See Geoff and the Fairlanes.

HARRY FOSTER

rock 'n' roll icon and comedian

A modest Bradfordian, Harry was a popular member of one of Bradford's iconic groups in the 1960s, the Tomboys with Helen. Then in his mid-thirties, Harry had seen life before some teenage rock 'n' rollers had been born!

Harry Foster was born in 1925 in Beck Street, off Leeds Road, Bradford, and attended St Peter's RC School. Leaving school aged fourteen, he started work at Ripley's Mill, Laisterdyke, as a bobbin fetcher. Aged seventeen, in 1942, he volunteered to join the Northampton Regiment as Private H. Foster. During his basic training at Hythe, Kent, he boxed for the battalion, winning three consecutive fights, and was awarded with a 10s 6d voucher. Harry, now aged eighteen, was sent to India with his regiment, and after acclimatisation was moved up into Burma. They were soon in the thick of fighting the Japanese, and in June 1944, on the infamous Silchar Track, Harry was wounded. After spending time in Camila and the Bay of Madras convalescing, he was moved to Poona and Deolali, then home to be demobbed in late 1945.

Harry was soon in full employment at Dawson's Cashmere Works. Over a few years he had developed a fine singing voice, in the style of a crooner – which was all the rage at the time. He soon became very popular, performing at many venues throughout Yorkshire. With the advent of rock 'n' roll, and now in his thirties, he was snapped up by The Tomboys. He was their oldest member, Tommy Butler being six years younger.

Harry's talent was exceptional, either as a soloist or providing backing vocals. Although he did not play an instrument, he was also a good frontman for the group, sometimes shaking maracas (as did Garth Cawood with The Dingos). His five years with the Tomboys with Helen, were one of the best eras for Harry.

When the group folded in 1964 Harry went on with the second chapter of his life in entertainment, that of comedian. He did not tell stories, just one liners, reminiscent of Bob Monkhouse. His jokes and his wonderful voice brought him many accolades for the next fifty years as one of the best comedians in the North of England and Scotland. With seasons at Butlin's and

Harry Foster is centre stage, with the Tomboys and Helen. At that time Harry was Bradford's oldest star, nearing forty. He was and still is a credit to the Bradford rock 'n' roll scene.

Blackpool, he appeared with many stars, including Joseph Locke, David Whitfield, Helen Shapiro, Eddie Calvert and Max Wall – among many others.

A good footballer in his younger days, Harry is still president of Tyersal Football Club and life member of both Bradford and District FA and West Riding County League. He has had a truly remarkable life and career.

Harry still lives with his lovely wife Doreen in the Tyersal area of Bradford, and, now in his eighties, he is still on for a song and a joke at his local.

I have always remembered Harry from those years with The Tomboys: he was always smiling and joking, and is now a legend in his own lifetime. I do hope he has forgiven me for calling him Tommy throughout our recent chat and again at the Bradford rock 'n' roll reunion! Harry Foster, a lovely man.

THE HI-TI'S

rock 'n' roll

For a few months in 1959 and 1960 a new group surfaced called The Hi Ti's, their name chosen because three of the group members, Tony, Terry and Mick, were of Italian descent. Mick Judge was on vocals and rhythm guitar, Neville Harrison on lead guitar, Tony Minchella on drums and Terry Hall on the piano. After many practices they only had a repertoire of eight rock 'n' roll numbers. At most of the venues at which they played no one complained or seemed to notice; as it was said at the time, the alcohol probably dimmed their audiences' senses.

The Hi-Ti's played at local clubs and pubs, and the manager of the King's Head in Westgate gave them a block booking twice weekly for three months. They were beginning to attract fans, even though the same eight numbers were played over and over again. What they lacked in their choice of music, they made up for by being immaculately dressed, the vocalist in a grey suit and the other members in dark suits.

After just nine months The Hi Ti's decided to call it a day, although they had proved very popular and had made their mark.

Michael (aka Mick) Judge (b. 1940, Bradford) vocals and rhythm guitar

Of Italian descent, Mick attended St Mary's RC School. Leaving aged fifteen, he became an apprentice tailor's cutter for Robert Hirst, Raincoats of Bradford. After learning the trade he decided to go into business on his own, working in the local markets and selling raincoats (seconds), including many other products. He had such entrepreneurial skills that he soon developed a successful business.

A good vocalist and a get-by rhythm guitarist, Mick's introduction to rock 'n' roll was when he helped to establish The Hi-Ti's in 1959. Although this only lasted a few months, he was soon back on the scene with his own group, Mick Judge and the Jury Men. In early 1965, when the group disbanded, he was the DJ at the Somerset ballroom on Idle Road for a time. Although still running his clothes business, he was soon doing the circuits in Bradford: he was an

The Hi-Tis. Some members were of Italian descent, hence the name. Although only in existence for a few months, their name and music are still remembered. Back row, left to right: Mick Judge, Tony Minchella, Neville Harrison. Front: Terry Hall.

accomplished vocalist with a flair for singing like Elvis Presley (ballads only), and was accompanied by his own mobile backing. He followed other Bradford performers like Dave Lee and Harry Foster, around venues including the Cock and Bottle, The Churchill, The Peckover and Hoffman's Club, all in the 'Little Germany' district.

In the early 1990s, when karaoke became popular, Mick hired six top of the range karaoke machines to franchise around Yorkshire, and he turned this into another successful business. Having suffered rheumatoid arthritis in his hands for some years, he soon went into semi-retirement, but with his daughter Maza he is still working in the world of personalised gifts.

Mick is as active as ever, and lives in Greengates with his family

Neville Harrison (b. 1939, Bradford) lead guitar.
When The Hi-Ti's folded, Neville went on to play with a few groups in and around Bradford.

Tony Minchella (b. 1940, Bradford) drums
Born into a well-known local Italian family, Tony attended St Bede's Grammar School, spent some time at Grattan Warehouse and later went into the printing industry. He still lives with his family in the Bradford area.

Terry Hall (b. 1939 Bradford) piano
Terry was of Italian descent. He attended St Bede's Grammar School and later had a career in engineering. He still lives in the Bradford area.

The lovely Carolanne surrounded by the Hornets, some of Bradford's most talented musicians. Left to right: Mick Duffy, Peter Newlove, Dave Marshall, Francis Ann Robertshaw (Carolanne), Paul Young.

WISHING YOU ALL A
MERRY CHRISTMAS AND
A PROSPEROUS NEW YEAR

FROM

THE HORNETS AND CAROLANNE

199 LEGRAMS LANE.
LIDGET GREEN.
BRADFORD 7.

TEL. 74956 OR 62699

THE HORNETS AND CAROLANNE

rock 'n' roll

In the mid 1960s a new group was born that mostly consisted of former members of other successful groups. The line-up of the Hornets and Carolanne was Paul Young, lead guitar, Mick Duffy, rhythm guitar, Pete Newlove, bass guitar, Dave Marshall, drums, and a lovely female vocalist, Carolanne.

The sun was now setting on the rock 'n' roll era, but the group began to play rock 'n' roll numbers by artists that most groups of the time had overlooked. This move was an overnight success, and for two years they proved to be very popular on the club circuits, with many fans. Until 1968 they were one of the finest club groups in Yorkshire, but as the music scene changed they decided to call it a day while still at the top.

Paul Young (b. 1948, Bradford) lead guitar
See Geoff and the Prosecutors.

Mick Duffy (b. 1948, Bradford) rhythm guitar
See Geoff and the Prosecutors.

Pete Newlove (b. 1943, Bradford) bass guitar
See The Caravelles.

Dave Marshall (b. 1944, Bradford) drums
See Vince Wayne and the Falcons.

Frances Ann Robertshaw aka Carolanne (b. 1948, Bradford)
Frances lived in Buttershaw. She married Paul Young, the guitarist, and in 1970 they went to live in America.

Ian Waller – deep in thought.

Ian again, second left, holding his guitar, with lots of volunteers to form a skiffle group, 1957.

IAN WALLER

pop musician

Ian Waller was born in Sheffield in 1938 of Bradford parents, who later returned to the city. He attended Grange Primary and Grammar School. Leaving school, he was employed as a dental technician.

In the mid 1950s Ian taught himself the guitar, and later tried to form a skiffle group. Becoming very proficient on the guitar, he was not with a rock 'n' roll group permanently but was coveted by many as a session player. Among the many groups with which he performed were Clay Martin and the Trespassers, Margie and the Sundowners, Dave Arran and the Crusaders, and Brenda and the Dominators.

After service with the RAF in the 1960s Ian was again in great demand, averaging over 150 engagements a year. For some time in the mid-1970s he was a member of the famous Overlanders, famous for the number one 'Michelle' in 1966. During this period Bradford's own Dave Lee asked Ian to join him, but he declined because of other commitments.

In 1985, after two decades of non stop music, Ian decided to call it a day. He has rock 'n' roll in his blood, and is a multi-instrumentalist capable of playing lead or bass guitar, banjo, piano, ukulele, eight string lap steel, harmonica, acoustic guitar, keyboard and mandolin. Something of an unsung hero, he has been called one of the best rock 'n' roll musicians to come out of Yorkshire by several of the singers and musicians he has worked with over the last four decades. He is a legend for his dedication to the music scene. Besides being modest about his achievements, Ian is also one of the nicest guys you would wish to meet. Today he lives in Queensbury with his wife Karin, and although he is retired he is still in demand as a performer in his own right.

Josie Meehan, 1964. She was also known as Jo White of the popular Bluenites.

JO WHITE AND THE BLUENITES

rock 'n' roll

In 1960 Jo White and the Bluenites came onto the rock 'n' roll scene. Although the group was short lived, it produced good rock 'n' roll music and also had a wonderful female singer, Jo White (Josie Meehan).

The group's original name in the late 1950s was Dollars - with Jo White was on vocals and an assortment of other musicians. They played mostly skiffle at most of the small cinemas in and around Bradford. In 1960 there was a new line-up and they played all rock 'n' roll. The group became very popular for eighteen months.

Jo White and the Bluenites consisted of Josie, vocals, Keith Worsnop, bass and vocals, Alan Cockroft (aged eleven), drums, and Paul White (Josie's brother), lead guitar. They practised at Josie's parents' house in Hampden Street (they had very understanding neighbours!). Influenced by Buddy Holly and the Everly Brothers, Keith and Josie practised for hours to achieve perfect pitch and harmonisation.

Many bookings followed, at the Majestic and Gaumont ballrooms, the Queens Hall, and every other week at the famous Students Club. Further bookings were obtained at the popular Imperial ballroom, Nelson, the Gaumont in Barnoldswick, and many working men's clubs in Yorkshire.

In late 1961 all was going well, and they were thinking about turning professional. It nearly happened! They were approached by the owner of a nightclub who was looking for supporting acts to perform on the same bill as Ray Ellington and his Band, who were going on an extended European tour. Unfortunately they were all committed, to work, college and, in drummer Alan's' case, school. The deal fell through, leaving them very disappointed – and it was not long afterwards that group members went their separate ways.

Josie Meehan aka Jo White (b 1939, Bradford) vocals

Josie attended St Joseph's RC School and later St Josephs College. Leaving school at sixteen she went to work for one of the North of England's leading confectioners, Silvio's on Arthington Terrace, Bradford, until 1960. When she moved on she remained in the confectionery business.

It was during these early years that Josie entered the world of skiffle with her brother Paul. In her early teens, she was one of the first local female rock singers, and could also play the saxophone. She was soon singing with Dollars, later progressing to Jo White and the Bluenites, but after this her showbusiness career ended.

Josie worked for the *Telegraph and Argus* for a few years in advertisement sales, then joined the magistrates office in Bradford's Town Hall and even spent some time working in Kingston, Jamaica. She finished her working life at the National and Provincial Building Society in Centenary Square. When it was taken over by Abbey she took early retirement.

Josie still loves the rock 'n' roll era, and is well remembered by many ex-band members, so much so that she was asked to join The Dakotas when they reformed in 1994. For the next twelve years she was an integral member of that group, helping to raise thousands of pounds for charity – but she had to give up because of ill health in 2008.

Josie still lives in the Allerton area with her husband Gerald, children and grandchildren. Music is in the family: her young grandson Charlie Meehan is a rock guitarist of some standing and a quality musician of the future – with Josie as his number one fan.

Paul White (b. 1941, Bradford) lead guitar

Brother of Jo White, Paul attended St Joseph's RC School and later St Bede's Grammar School. Aged sixteen he was employed by the BDA (Bradford Dyers Association) as a clerical assistant. A self-taught guitarist, in 1957 he played at the Topic Folk Club, then based in the Red Café, later the Buffs Lodge, in Bradford.

Paul first joined Dollars, which became Jo White and the Bluenites. In 1962, after sitting in with one or two forgotten groups, he joined The Dakotas, taking over lead guitar from Dave Arran, who had left to turn pro with The Crusaders. When The Dakotas folded Terry continued his career, retiring aged fifty-eight as financial director of a large European auto component group.

Since 1994 Paul has been playing with the original Dakotas, helping local charities. Like other members he is a credit to his generation. He still lives in the Bradford area with his wife Susan.

Keith Worsnop (b. 1941 Bradford) bass guitar and vocals

Keith lived on Blackshaw Drive, Buttershaw, and attended St Bede's Grammar School from 1952 to 1957. He joined Jo White and the Bluenites as a singer and subsequently bass guitarist. Keith had a really good voice in the Ricky Nelson mould, and was also noted as being the good-looking one. He was also known as a great Ava Gardner fan, and watched her films time and time again. It is not known if Keith played with any other groups after the demise of Jo White and the Bluenites.

Alan Cockroft (b. 1949, Bradford) drums

Alan lived on the Buttershaw estate. Charlie Cockroft, his father, was a popular drummer who played at many local working men's clubs, and it was he who taught Alan to play. By the age of eleven he was quite a proficient drummer. It was probably unique that one so young played with a semi-professional group – but whenever Jo White and the Bluenites performed Charlie was in attendance! When the group folded Alan continued with his school education, and played for a few months with Lorraine and the Baht'ats. Later, in the mid-1960s, he was still in the music business – working for the well-known Moore's music shop in North Parade.

A young John Verity with his Fender Stratocaster: the shape of things to come.

JOHN VERITY

rock star

John Verity was born in Great Horton, Bradford, in 1949. He attended Great Horton Infants and Primary School and later Grange Boys Grammar School. During his latter schooldays he taught himself to play the guitar, and found that he had a flair for the instrument, as well as being an equally good vocalist. By the mid-1960s his musical career had kicked off, and he was soon in demand playing with many local groups, including The Crusaders, Allen Pounds Get Rich, Mick Judge and the Jurymen and the Dave Berry Group.

By 1969 John was living and working in America. While there he formed the first ever line-up of the John Verity Band, who supported many of the big names of the day. Returning to the UK in 1971, he began work with producer Steve Rolland in a new version of his band, Family Dogg. By March 1972 John was back in Bradford, building his homemade SHY studio in a cellar, helping to produce demo tapes for local bands. He also formed the second version of the John Verity Band with other local musicians. They recorded and released their first LP, *John Verity Band*, on Probe Records.

The band secured a management deal with Argent's manager Mel Collins, and over the next few years they gathered a large loyal local following from their constant gigging. That line-up played its last gig at the Tavern in the Town Rock Club in December 1974, after which John moved on to join Argent, replacing their guitarist and singer Russ Ballard. He stayed until they finally split in 1976, after which he formed Phoenix with ex-Argent bassist Jim Rodford and drummer Bob Henrit. Phoenix released an LP on CBS and later played at the Princeville Rock Club in Bradford. After joining rock band Charlie in 1980, John formed Verity in 1981 and released a come-back album, *Interrupted Journey*, on PRT Records.

In 1992 John relocated from his native Yorkshire to rural Bedfordshire. Since his move south the John Verity Band gigs have continued, although with different line-ups. At the 1994 Manchester Festival Fender Stratocaster Fortieth Anniversary concert, he guested along with many rock legends past and present, including Sonny Curtis, Frankie Miller and Rory Gallagher. John's performance of 'Stay with Me Baby' was one of the high spots of the evening, bringing the capacity crowd at the Manchester Free Trade Hall to its feet. He has also done vocal sessions for three episodes of the Granada series *Full Stretch* (1991) and another guest spot with the Strat Pack for the 1995 Australia Day celebrations at the Hippodrome in London's West End.

In 2000 there was a major gigging project with a thirty-two date UK tour, opening the show on the Jools Holland Sex, Jazz and Rock and Roll Tour at major venues, including Manchester Opera House, Birmingham Symphony Hall and London's Albert Hall.

Still living in Bedfordshire with his wife Carole, John writes and records at home, and is still gigging in the UK and Europe. Much of his recorded back catalogue has now been re-released worldwide. Who knows what's next?

JOHNNIE CASSON

from rock 'n' roll to Britain's top comedian

Johnnie Casson, who appears on numerous occasions on British TV, was in his early days an outstanding local rock 'n' roll drummer, who created a second showbusiness career as a highly rated comedian.

Johnnie Dorsey Casson was born in Halifax in 1943 and lived at Carlton House Terrace in the Kings Cross area. His father had been the *Melody Maker* champion trombone player, and he tried to teach Johnnie to play. His son found the instrument too cumbersome for a small lad, however, and he really fancied the drums. Later, at St Bede's Grammar School in Bradford, Johnny formed a skiffle group with a few local lads. They played at local dances and went everywhere by bus. On the journey to Bradford on the Hebble bus, a drum kit could be stored under the stairs. On the same bus Keith Artist, of Dal Stevens's group, put his drum kit in the same place!

As time went on Johnnie set his sights on rock 'n' roll, after seeing many of the top stars at the Gaumont in Bradford, including Buddy Holly, Bill Haley and the Comets, Eddie Cochran and Gene Vincent. Moving on from skiffle he started playing at the Sportsman's Inn in Ploughcroft with some local lads. At Southward Working Men's Club he was approached by Jimmy Boocock, from one of Halifax's premier groups, The Avengers, and asked if he would like to join the group. He accepted, and was introduced to many new venues. In 1961 they auditioned for Butlin's but were turned down, but in 1962 they were booked for a five month season at Butlin's in Bognor Regis.

After a short time with the local Ray Kennan Combo, in 1963 Johnny joined The Cresters to replace Colin Houghton. He was with them for around twenty years, playing at practically every dance hall, cabaret and rock 'n' roll venue in the British Isles. It was while on this circuit that Johnnie started to perform comedy, which became more popular than the music.

In 1983, while on holiday at Butlin's, Johnnie's wife entered him in the Star Trail talent competition as a solo act. He won the contest, which meant a free holiday during which he would appear in the regional finals – which again he won. The grand final was held at the London Palladium, and Johnnie was again the judges' choice. This encouraged him to leave The Cresters and set off

Johnnie Casson—music or comedy, always an entertainer.

on the path as a solo performer. Television soon followed, and an appearance on *Opportunity Knocks* prompted Bob Monkhouse to say that he was 'one of the top four comedians in the country'. A chance to take part in Granada TV's remake of the historic *Comedians* show found him being featured on all six shows, and he was critically acclaimed as the find of the series.

Johnnie's first appearance on ITV's *Des O'Connor Tonight* was so successful that it was followed by a further four appearances. This continued with the daytime TV *Des and Mel*, on which Johnnie appeared four times. Johnnie is a tireless worker for charities and is still working the theatres, with a following drawn from all age groups.

It is not alternative comedy (as in an alternative to laughing) for the great Johnnie Casson, whose style is reminiscent of those other greats, Les Dawson, Eric Morecambe, Benny Hill and Frankie Howerd. Like Halley's Comet, such comedians are with us on rare occasions. Johnnie now lives in Brighouse, the

‘Las Vegas of the North’, with his wife Jean and three grown-up daughters, Lucy, Lindi and Amy.

A fifteen-year-old Josie McCann, one of Bradford's earliest pop singers.

JOSIE Mc CANN

pop singer

Josie McCann was born in Bradford in 1944 and attended St Patrick's School, Westgate. She left school aged fifteen and was employed in the offices at Grattan Warehouse (Mail Order) Ingleby Road. A very accomplished rock 'n' roll singer, Josie had a very upbeat style like Connie Francis. Her tone varied from touching, soft and sweet to soaring and powerful.

Josie was a young girl with a wealth of talent. She came third in the Aim for Fame competition at the Alhambra in 1959, singing the Connie Francis hit numbers 'Stupid Cupid' and 'Lipstick on your Collar'. Pauline Matthews (later Kiki Dee) was the winner. Josie sang with many local groups in the late 1950s, but by the early '60s she had faded from the scene. Alas, she did not follow in Kiki's footsteps. She could and should have done, such was her ability.

Josie now lives on the East Yorkshire coast at Withernsea, with her husband Trevor and family.

Northcliffe playing fields,the venue for the K D's publicity photograph. Back row, left to right: Maxine, Mick Craven. Front row: Dave Lawson, Keith Duckworth.

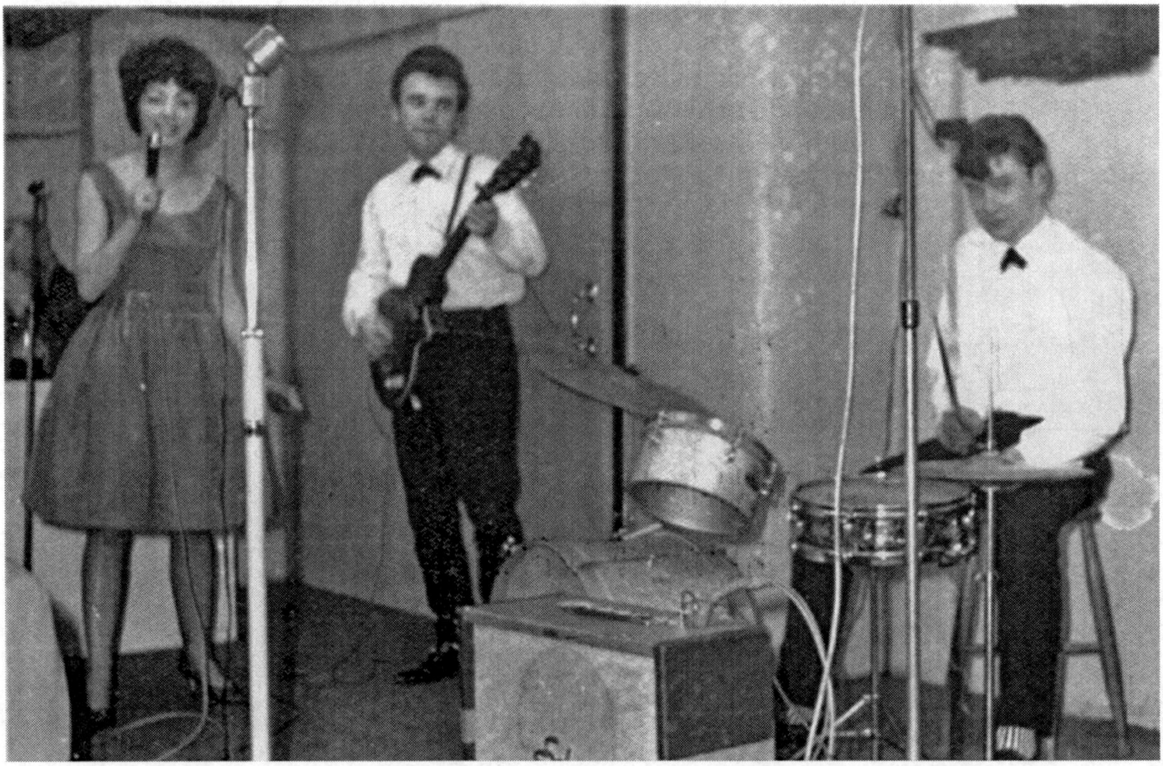

Maxine and two of the boys entertain at a working men's club. Left to right: Maxine, Dave Lawson, Mick Craven.

THE KD's WITH MAXINE

rock 'n' roll

It was in the early 1960s that a group of lads and a lass decided to form a rock 'n' roll group and give it a go. None of them had any experience. Their name was the K D's with Maxine. The K and the D were the initials of members Keith and Dave: the group was made up of Keith Duckworth from Leeds, lead guitar, Dave Lawson from Bradford, rhythm guitar, Keighley lad Mick Craven, drums, and Maxine Lawn from Halifax, vocals. How the four group members managed to meet to practise and get to bookings when they lived in four separate towns is not recorded. They must have clicked, however, as through their manager, Maxine's father George Lawn, they got their first booking in 1961 at the Halifax bingo hall, playing to a surprised audience during the interval.

Like most groups during this period they were soon playing at pubs and clubs with the odd spot in the local dance halls, and this continued until early 1963, when they fell out and went their separate ways. Although this foursome never really graduated like other groups, in some small way they were part of the rock 'n' roll scene.

Maxine Lawn (b. 1945, Halifax) vocals

Maxine lived in Halifax. Her father George managed the group.

Dave Lawson (b. 1945, Bradford) rhythm guitar

Dave worked in the jewellery trade before moving to Bowness in the Lake District. Later he lived in Lanzarote and ran a bar there.

Keith Duckworth (b. 1945, Leeds) lead guitar

Keith lived in Rodley.

Mick Craven (b. 1944, Keighley) drums

After Mick's birth the family moved to Frizinghall. He attended Bradford Boys Grammar School, then joining G.R. Herron and Son, top makers, in Little Horton Lane, Bradford, as a sample room boy. It was around this time that he became a member of the K, Ds with Maxine. He then went on to play drums for

Northcliffe playing fields, again in 1963. Left to right: Keith Duckworth, Mick Craven, Maxine Lawn, Dave Lawson.

the popular Dave Lee until 1968, leaving when Dave turned professional. It was in that year that Mick married Elizabeth; they had two children, Robert and Julie. After his Dave Lee days Mick did 'fill ins' with other groups for a short while, but with work and family commitments his drumming days soon came to an end.

In 1966, in the early days of computers, Mick was employed as a computer programmer by E.J. Arnolds of Leeds. Later, still in computers, he joined Empire Stores on Canal Road, Bradford. In 1989 he moved to Edinburgh, working on computer systems for John Menzies, the stationers, but this was short lived as he was made redundant in 1991. Back in Yorkshire, he took an off -licence business in Silsden before establishing a residential letting agency business in Keighley.

Now semi retired, Mick spends most of his spare time playing squash, golf and snooker, and he is a member of Keighley Bridge Club. He continues to play five a side club football twice a week at Nab Wood Sports Centre. Mick and Elizabeth live in East Morton, Bingley, where he is the treasurer of East Morton War Memorial Trust.

KEITH ARTIST

drummer

Keith Artist was born in St Luke's Hospital, Bradford, in 1941, and lived in Wilsden and Thornton before moving to Swaine House estate, where he attended the local primary school. He later went on to Belle Vue Boys School, during which time the family moved to the Delph Hill estate in Wyke.

Leaving school, Keith worked in the office of a wholesale fruit and vegetable merchant in Bradford. He became interested in early skiffle music, and while living on the Delph Hill estate he made friends with three other musically minded lads. They formed the 789 Skiffle Group, practising in the front room of one of the members on Sunday afternoons. At one time he had wanted to play the guitar, but he gave up this idea because a rhythm section was required – and he was able to play the washboard.

After the demise of the Delph Boys Keith became hooked on rock 'n' roll and decided to teach himself the drums in 1959. He bought a drum kit from Harmony House in Bridge Street Bradford for £24 10s 0d, and around this time left his job in the market to join the Atlas Haulage Company as an assistant in the traffic office. He spent most of his free time practising the drumming sequences of all the hits of the 1950s. This paid off, and he was soon a very proficient drummer. For a short time he joined the seven-piece Sobey Dance Band, which was soon reduced to a quartet.

In 1959–60 Keith made his first move to rock 'n' roll when he joined Dal Stevens and the Four Dukes, although at the beginning he nearly did not make it to his future career. When he first joined the group they had to find somewhere to practise, and for the sum of 5s Dal procured the local swimming baths in Storr Hill, Wyke, on Sunday mornings from 10 o'clock until noon. The first practice went very well, but come the second Sunday and local residents had had enough: they didn't want an up-and-coming rock 'n' roll group to spoil their Sunday morning lie-ins! The group had barely got through Cliff Richard's 'Move It' when a deadly missile in the shape of a half-brick came crashing through one of the windows, narrowly missing Keith's head and his prized drum kit. No second barrage was needed, because no group has ever dismantled guitars, amplifiers and drums quicker. They soon left Wyke behind, probably with the sound of laughter from the residents of Storr Hill, who put them to flight with just one missile.

The next group that Keith joined, between 1961 and 1962, was The Crusaders, a tip-top band with excellent musicians coordinated by the popular Cliff Dutton. The group obtained a season in Germany, but Keith had to decline the invitation because of family and career commitments.

It was in 1963 that Keith decided it was time to form his own group, the Four Musketeers. They were very popular on the local circuit and at clubs in South Yorkshire, with their Beatles, Rolling Stones and Chuck Berry covers. At the end of 1965 the group folded.

In the mid 1960s Keith was playing with Dave Lee (piano) and Dennis Oliver at the Red Lion pub in Bankfoot. From the 1970s onwards he played with Tony Earl and the Revelation and a band called Shambles. In the 1980s he re-formed the Four Musketeers under the new name Resurrection, and once again in 2002–4. Keith played with many groups until his retirement from the Atlas Haulage Company, after forty-four years' continuous service, in 2006.

After all those years drumming, Keith is now learning to play the guitar, and is even having a bash at the ukulele, harmonica and keyboards. He is also a fair-weather cyclist. When he has some spare time Keith and Anne, his wife of forty-six years, spend it at their caravan in Cumbria; they still have their family home in Queensbury.

Keith Artist is one of Bradford's original and well-respected rock 'n' roll musicians. An exciting, incisive, inventive drummer, he could perfectly recreate parts that he heard on early rock 'n' roll records. His drum solos were memorable. Keith is quite shy and a man of not too many words, but he has a great talent. He has been a good friend of mine for over fifty years.

Keith Artist, one of Bradford's premier drummers, with his new Premier drum kit.

A rare photograph of Keith standing: most of the time he was sitting down!

The man behind the drums, the talented Ken Hickey.

KEN HICKEY
vocalist and percussionist

Kenneth (Ken) Hickey was born in Manningham (close to Bradford City AFC) in 1947, and was educated at Midland Road, Green Lane and Frizinghall schools. He was also encouraged by his mother to sing with St Aidan's Choir. He was only eight when he became obsessed with drums. His father, who was a drummer in a combo, taught him the basics, and he was hooked!

Seven years later, aged fifteen (in 1962), he was with his first group, The Wingbeats. When this group folded he joined The Chessmen, later known as Alan Knight and the Chessmen, and later again Chad Wayne and the Chessmen. While all this was taking place he had begun an apprenticeship as a wool sorter with Hey and Shaw's (Bradford) Ltd. This only lasted two years, however, as he was approached by Cliff Dutton of The Crusaders to join them, as they were turning professional. Ken lost no time in giving up his job to secure his place.

It was a good move, as in 1964–6 the group went on to play all over West Germany for two or three months at a time. On their return to the UK they played at nightclubs and US army bases, and backed many stars, for example Jess Conrad, Gerry Marsden and Joe Brown. When The Crusaders folded in late 1966 Ken continued with many groups and bands well into the 1970s, '80s and up to the present day, including nine years with Mecca bands. Ken owes his lead vocals to Doc Parkin, the Leeds Mecca bandleader who was so supportive.

Ken is still a freelance session drummer, vocalist, percussionist and one-man entertainer, and today he is still on call for twelve jazz bands, dance bands, trios and combos. For over two years he worked as a romantic singergram for an agency called Huby Baby Strippergramme. Today Ken's one man show entertains the elderly, special needs and Alzheimer's sufferers, twenty groups in the Bradford area. Ken, who still lives in Cleckheaton with his wife Cynthia, celebrated his sixty-fifth birthday and fifty years in showbusiness in April 2012, a lifetime since The Wingbeats.

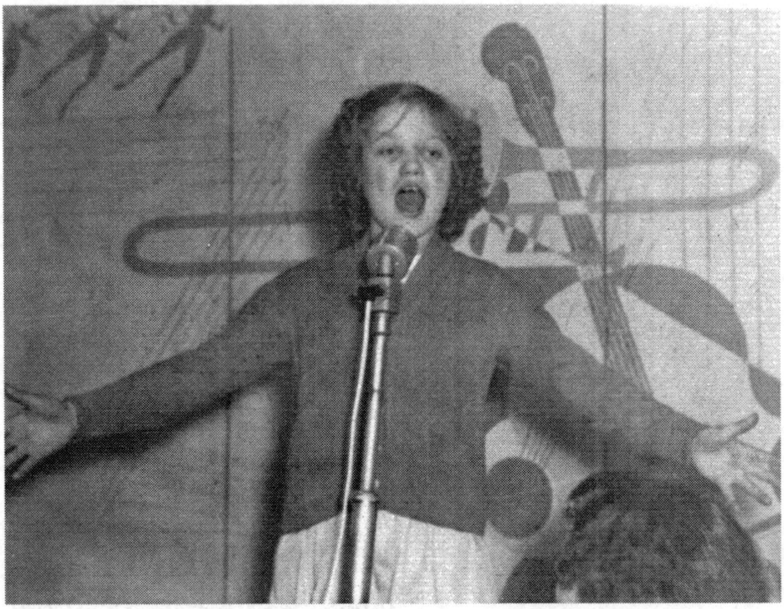

A young Pauline Matthews (Kiki Dee) delights the audience at Dudley Hill Cricket Club, 1956.

On stage at the Gaumont theatre, 1959. Pauline, aged twelve, wins yet another talent contest. Second left is the well-known theatre manager of the time, Phil Ridler. The prize, a cheque for £25, is being presented by the Lord Mayor, Councillor Ernest England, with his wife. Note a young Spike O'Brien on the right of the Lord Mayor.

KIKI DEE

pop singer

Kiki Dee was born Pauline Matthews in 1947 at the family home, 146 Marsh Street, Little Horton, Bradford. She attended Saint Oswald's Primary School, then Wibsey Secondary School. From an early age she was encouraged by her father to sing (she was a natural), and by the age of ten she was winning local talent contests and establishing herself as a star in Yorkshire. After leaving school she worked as a counter assistant in Boots the Chemists, and sang in local groups and dance bands in the evening. Many of Bradford's rock 'n' roll groups in the early 1960s claimed that Pauline sang with them at some time.

In 1963 Pauline was scouted by Philips Fontana, who released her debut recording of Mitch Murray's 'Early Night' the same year. It was during this time that she adopted her stage name, Kiki Dee, from the knee-high 'kinky boots' that were fashionable at the time and the American actress Sandra Dee's last name. After a slow start she made her debut album *I'm Kiki Dee* in 1968. In 1970 she became the first white British female singer to sign for the Motown label.

In 1973 Elton John signed Kiki to his Rocket label, and her single 'Amoureuse' reached number thirteen in the charts. A year later she formed her Kiki Dee Band, and her first album, *I've Got the Music in Me*, went gold in the USA. In 1976 she recorded a duet with Elton John, the world smash hit 'Don't Go Breaking My Heart'.

In 1978 Kiki recorded her final single for the newly RCA-renovated Rocket Records, 'Stay with Me'. In 1984 she made her West End debut in the international production *Pump Boys and Dinettes*. She received rave revues, and then an Olivier Awards nomination for her performance as Mrs Johnstone in the revival of the hit musical *Blood Brothers*.

After several years in and out of the spotlight, Kiki returned to the charts in 1993 with a Top Ten duet with Elton John: they sang the Cole Porter classic 'True Love'. She followed this up with an album of songs from throughout her career. With her musical partner, guitarist and songwriter Carmelo Luggeri, she has been creating original music for the last few years. While touring in 2011 she was thrilled that many people in the audience commented to her that she had never sounded better, and her writing is still moving forward creatively.

Kiki's impeccable vocal abilities have established her impressive credentials as a musician during a career that covers nearly five decades. This daughter of a weaving overlooker, who as Pauline Matthews turned her back on a job as a counter assistant at Boots in Broadway, Bradford, became the queen of British rock and a world star.

LEE CHEVIN AND THE RAVERS/THE RIDERS

rock 'n' roll

Lee Chevin and the Ravers were another of Bradford's very successful groups who were part of the scene from 1959. The original members were Ian Normington, lead guitar, Dave Archer, drums, Kenny Raper, rhythm guitar, and Dave Pannett, bass guitar. They were known simply as The Ravers, One of their first bookings was a staff dance in 1959 at the Queens Hall. As with all new groups, a corner of the ballroom was found for the Ravers to make their mark – and it was not a very encouraging start!

For a short while in the early days they were managed by local lad and entrepreneur Tony Gilfoyle. Some members left and new ones joined, and the line-up changed to Dave Pannett, bass guitar, Brian (Baz) Bastow, rhythm guitar, Rod Wright, lead guitar, Dave Archer, drums, and Lee Chevin, vocals. This line-up continued for the next four years; the group was known first as Lee Chevin and the Ravers and then The Riders.

Local venues and dance halls were entertained many times by these young Bradford lads, who made lots of friends and fans – especially at the Majestic dance hall, where they probably played more often than any other group.

Becoming quite successful, the group was only a few months old when it was offered work in Germany; but for this they had to have a girl singer as well as Lee. They auditioned one or two, but the girl who got the job was Pauline Matthews (later Kiki Dee). However, the tour was called off before it began, as Pauline was not only too young but also had other commitments.

The group's first real break came in early 1963, after a chance in a million meeting with Russ Conway on the forecourt of the Central Garage in Bradford town centre. They had stopped for petrol when they saw Russ's Rolls-Royce convertible. Soon they had told him all about the group, and a few weeks later Lee Chevin and the Ravers had passed an audition for George Martin (of Beatles fame). In July 1963 they made a record at the famous Abbey Road Studios in London. This was released in November 1963. The A-side was 'Darling Jean', written by Brian Bastow and Dave Pannett, and this was

The Ravers perform one of their first bookings: the *Telegraph and Argus* staff dance at the Queens Hall, December 1959. Left to right: Kenny Raper, Ian Normington, Dave Archer, Dave Pannett.

L-R: Dave Pannett, Brian Bastow, Rod Wright, Lee Chevin, Dave Archer.

(above) A publicity photograph for EMI records. The group would now be known as Lee Chevin and the Riders. Left to right: Rod Wright, Brian Bastow, Lee Chevin, Dave Pannett, Dave Archer.

(right) Bass guitarist Dave Pannett relaxes during a break.

Manager Tony Gilfoyle, with Eileen, showed off his success with his Jaguar XK140.

Barry Fish (Lee Chevin), vocals, tries his hand with the guitar.

coupled with 'Memories of You', written by Lee Chevin. The record was released on the Parlophone EMI label. It was at this time the group had to change their name from The Ravers to The Riders, because there was already a group called Paul Raven and the Ravers (later Gary Glitter and the Glitter Band). The recording engineer who worked on the disc was Norman Smith, better known as Hurricane Smith, who had one or two hits in the British charts. 'Memories of You' was also recorded by The Applejacks, who were number one at the time with 'Tell Me When'. A song 'In Love with an Angel', written by lead guitarist Rod Wright, was put on a disc by a singer called Draffi and released in Germany. About this time the group was offered a five year contract by impresario Tito Burns, who was the manager of Cliff Richard and the Shadows, Shirley Bassey and many more stars. Needless to say, The Riders signed.

For the next few years the group travelled throughout the UK, appearing with many of the pop stars of the time, notably Lulu, Manfred Mann, Merseybeats, Applejacks, Jess Conrad, Vince Eager, Mike Sarne and Edna Savage. They were the type of group that always drew a good crowd and had many teenage fans. After four years, however, and with music and fashions changing, in 1964 one of Bradford's premier groups finally called it a day.

Barry Fish aka Lee Chevin (b. 1943, Leeds) vocals

When he was two, Barry's family moved to Bradford, where he attended Usher Street Primary School, Dudley Hill Junior School and Carlton Grammar School. His first job was with Chanters Dental Engineering, followed by a spell with Brown, Muffs transport and then Fags vending machines.

While he was sorting out a career Barry joined the Blue Star Skiffle Group as a vocalist, but was soon converted to rock 'n' roll. He was a great asset to The Ravers, whom he joined in 1960, and he was with them when they made the record of 'Memories of You', which he also wrote.

When the group disbanded in 1964 Barry joined up with Dave Pannett as a duo called the Two Chimes. They played on the club circuit in the Leeds and Bradford area. In 1967, now married to Pat, he moved to Ellesmere Port, still with Fags, the vending machine company, and after a short time with Lyons Catering as a representative, he found his niche when he joined Chester City Council and later, in an executive position, Cheshire County Council.

Barry retired in 2006 and lives in Cheshire. He now has time to enjoy travel, walking, watercolour painting, dancing and socialising with friends, but most of all spending time with his wife Pat, his family and his granddaughter, born in 2009.

Dave Pannett (b. 1944, Ilkley) bass guitar

Expectant mothers living in Bradford were evacuated towards the end of the Second World War to avoid the bombing, and Dave was born at Semons Home in Ilkley. He was brought up on Rooley Lane, Dudley Hill, and his first school was St John's Infants School in Bierley. From St John's he moved to Highfield Secondary Modern on Tong Street, Bradford.

In 1957 Dave purchased his first acoustic guitar, and twelve months later formed a skiffle group at school. This consisted of a tea chest bass player, a drummer and washboard player and Dave singing and playing the guitar. Their first and only performance was at the Christmas school concert.

Dave started work in 1959 at Brown, Muffs in the decorating department. This job only lasted a few months, and Dave found himself redundant when the department closed down. His next job was at Christopher Pratts and Sons' furniture shop on North Parade, Bradford, where he started as an apprentice French polisher.

Still learning and playing guitar, he started a group with his friends Kevin Darby and Lee Chevin, the Blue Star Skiffle Group. In 1960 he was invited to join The Ravers as the rhythm guitarist. The group became Lee Chevin and the Ravers, who were soon very successful. Later, when they became Lee Chevin and the Riders, he was with them when they recorded 'Darling Jean' and 'Memories of You' in November 1963. Dave co-wrote 'Darling Jean' with Brian (Baz) Bastow, the bass player.

After the group disbanded in 1964 Dave and Lee Chevin performed on the nightclub circuit as the Two Chimes. In 1963, while playing at a dance at Armley Baths, Dave met Mary. They were married in 1967 and have two children, Lisa and Richard, and two grandchildren, Joshua and Chloe. Dave started his own french polishing business in 1973, which he still runs. His hobbies are playing the guitar, listening to music, walking and reading. Dave and Mary still live in the Bradford area.

Brian (Baz) Bastow (b. 1941, Bradford) rhythm guitar

Brian joined Lee Chevin and the Ravers in 1960. He played bass on the record 'Darling Jean' and 'Memories of You' in 1963, co-writing the former with Dave Pannett. Later he went to live in America. See the Stormsville Five.

Rod Wright (b. 1942, Huddersfield) lead guitar

Rod lived in Huddersfield, and was educated at Bradley Junior School and Huddersfield New College. After leaving school he went to Huddersfield School of Architecture. At an early age he took piano lessons, but with the advent of skiffle and rock 'n' roll he soon progressed to the guitar, and by the age of fourteen he was quite proficient at playing lead. He joined a Huddersfield group called Del Barry and the Downbeats and, after much success, along with several other Huddersfield groups they appeared on a teatime music show recorded by the BBC in Manchester. After this they were signed for tours in France and Germany by a French management agency. As Rod was still a young teenager his father said no, saying that he had to continue with his career.

After he left The Downbeats, Rod was a founder member of another Huddersfield group, the Four Escorts, playing lead guitar and contributing vocals. Again he was with another successful group, which was offered a season at Butlin's in Skegness. It was unfortunately another no-go for Rod: it would not have gone down well at home! His career again took priority.

So it was that in 1960 Rod joined The Ravers. He was highly regarded as an excellent lead guitarist, and went on to play lead on their recording of 'Darling Jean'. He continued with them until they folded in 1964. From 1964 until later in the decade Rod played with a Huddersfield group called Denny and the Witchdoctors.

Rod's daytime career had now taken off, and he worked for Wimpy Homes at their main office in Leeds until he moved to Asda's head office, also in Leeds, as design manager. In the mid-1970s he moved to Wolverhampton, working for Tarmac Midland, but after a few years he was back with Wimpy in Leeds, until he was made redundant in 1991. During these two decades Rod kept his hand in by playing with all sorts of groups, adapting to the musical changes that were taking place.

In 1991 he set up his own business, making architectural drawings for home extensions and business premises. Now semi-retired, he plays league table tennis and supports Huddersfield Rugby League, and still plays the guitar for pleasure. He has fully recovered from colon cancer a few years ago.

Rod lives in the *Last of the Summer Wine* area of Holmfirth with his wife Christine. He still wonders just how much his life would have changed if he had gone to France or to Butlin's as a young teenager all those years ago.

Dave Archer (b. 1943, Bradford) drums

Dave lived in Lidget Green. Hewas one of the original Ravers and played the drums on the record 'Darling Jean' and 'Memories of You'. After the group disbanded he played for a short time with Vince Wayne and the Falcons. He then spent some time in America working with the Tomboys with Helen, then known as The Bradfords. He now lives in Washington.

Ian Normington (b. 1942, Bradford) lead guitar

Ian attended Tyldesley Boys School in Blackpool and later Bradford College of Art. Although a modest person, he was a self-taught guitarist of some distinction, who practised in the early days with drummer Dave Archer of the Ravers – and he spent a short time with The Ravers before joining the newly formed Mick and the Tornadoes in 1960. It was during this time that Ian was noted by other local group members, and he became a very prominent guitarist, especially with The Tornadoes. His ability was demonstrated when the group was booked to play at the Corner Café in Scarborough, and Mike Berry and the Outlaws were on the same bill. The Tornadoes played the first session and Mike Berry was on later. When their lead guitarist did not turn up, Mike asked if Ian would stand in. He did, and played the full session with Mike Berry and the Outlaws (unpaid!).

When The Tornadoes folded in 1963 Ian's priority was his career. For a short while he worked for Whitaker and Mapplebeck (Cycles) Ltd building bicycles, especially the racing cycles that the business was famous for. Ian later moved into engineering and then industrial sales until the late 1980s. It was then that he formed his own business, West Yorkshire Electronic Security Group, for security services to business and industry. He has continued in this business until today; it has been renamed Detronic.

Now semi-retired, Ian has converted and developed three private nursing homes in the Bradford area, and in his spare time he and his wife Ann spend time at their villa in Portugal and touring the UK in their caravan. Still very modest about his rock 'n' roll days, he remembers the good times – although

A young couple in the early 1960s: Ian Normington with his future wife Ann.

musically he has a broad spectrum of interest today, including jazz and classical music. He still lives in the Bradford area with his wife of fifty years. They celebrated their golden wedding in 2012 with his loving family, including four grandchildren.

Kenny Raper (1942–80s, Bradford) rhythm guitar

Kenny lived on Aberdeen Place, Lidget Green. He was a popular and natural guitarist. After The Ravers he moved around, playing with other local groups. In the 1970s and '80s Kenny was employed as a continental coach driver, and it was in the 1980s that he sadly passed away.

Tony Gilfoyle (b. 1940, Bradford) roadie, manager and entrepreneur

Tony lived in Legrams Street, Listerhills, and attended St Patrick's School in Westgate. Leaving school aged fifteen he became an apprenticed plumber, serving out his time until he was twenty-one. Even while serving his apprenticeship Tony made inroads into the world of rock 'n' roll, acting as a roadie who transported The Dingos to venues in his Zodiac estate with a trailer. (Not many teenagers had a driving licence at that time, let alone a Zodiac estate!) His entrepreneurial skills soon turned to group management, and he was soon claiming much success with Lee Chevin and the Ravers.

Tony was soon on a par with other local agents, such as the well-known Mrs Miller and Owen Hammond, with whom he had a very good working relationship. He was later involved with the Del Rio Four, who went on to become The Chapters. His easy manner and business acumen continued into the final days of rock 'n' roll, when he found another business niche. This was selling women's skimpy outfits, all the rage for discos and clubbing. Tony's business was a tremendous success, culminating in five shops named GranniesWouldn't Like It. Later he went on to work in the building industry and the motor trade, and had more than a passing interest in antiques.

Tony is now semi-retired and spends most of his time in Alanya, Turkey. Back in the UK his time is taken up with his family, daughter Amanda and two grandchildren Marsha and Faris.

LINDA RUSSELL AND BRUCE

duo

Linda and Bruce Russell became a double act in September 1965 – Bruce switching from bass guitar to lead guitar, since this fitted the duo formula better. It was during this time that Linda made several records at the EMI studios at Abbey Road, including a demo in the famous small studio that had been used by the Beatles. This was a song written by Kenny Lynch in 1965 entitled 'Under the Smile of Love', on which a young and unknown Jimmy Page (later of The Yardbirds and Led Zeppelin) was the session guitarist.

The duo Linda Russell and Bruce continued playing the Northern club circuit from July 1965 until 1968, including the large clubs such as the Greaseborough in Rotherham and the Scala Club in Doncaster. These clubs booked two or three artists for eight shows during the week, seven evening performances and Sunday lunchtime. Linda and Bruce supported acts such as Kenny Ball and his Jazzmen and Acker Bilk.

Linda's first TV appearance was in December 1967 when she appeared on the Granada programme *First Timers*, a Muriel Young production. Linda sang the Bobby Hebb hit 'Sunny', and Bruce accompanied her on guitar, out of shot.

In 1968 their agent Bernard Hinchcliffe took Jimmy Corrigan and his wife Betty to see them at the Kon Tiki nightclub in Wakefield, and the following day they received an offer to be resident artistes at the newly opened Batley Variety Club. They were to perform in total for over seventy-eight weeks, along with other residents, compère Gerry Brooke and singer-dancers the Deb Set. They appeared with most of the big acts of the day, including Shirley Bassey, The Hollies, Billy J. Kramer and the Dakotas, Des O'Connor, Louise Armstrong, Lulu, the Walker Brothers, Bruce Forsyth, Norman Wisdom, Gracie Fields and Cilla Black.

In July 1969 Linda Russell represented Britain in the Golden Orpheus Song Festival in Bulgaria, where, backed by a forty-piece orchestra, she won a prize in the category 'best interpretation of a Bulgarian song by a foreign artiste'. Later this led to a ten-date tour, which culminated in playing at the Bulgarian State Circus Auditorium in Sophia.

Linda Russell and Bruce, a popular local duo that went on to national fame.

Linda and Bruce had their first child, Gabrielle, in 1970. During the last two months of Linda's pregnancy Bruce worked on the film *The Railway Children*, helping to create the famous landslide. Linda and Bruce continued to play the local clubs until the birth of their second child, Simon, in 1973.

In 1973 a group called Peppercorn was formed when Bruce and Linda merged with another duo, David and Joyce Kilvington. Peppercorn played until 1980 when the two duos separated, and Linda and Bruce continued playing together until 1995.

Linda Russell, née Nixon (b. 1942, Keighley)

Linda attended Highfield School, Keighley. Aged fifteen she was soon on the local rock 'n' roll scene as a vocalist with The Presidents and the Beat Squad. In 1962 she left Peter Black's in Keighley, where she had worked as a sewing machine operator, to play on several American military bases in France with the Beat Squad.

It was in 1964 that Linda married the Beat Squad's bass guitarist Bruce Russell. In 1965 she joined a new group called Linda Russell and the Keymen, and later that year that she and her husband Bruce formed the Linda Russell and Bruce duo. Linda retired after a career of thirty-five years. She occasionally comes out of retirement at charity shows, the latest being at Christmas 2009 when she appeared with the Haworth Brass Band and a group called Musical Youth.

Bruce Russell (b 1939, Keighley)

Bruce attended Keighley Boys Grammar School .As a young teenager from 1957 he played bass guitar with The Presidents and the Beat Squad. He was working as an apprentice wool sorter, but in 1962 he left to play on several American military bases in France with the Beat Squad. Bruce was engaged to Linda at this time, and they married in 1964. In 1965 he was with Linda in Linda Russell and the Keymen, and the same year they became the Linda Russell and Bruce duo.

After many years in showbusiness, in 1989 Bruce went back to college, gaining a BA Hons degree, a PGCE (teaching qualification) and a Master of Philosophy degree, which resulted in him becoming a teacher of psychology, criminology and forensic psychology at Keighley College.

In 1996 Bruce joined a band called Replay, a retro band playing mostly 1960s music, especially Beatles songs. He was on vocals and played lead guitar. The group was voted best group at the Huddersfield Clubland Command Performance in 1998. In 2002 they disbanded.

Linda and Bruce together with Ricky Hardacre played a few dinner dance venues as We Three in 2005, but disbanded as Ricky had health problems. Bruce continued to play at jam sessions around Keighley, and in 2009 joined an established comedy-musical trio called the Beer House Boys, although the term boys was rather inept since their combined age was nearly 200!

Linda and Bruce now live in retirement in Haworth after a lifetime in showbusiness, and have wonderful memories of over fifty years as artists at the top of their profession.

Linda Russell and The Keymen at an American military base in France. Back row, left to right: Bruce Russell, Linda Russell, Richard Hardaker, Ted Earle, Dave 'Murph' Mirfield.

LINDA RUSSELL AND THE KEYMEN

rock 'n' roll

This group started at the beginning of 1963. Its members were gathered together from former groups, and were already of professional status. They included Linda Russell, vocals, Bruce Russell bass guitar and vocals, Edward (Ted) Earl, drums and Dave (Murph) Mirfield, electric keyboard.

In May 1963 Linda Russell and the Keymen played their first professional season at Butlin's in Filey. At the end of the eighteen week season, in September 1963 they were in France, playing at the American airbases in La Rochelle, Toul, Verdun, and Orlean, until the spring of 1964. On returning, they were back at Butlin's in Filey for a second season.

Later there was a brief spell playing locally, during which time they supported the Bradford group The Cresters. Before they returned to France lead guitarist Ricky Hardacre, formerly of the Beat Squad, rejoined the group as an extra musician, having taken a year out from his studies at Leeds University.

During this time Linda was offered a recording contract with HMV records, and signed up with the Bernard Hinchcliffe Agency, which managed the group in conjunction with Wally Rideley, a HMV A&R man.

The group finished their final summer season show at Skegness's Arcadia Theatre in 1965, supporting Ronnie Hilton and Norman Collier. During this time they also supported Des O'Connor and the Four Pennies. However, Linda Russell and the Keymen disbanded at the end of the season in 1965, although later, with new members, the group renamed The Keymen carried on until 1970. In 1966 Michael Jackson (later of Love Affair) played bass guitar with them for a short while.

Linda Russell (b. 1942, Keighley) vocals

See Linda Russell and Bruce.

Bruce Russell (b. 1939, Keighley) bass guitar and vocals

See Linda Russell and Bruce.

Edward (Ted) Earl (b. 1940, Keighley) drums
See The Presidents.

Dave (Murph) Mirfield (1938–2003, Keighley) electric keyboard
Dave carried on playing into the 1970s with The Keymen.

Richard (Ricky) Hardacre (b. 1943, Keighley)
See The Beatniks.

LORRAINE AND THE BAHT'ATS

rock 'n' roll

Lorraine and the Baht'ats were formed in 1964 with a title synonymous with Yorkshire. In the song 'Ilkley Moor Baht'at', the 'baht'at' means 'without a hat.' The line-up consisted of Lorraine Burns, vocals, Jack Wells, lead guitar, his brother Roger Wells, rhythm guitar, Jack Shaw, bass guitar, and Hugh Donnelly, drums. Throughout 1964 and 1965 they played at many of the popular local venues and beyond. In 1965 Jack Shaw was replaced by Mike Berry, and Alan Cockroft replaced Hugh Donnelly. After winning the April 1965 Top Town Competition at St George's Hall, Lorraine and the Baht'ats were given the chance to be the first group to appear on Hughie Green's *Opportunity Knocks* TV show. This they did in 1966, but without success. A short while later the group folded.

Lorraine Burns (b. 1942, Bradford) vocals
See The Caravelles.

Jack Wells (b. 1945, Bradford) lead guitar
See The Caravelles.

Roger Wells (b. 1942, Bradford) rhythm guitar
See The Caravelles.

Jack Shaw (b. 1943, Bradford) bass guitar
Jack left the group in 1965.

Hugh Donnelly (b. 1944, Bradford) drums
Hugh left Lorraine and the Baht'ats in 1965.

Mike Berry (b. 1944, Bradford) bass guitar
See The Caravelles.

Alan Cockroft (b. 1944, Bradford) drums
See Jo White and the Bluenites.

Mel Clarke, a name synonymous with Bradford's rock 'n' roll era, aged sixteen.

The original Mel Clarke Four, 1958. Left to right: Mel Clarke, Drew Charles, Colin Houghton, Steve ('Red') Williams.

THE MEL CLARKE FOUR

rock 'n' roll

In April 1958 four young men entered a talent audition at Girlington Hall, Bradford: Mel Hogan, straight from Grammar School, guitar and-vocals, Steve (Red) Williams, bass guitar, Colin Houghton, drums, and Peter Williams, rhythm guitar. They were called the Unknown Four. After this audition Peter Williams dropped out and joined the Royal Marines. He was replaced not by another rhythm guitarist but by a talented young pianist, Drew Charles. This turned out to be a step in the right direction. A pianist with a rock 'n' roll band in those days was indeed a rarity, as the usual line-up was three guitarists and a drummer, but what an asset Drew proved to be! He quickly introduced his raw boogie blues influence to Mel's Chuck Berry-style guitar playing, which set the band apart from most local group's usual rock 'n' roll sound.

After about six weeks of rehearsing, a letter arrived that confirmed the group had passed the audition at Girlington and was to appear at the Top Talent Show at St George's Hall, a highly prestigious (if unpaid) venue, where top names in the pop world appeared.

The band performed three numbers, a guitar instrumental called 'Haunting' written for the occasion by Mel, a Chuck Berry number 'Johnny B Good' and a brilliant rendition by Drew of the Jerry Lee Lewis classic 'Great Balls of Fire'. They came second, and were no longer unknown: the name Unknown Four was subsequently dropped! Mel Hogan became Mel Clarke, and the Mel Clarke Four was born. The group soon became very popular, and performed regularly at the Majestic, Gaumont and Gaiety ballrooms, and many times at the famous Students Club.

The band played continuously from the late 1950s well into the 1960s with almost the same line-up, except for drummers who were too numerous to recall – after they lost the very talented Colin Houghton in the early 1960s to the Cresters. Included from time to time was the talented vocalist Sandra Day, with her wonderful interpretations of the Connie Francis numbers 'Stupid Cupid' and 'Lipstick on your Collar'. Mel and the group cut three demo discs at Excel Studios, two singles and an EP – which local DJ Jimmy Savile plugged on his new radio show. Sadly it was never taken up by the major recording companies.

The Mel Clarke Four went on to support many of the top groups and stars who came to the area and travelled throughout the north of England, playing full weeks in cabaret at the Huddersfield Empire, then known as The Continental, the Imperial ballroom in Colne, Christie's in Selby, and many others. This was all despite their lack of agent: they preferred to accept work as it came up. Sometimes they worked five nights a week, alongside their daytime jobs.

The group broke up for some time, the members going on with their careers, but they still get together sometimes, and are still in great demand. The Mel Clarke Four is a very well-respected group, and it has given enormous pleasure over the years.

Mel Hogan aka Mel Clarke (b. 1942, Saltaire) lead guitar and vocals

Mel attended Bingley Grammar School, and was only fifteen when he came onto the local rock 'n' roll scene. The Mel Clarke Four were always one of the top three popular local groups, the others being Mike Sager and the Cresters and The Dingos. As well as being an adept lead guitarist, Mel was also an accomplished vocalist, performing Chuck Berry and Little Richard numbers just as well as their originators. When the group folded Mel went on to play with The Dingos for a while.

When not playing, Mel spent most of his life in engineering and the auto industry. He is a very modest individual, but it has to be said that he was at the forefront of Bradford's rock 'n' roll scene, with something approaching celebrity status.

Now retired, Mel lives in Baildon with his wife Betty. He still plays at the odd venue, and with the Mel Clarke Four has had top billing at the annual Bradford rock 'n' roll reunions.

Steve (Red) Williams (b. 1942, Shipley) bass guitar

Steve attended Frizinghall Junior School and Northcliffe Secondary Modern School. Leaving school aged fifteen, he joined Arthur Blair's Plumbers as an apprentice, but this was not to his liking – and he was soon working with his father as an apprentice painter and decorator.

It was about this time that, like most teenagers, he was influenced by the new rock 'n' roll music. His mother was a talented pianist, as his grandmother had been; she was one of the Arcadians, a popular musical troupe that had performed in a large marquee on spare land in Legrams Lane. In 1940 this land became the site of one of the city's cinemas, The Arcadian.

The family's musical ability was passed onto Red, as he soon became known because of his large mop of red hair. Becoming quite proficient as a rhythm guitarist, he joined the newly formed Mel Clarke Group. However, Mel needed a bass section – and as no bass guitars were available Mel and Red used the large strings from a cello and incorporated them onto Red's rhythm guitar. Heath Robinson it was, but it worked, until a bass guitar was available. Red soon became an excellent bass guitarist.

When the group finally folded, Red and Kenny Fowler, formerly of The Dingos and Sandra Day, formed their own group, Sandra and Blue Flames. After a short period Red, now married, became part of Cliff and Brenda with the Dominators, again with Kenny Fowler. In the early 1970s, living in Denholme, Red formed a duo with lead guitarist Barry Pyatt, who ran a recording studio (Studio 21) close by in Denholme. With Red on bass and vocals, they called themselves the Last Chance. Later drummer Keith Artist came along, and their name was changed to Treble Chance.

After the usual bookings in pubs and clubs Red decided it was time to have a break and concentrate more on his painting and decorating business, which had supported him throughout his playing career. In the late 1980s he was asked by the rock 'n' roll pianist Spike O' Brien to join him and guitarist Barry Pyatt. The group only lasted a short time, but their name must have caused much amusement at local venues. The Goolies soon disappeared!

In the early 1990s, with the help of his former colleagues Drew Charles and Kenny Fowler, Red formed The Bilberries – the forerunner of today's popular group The Elderberries.

Sadly, in 2003 Red had a stroke, which left him slightly incapacitated and in a wheelchair. He has lost none of his enthusiasm for life, however, and carries on much as before. With his son David he helped to build a motor special for hill-climbing, and has recently been awarded a City and Guilds certificate for gardening, while his knowledge of computers and photography is limitless.

Red still lives in the Denholme area with Peggy, his wife of nearly fifty years, who met him at a Monday teenbeat night at the Mecca Locarno.

Andrew (Drew) Charles (b. 1942, Glasgow) piano

In 1947 Andrew's family moved to Bradford, because of his father's tailoring business. Andrew attended Frizinghall Junior School and later Bradford Boys Grammar School. Leaving school aged sixteen, he worked for a time in the clothing industry in Leeds. It was during his journeys by train to Leeds that he met a former Grammar School friend, who told him that a new rock 'n' roll group was being formed by Mel Clarke. Drew, as he was now called, had taken piano lessons and was quite a virtuoso on the keyboards – so he was asked to join what became the Mel Clarke Four.

Drew was soon a popular member of the group, not only with his colleagues but also with the group's many teenage fans. Drew's interpretation of Jerry Lee Lewis and Fats Domino songs were spectacular, and were much admired by members of other local groups.

After the Mel Clarke Four disbanded, Drew worked at Grattan Warehouse on Ingleby Road. He was soon back in showbusiness, leaving Grattan and turning professional with the Ray Kennan Combo. After a short time he was back with a daytime job, and was soon in a managerial position at Brooksbank China wholesaler in Bingley, later moving to their larger shop in Keighley. He even found time to manage the popular Mojo Club (Market Tavern) in the late 1960s. For the next few years he worked in the china industry, this time at the popular shop called Jackson's in Sunbridge Road, later moving to Darley

Street. After leaving this position he worked as a representative for DER Television, and also spent some time with JITV in Bradford.

Drew still found time to play at local venues, although he went back to his first musical interest of playing r&b. In the early 1990s, with former colleagues, he helped to form The Bilberries, who later became The Elderberries.

It appears that old age has passed Drew by! He still has the same personality, temperament, style and looks that he had in the late 1950s, and his name will always be synonymous with Bradford's rock 'n' roll years. He retired in 2005, and now lives in the Tyersal area of Bradford with his wife Christine.

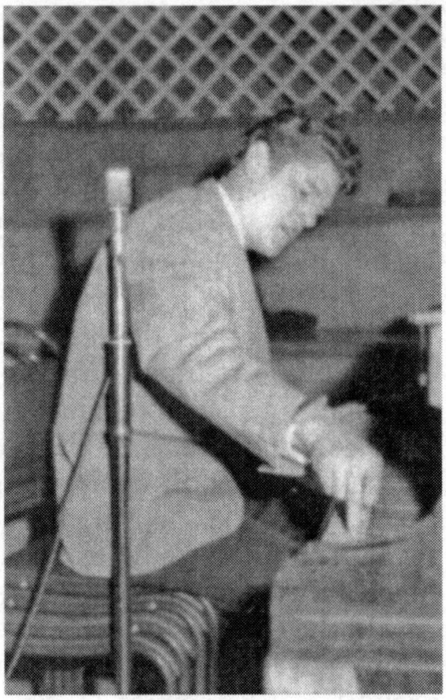

The much respected Drew Charles, early 1960s.

Peter Williams (b. 1940, Bradford) rhythm guitar

Peter left the group after a few months to join the Royal Marines.

Sandra Ainsworth aka Sandra Day (b. 1942, Batley) vocals

See profile.

Colin Houghton (1943–90, Bradford) drums

See profile.

MICHAEL JACKSON

Bradford's first artist to make number one

Michael Jackson was born in Bradford in 1950 and attended Hanson Grammar School. As a young bass guitarist, Michael (Mick to his mates) spent some time with local groups The Spell and The Keymen, from Keighley. In late 1966 he answered an advert for a bass guitarist in the music paper *Melody Maker*. He got the job and his musical career with Love Affair began. The group had been originally formed in early 1966 by a successful handbag manufacturer, Sid Bacon, as a vehicle for his fifteen-year-old drummer son, Maurice (Mo).

The group enjoyed a residency at the Marquee Club in London before turning professional in 1967. Their second single was a cover of the soul singer Robert Knight's 'Everlasting Love' in January 1968, on CBS records, which got regular airplay on Radio Caroline. The single climbed the charts and shot to number one, becoming a classic pop song of the day. Fresh from their chart success, Love Affair toured Europe and the UK, including two home-town shows for eighteen-year-old Mick in October 1968 at the Gaumont, supported by Scott Walker, The Casuals and the Paper Dolls. Love Affair's next single for CBS was 'Rainbow Valley', which reached number five in the charts. Their next few singles, 'A Day Without Love', 'One Road' and 'Bringing On Back the Good Times', all became top twenty hits. Between 1967 and 1969 they enjoyed massive success, and were one of the UK's biggest pop groups. The boys' photos were on many a teenage girl's bedroom wall, courtesy of magazines like *Jackie*. In 1969 Mick also found time to manage one of Bradford's local groups, 'Igginbottom.

Love Affair became the first UK group to tour Poland. When singer Steve Ellis quit and went solo in late 1969, they recruited a new vocalist called Gus Eadon. Despite a short-lived name shortening to LA for their second album, the group continued until 1971, when Mick left, saying he was 'tired of the constant touring and general music-biz clap-trap'. The same year he married his long-term girlfriend Patricia Speight of Shipley. They had originally met as young teenagers at the coffee bar/disco the Hole in the Wall in the early 1960s. Later, Mick became the UK sales director of Alfa Romeo.

In 1999 Mick, Mo and Morgan re-formed the group for a charity single and video on behalf of Bradford Royal Infirmary's ward seven specialist unit, which deals with rare blood disorders.

The wonderful and popular Mick and the Tornadoes. Left to right: Dave Murgatroyd, Dave Gallagher, Mick Kershaw (Mick Novac), Mick Stephenson, Ian Normington.

MICK AND THE TORNADOES

rock 'n' roll

Extremely popular, Mick Kershaw and the Tornadoes performed at almost every local venue during Bradford's rock 'n' roll years. Versatility and outright professionalism ensured they were consistently popular, especially with female fans.

Originally the group was called The Sansovenos, but in the early 1960s changed its name to Mick and the Tornados. At the same time Mick changed his stage name to Mick . The group had been consistently mistaken for the Tornados of Telstar fame, so it was agreed to add an 'e' to their name. There was an American group called The Tornadoes that was popular during the surfing music period, but Mick and the Tornadoes were never challenged by them.

After the changeover only two original members of the group remained, Mick Kershaw, vocals, and Mike Stephenson, rhythm guitarist. New members were Dave Murgatroyd, drums, Dave Gallagher, bass guitar, and the well-known Ian Normington, lead guitar. It was a solid line-up of professional young men who, with Mike Stephenson acting as manager, obtained many top bookings in and around Yorkshire. When Mike Stephenson left, a young Brendan Crowe took his place. The group folded in 1963.

Mick Kershaw aka Mick Novack (b. 1942, Bradford) vocals
See Sansovenos.

Mike Stephenson (b. 1938, Bradford) rhythm guitar
See Sansovenos.

Ian Normington (b. 1942, Bradford) lead guitar
See Lee Chevin and the Ravers.

Dave Murgatroyd (b. 1941, Bradford) drums
Dave attended Bingley Grammar School, after which he held many positions including fire insurance clerk and licence road tax clerk. Early music days

consisted of playing a washboard with a skiffle group, then borrowing a drum kit to play with his Bingley Grammar School friends, who called themselves the Canal Street Jazz Band. In 1960 Dave joined Mick and the Tornadoes, and was with them on and off for nearly two years, during which time he played for short periods with other groups, including many jazz groups. He even spent a short time in London, but couldn't settle and came home.

In 1962 Dave joined The Dakotas, and was an integral part of this popular group for the next three years. However, during quiet spells with The Dakotas he still filled in on the jazz scene with local or visiting jazz musicians.

In 1966 Dave joined the organist Bruce Howell at Thornton Working Men's Club as a backing drummer. They backed three professional acts each night, working through Owen Hammond, co-owner of the Lyceum Night Club in Bradford. Later Dave and Bruce moved to Low Moor Working Men's Club, where they backed Ruby Murray, David Whitfield, the Caravelles and many others. Eventually Bruce went back home to New Zealand.

From the 1970s Dave played with a succession of organists and pianists at different clubs, however the standard got worse. It was during these years from 1969 until 1990 he became an assistant teacher at Exley Secondary School, Halifax and was later the head of history, until 1990. After a few office jobs Dave finally retired in 1999 – and was then able to pursue his hobbies.He is a member and ex-chairman of Bygone Bikes, a Yorkshire bicycle restoration club, and is also a member of the re-formed (1994) Bradford Dakotas. Married to Rosalie in 1962, he still lives with this family in the Bradford area.

Dave has had a marvellous musical career, being well respected as a gifted drummer on both the rock 'n' roll and the jazz scene.

Dave Gallagher (b. 1942, Bradford) bass guitar

Dave was formerly with the Rhythm Rebels and was an integral part of the Tornadoes during its formative years. His credentials were impeccable: he had played with the Del-Rio-Four, The Chapters, the Quiet Three and many others. He now lives with his family in Tayside, Scotland, and still plays bass guitar. At one time he was with a popular Scottish folk band called Callanish.

Brendan Crowe (1944–85, Bradford) rhythm guitar, vocals

Brendan lived in St Wilfred's Crescent, Lidget Green. He attended the local RC school, St William's, Ingleby Road, and on leaving aged fifteen was employed for some years at Grattan Warehouse in Ingleby Road. During this time he taught himself to play the guitar, and with his good looks, vocal style and easygoing ways he was snapped up as a rhythm guitarist with Mick and the Tornados, to replace Mike Stephenson.

In 1964 Brendan joined the popular Caravelles. In 1965 he was asked to join The Rattlers, headed by Spike O Brien, on their six month summer season at the Villiers Hotel, Douglas, Isle of Man. Brendan played with many other groups well into the 1980s, but in 1985 after a short illness he passed away, aged just forty-one. He was a very popular young man, a good guitarist and vocalist, who would have gone on to better things.

MICK JUDGE AND THE JURYMEN

rock 'n' roll

With a title apparently from a Wild West film, they could not fail – and from 1962 until early 1965 they were successful. The group members were talented musicians: Mick Judge, vocals and rhythm guitar, John Powell, bass guitar, Brendan Wynne, drums, and the jewel in the crown Allan Holdsworth, lead guitar.

With a top repertoire of rock 'n' roll numbers, they were playing at many clubs and dance halls in the Yorkshire area throughout 1963. Later they attracted the Owen Hammond Agency, which immediately signed them up – and in early 1964 got them a booking (without an audition) at Butlin's

With almost a Beatles pose, Mick Judge and his Jurymen hold court. Left to right: John Powell, Brendan Wynne, Mick Judge, Allan Holdsworth.

Skegness. On their return they appeared at the newly opened Silver Blades Ice Rink in Bradford, with advertising in the foyer and publicity in the *Telegraph and Argus* referring to 'their successful season at Butlin's'. The same happened at The Mecca (Locarno) on Manningham Lane. Such was the popularity of the group that Owen Hammond really pushed them forward, and they backed the young Pauline Matthews (Kiki Dee) at many local venues.

Then came the crunch. Owen Hammond wanted the group to tour Germany. Mick Judge jumped at the chance as did Allan Holdsworth, but the other two members, drummer Brendan Wynne (who was married with two children) and bass player John Powell could not accept. The group folded early in 1965.

Michael Judge aka Mick Judge (b. 1940, Bradford)
See The Hi-Ti's.

Allan Holdsworth (b 1946, Bradford) lead guitar
See profile.

John Powell (b 1943, Addingham) bass guitar.
Later John had a successful business, selling caravans in Scotland.

Brendan Wynne (b 1938, Shipley) drums
Brendan was the only group member to be married.

MIKE SAGAR AND THE CRESTERS

rock 'n' roll

The popular Cresters were synonymous with the Bradford rock 'n' roll scene – despite its fantastic guitarist, Richard Harding, being born in Bramley and a later member, Johnnie Casson, being born in Halifax. Most group members were Bradford lads, and The Cresters' early days were spent playing in and around the Bradford area.

Richard Harding, lead guitar, and Mike Sagar, vocals, had both been with The Tennesseans in the late 1950s, and it was they who brought together the others: Colin Houghton, drums, replacing Kenny Gough, Malcolm Clark, rhythm guitar and vocals, and David (Emil) Hardacre, bass guitar. Emil was about to go to university, however, so a replacement for him was needed: the excellent David Butterfield filled the slot for a short period until he left to join The Dingos. He was replaced by Ian Bannister, formerly of The Dingos. During this transition the group's name changed to Mike Sagar and the Cresters. Within weeks their professionalism and fantastic musical ability soon made them the best rock 'n' roll group in the area. After playing at many local venues, including the Gaumont, the Majestic and the Students Club, it was in October 1960 that their manager Steve Black arranged a test recording at EMI. This led to the recording of 'Deep Feeling', which was not really a success. It hit some regional charts but only reached number forty nationally, so did not feature in what was then the Top Thirty. After it was voted a hit on *Juke Box Jury*, people tried to buy it – but EMI had commissioned all the pressing plants to produce Rolf Harris's 'Tie Me Kangaroo Down, Sport'. By the time 'Deep Feeling' was pressed, three weeks later, the chance of a hit had gone. It was also said that the number was not popular with other groups, as they found it too difficult to play – so there was less exposure than a hit needed.

It was just after this that Colin Houghton, the group's drummer, had to go into hospital for a heart operation, and his place was taken for the next two months by Kenny Gough. Within a few months the group had appeared in the North of England and in Scotland at the Glasgow Empire. Later they got the job of backing Freddy Cannon and doing a spot on their own. Although still only semi-professional in the early 1960s, they had many engagements,

(above) The original Mike Sagar and the Cresters. Back row, left to right: Malcolm Clark, Ian Bannister. Front row: Colin Houghton, Mike Sagar, Richard Harding.

In 1961 the Crestas were joined by three young ladies for backing vocals: Linda Wilkinson, Mona Hurley and Malcolm Clarke's girlfriend Anne Harrison. Shown right are Linda and Mona.

The new line-up of The Cresters, 1963. Back row, left to right: John Harding, Malcolm Clark, Richard Harding. Front: Johnnie Casson.

The Harding brothers, Richard and John, at home in the studio, Hough Lane, Bramley, 1964.

including at Kendal, Morecambe, Skegness and Bridlington. In 1961 they played at the Old Queens Theatre, Blackpool, being on the same bill as Emile Ford and John Leyton. It was during this time that three local girls, Linda Wilkinson, Mona Hurley and Malcolm Clark's girlfriend Anne Harrison, joined the group to augment the backing vocals. This meant they could broaden their repertoire to include numbers in Ray Charles style, and also harmony numbers such as 'Volare' and 'Something's Got to Give' in Ray Conniff style. The group was also playing Brubeck's 'Take Five' and other instrumentals.

Towards the end of 1961 the decision was made to turn professional, which meant the group gave up their day jobs. Two of the girls, Linda and Mona, reluctantly left the group, leaving Anne on backing vocals for a short time. The group came under the agency of Tommy Sanderson, which meant they could play nationwide, particularly in London. They were based in Kilburn, and had regular venues in Lewisham, Camberley and Edmonton. They also travelled all the way to Ventnor, Isle of Wight, for a one date package show – and played to about twenty people! For a time they had digs in Salisbury, so they could cover the south-west of England. Regrettably Mike Sagar suffered a growth on his vocal cords which required an operation, and meant he had to be away for several months. During this time they were billed as The Cresters.

Three radio broadcasts followed, on the *NDO Show* (BBC Northern Dance Orchestra) from Manchester, and two TV shows, first in London (*Talent Showcase*) and the second from Bristol, the Jimmy Young *6-25 Show* (they were all live in those days). It was in 1962 that The Cresters left the Tommy Sanderson Agency for Jack Fallon's Variety Agency. In October 1962 they made their first tour of Scotland. Half-way through they realised they had forgotten their stage suits at the previous venue, and it was too late to turn back. Arriving in Elgin, they made a quick visit to the local Burtons, and purchased grey trousers and different coloured shirts. At one venue, at Bridge of Allan in Stirling, all the girls crowded round the stage when they were performing. The local boys were jealous and threw coins at the group, and the curtains had to be closed.

The group's second visit to Scotland did not start well. After playing at Aylesbury in Buckinghamshire, on a Saturday, they left at 1am to travel to Aberdeen, with no motorway to speak of and one driver (road manager Brian Scott). There was no Forth Bridge, just a ferry. Seventeen hours and 530 miles later they arrived at the Beach ballroom in Aberdeen, and played one small spot at a seated concert. At least the following night they were playing at the same venue for dancing, so it was not a totally wasted journey.

Perhaps 1962 was the most prolific time for the original Cresters, probably not financially, but certainly in terms of the many venues they played. Mike Sagar had returned from his successful operation, but only for a short while before he left the group and returned to Bradford. Things were changing! In early 1963, as the bad winter set in, the stalwart road manager Brian Scott left, taking his van with him. It was down to the Cresters' long-time manager, Steve Black, to purchase a van and act as driver. Furthermore all the group members were becoming disillusioned with their low wages and the incessant travelling, and they were starting to argue. Suddenly the bass guitarist Ian Bannister left, to be replaced by Richard Harding's brother John, as did drummer Colin Houghton, whose place was taken by Johnnie Casson.

In October 1963 the new line up was back in Scotland on a three day tour with The Beatles, a tour that also featured The Overlanders and the female duo The Caravelles (not the Bradford Caravelles), who had just had a Top Ten hit with 'You Don't Have to Be a Baby to Cry'. The Cresters went on to appear at the famous Batley Variety Club many times, working with Lulu and George Hamilton IV, and even backed Tammy Wynette at the Maltings in Norfolk.

The group was as popular as ever, especially on the cabaret circuit, where with the help of Johnnie Casson they introduced a comedy routine. In fact, the comedy almost became as popular as the music. Still at the top in 1983, the group eventually folded, with Richard Harding the only original member. Today The Cresters, with its two original members Mike Sagar and Richard Harding, still perform at many venues, and top the bill annually at Bradford's rock 'n' roll reunion.

Mike Sagar (b. 1940, Bradford) vocals
See profile.

Richard Harding (b. 1943, Bramley) lead guitar
See profile.

Colin Houghton (1943–90, Bradford)
See profile.

Malcolm Clark (1943–68, Bradford)
See The Dingos.

David (Emil) Hardacre (b. 1937, Bradford) bass and lead guitar, vocals
David attended Carlton Grammar School, and later Durham University. He was quite an accomplished rhythm guitarist in his early days, but played bass when he joined The Tennesseans from the late 1950s until joining The Tomboys in the early 1960s as both lead guitarist and vocalist. David was known throughout Bradford's rock 'n' roll era as one of the most accomplished guitar players in Yorkshire, and was always known as Emil to his peers. He was with The Tomboys until they disbanded, and later went to live in America.

David Butterfield (b. 1943, Bradford) bass guitar
David was educated at St Bede's Grammar School in Heaton. Like many teenagers, he started piano lessons, and maybe less conventionally followed this by learning to play alto sax in a dance band. After an introduction through Lonnie Donegan to skiffle, a guitar was bought for him by his parents, which led to him moving with great enthusiasm towards rock 'n' roll.

After starting up and playing with various groups in his locality, Thornton, he auditioned for The Tennesseans: Emil Hardacre was about to go to university and a replacement bass player was required. Within weeks of joining the group there was a name change, to Mike Sagar and the Cresters.

Dave truly believed that there was not a band in the country playing better rock 'n' roll than The Cresters. As time went by he found himself having to decide whether to stay with them and go professional, or stay with the job he had and make that his future. He decided to take the latter route, and found himself playing with another great group, The Dingos.

Dave is happy still playing the guitar regularly, wherever in the world his job takes him. His dental business, which he started with his wife Kathy, son Tim and daughter Tessa, now employs over 100 people in England, America and Mallorca. Travelling has allowed Dave to meet some great musicians, and have the opportunity to play alongside them. One such opportunity was the incredible meeting he had in the House of Blues, Las Vegas, where he was introduced to their new harmonica player – none other than Ian Atkinson, originally from Hebden Bridge, who had played with the Del Rio Four. Dave is now a member of the Las Vegas Blues Society, and every month gets invitations to take his guitar along and join in!

Dave lives in Ilkley with his wife Kathy, as do Tim and Tessa and their children, Danny, Sophie, Lauren, Claudia and Libby.

Ian Bannister (b. 1943, Bradford) bass guitar
See The Dingos.

Johnnie Casson (b 1943, Halifax) drums
See profile.

John Harding (b. 1946, Bramley, Leeds) bass guitar
John attended Swinnow Primary School and Hough Side Secondary School in Bramley. He was the younger brother of Richard Harding, and like Richard became a very competent guitarist. While still at school he used to go to the Students Club to see The Cresters, little knowing that one day he would be part of this famous group.

Towards the end of his time at school, having learnt to play lead guitar, John joined a group called The Thunderbirds. After a few months' experience he became rhythm guitarist with the Lucky Strikes. They had been formed to back touring artists, and were so successful that they turned professional. They backed most of the top stars and played at major venues in the UK.

It was now the early 1960s and John, now a very proficient guitarist, moved on to join the Ray Kennan Combo as lead guitar until 1963, when a dream came true and he joined The Cresters. Now playing bass guitar, he was part of The Cresters for the next twenty years, until the group finally disbanded in 1983. At that point he went solo, performing at the pubs and clubs as Chet Summers, playing the guitar and singing country and western music to backing tracks until 1988. That same year John became ill and after eighteen months was diagnosed with MS. Sadly he has not worked since, thus ending the remarkable career of a very talented artist who was able to play lead, rhythm and bass guitar.

John lives in Addingham, close to his daughter Zoe and grandchildren Lucy and Vincent in Ilkley. He is still active and mobile, enjoys working at the computer and still plays his guitar for fun.

John Harding was a great asset to The Cresters, but is sometimes overlooked as he had such a famous brother. He must have had something to play alongside his brother for over twenty years at the top.

Kenny Gough (b. 1941, Bradford) drums.
Kenny was one of those really good drummers who could be relied on to play his part whichever group he was with. He began as an early member of The Tennesseans, and in the 1960s was an original member of the Del Rio Four. When Colin Houghton of The Cresters had to go into hospital for a serious operation, Kenny, who had played with the group before, joined them until Colin recovered. Such was his ability that the call came just after The Cresters had released 'Deep Feeling', an important time for the group. Kenny went on to play with many groups, including for a short while Vince Wayne and the Falcons.

Mike Sagar's 1960 publicity shot for HMV records.

MIKE SAGAR

pop star

Mike Sagar, good-looking, strong voice and a marvellous sense of humour, had all the qualities to line-up with the Cliffs, Adams, Kennys and the rest. However, things were not to be, although his name is still recognisable to yesteryear's teenagers, especially in his home town of Bradford.

Mike Sagar (b. 1940) attended St James's School off Manchester Road and, passing his scholarship, went on to Grange Boys Grammar School. Aged sixteen, he became an apprentice wool sorter for G.R. Heron Ltd in West Bowling. It was during these early years that Mike taught himself to play rhythm guitar, although it was his vocals that brought him to the attention of the new rock 'n' roll groups coming onto the scene.

In 1957, aged seventeen, Mike joined The Tennesseans, who became one of Bradford's early successes. In 1960 he was with The Cresters when they recorded 'Deep Feeling'. His next record release came in 1961. 'The Brothers Three' was written by group member Richard Harding, who based it on John Leyton's song 'Johnny Remember Me'. The Cresters did not play on this record: the studio band of session musicians backed Mike. Like 'Deep Feeling', this record only had mediocre success. However, Mike and the Cresters were proving to be very popular, with many bookings throughout the UK, so much so they turned professional in 1961.

Regrettably Mike suffered from a throat problem, which was diagnosed as polyps on his vocal cords; this needed surgery and several months of recuperation. He rejoined them in 1962, but not for long. After an argument Mike stormed out of the band's digs in Kilburn, walked to Kilburn High Road and thumbed a lift home to Bradford.

Back home Mike turned his hand to the building industry, a complete contrast to singing rock 'n' roll – but it was not long before he was back with The Cresters. From 1963 he also played with Mick and the Tornados, the Quiet Three, The Toledos and, in the late 1960s, with Jinx.

In the 1970s Mike on vocals and Billy (Willie) Fenton guitar became the Mike Sagar Duo. After a short while, with two new members, this became the

Mike Sagar Trio. In 1979 he formed Dillinger, which, with the odd change in personnel over the years, is still popular today.

Today Mike is still actively involved in the music business and appears at many venues with The Cresters, he and Richard Harding being the only two original members. He still lives in the Low Moor area of Bradford with his lovely wife Tracey.

I have known Mike for over fifty years and never forget that in 1966, when I had just married Diana and was living in Wilsden, Mike and Ian Bannister built a large stone fireplace in our cottage as a wedding present. Thanks, Mike, and you can now stop asking when this book will be published.

THE NOMADS
rock 'n' roll

The Nomads were formed in about 1962. Originating in Oxenhope, they played at local youth club circuits, mainly the Crotona, Haworth and Central youth clubs. The band's name supposedly came from Patricia Dore, a leader at the Haworth Youth Club. The original members were Norman Crabtree, lead guitar, Robert Bailey, rhythm guitar, Mike 'Spike' Howley, bass guitar, and Joe Haigh, drums. Success was not long in coming, and regular bookings at ballroom venues soon established them. After some success and publicity, when they appeared with Freddy and the Dreamers at the Imperial ballroom in Nelson, they were booked to appear with The Searchers in 1963. Also on the same bill was The Beatles, but such was their popularity that they did not take part, much to the disappointment of The Nomads!

In 1964 the lead guitarist Norman Crabtree moved on to join the Mark Russell Four, as did the drummer Joe Haigh. The Nomads had no problem in filling their places as they were still very much in demand, with bookings months ahead. Ian Sanderson, late of The Spartans, became their lead guitarist, and drummer John Kirkham filled Joe Haigh's shoes. A fifth member was added: Malcolm Nixon had been in groups since 1958 and was an excellent lead guitarist. This particular line-up continued through the 1960s until 1980.

The Nomads never went out of fashion in the 1980s and '90s, and although group members changed they still have bookings in the twenty-first century. Some of their regular venues are the Snooty Fox, Bronte Hotel, Three Sisters, the Green Gables, and the usual wooden hut affairs! Thursdays, Fridays, Saturdays and Sundays used to see the band playing at least one of these venues, but the changing of music licensing laws had a detrimental effect on all live music, and pretty soon there was only the Green Gables licensed for bands.

The Nomads are still giving pleasure to their many fans – and, like some of the other original groups still playing, they have raised many thousands of pounds for a local cancer charity, Manorlands.

The Nomads perfom at an outdoor venue, 1962. All members of the group came from the Keighley area, and were still playing well into the twenty-first century. Left to right: Norman Crabtree, Mike (Spike) Howley, Robert Bailey, Joe Haigh.

The Nomads promote Ben Shaw's, one of Yorkshire's leading soft drinks manufacturers, at the Silver Blades ice rink, 1965. Left to right: Malcolm Nixon, John Kirkham, Mike Howley, Robert Bailey.

Norman Crabtree (b. 1944, Keighley) lead guitar
Norman joined The Nomads in 1962, but left in 1964 to join the Mark Russell Four.

Joe Haigh (b. 1944, Oxenhope) drums
Joe joined The Nomads in 1962. In 1964 he was invited to play with the Mark Russell Four.

Robert Bailey (1942–2007, Keighley) vocals
Robert was a founder member of The Nomads, their lead vocalist from 1962. His talent was well known and he had many a girl swooning over his renditions of Bee Gees and Four Pennies songs. He was also transport manager: he owned the van, and often refused to turn up the heater on cold journeys! Well educated, Robert later taught engineering at Keighley College, and also ran the family quarrying business after the death of his father. He never played in public again after he left The Nomads in 1972, and sadly passed away in 2007 after a short illness.

Mike (Spike) Howley (b. 1943, Keighley) bass guitar
Mike attended St Anne's School. He was front man, founder member and driving force behind the group, and famous for his rendition of 'Peanuts'. As a young lad he was quite a ventriloquist, and sometimes he incorporated his dummy called Jimmy Green into the act, to everyone's amusement. Spike later formed a dance trio called the New Hammond Sound, continued to play from time to time with The Nomads, and latterly appeared with the Brian T. Strollers.

Malcolm Nixon (1941–2004, Keighley) lead guitar
See The Presidents.

John Kirkham (b. 1940, Keighley) drums
John joined The Nomads in 1964. Also a very accomplished jazz drummer, he left the group in 1966.

Ian (Sandy) Sanderson (b. 1945, Keighley) lead guitar
See the Rocking Spartans.

The Phantoms, 1962. Left to right: Brindley Jardine, Chris Gibson, Peter Clegg, Roy Waterworth.

The Phantoms rock 'n' roll on a Saturday morning for youngsters, while mums went shopping. The venue was the Gaumont cinema stage.

THE PHANTOMS/BRANWELL AND THE BRONTEBEATS WITH CHARLOTTE

rock 'n' roll

The Phantoms began in 1962, originally as the Fabulous Phantoms. The group members were Brindley Jardine, drums, Chris Gibson, lead guitar, Colin Whiteley, bass guitar, and Peter Clegg, vocals and rhythm guitarist. Their manager for a while was Peter's father, George. One of their earliest bookings was at Bingley Grammar School, an event that received much publicity in the *Daily Mirror*. During their performance an elderly female teacher ordered them to leave the stage, as she said 'the group were sending the girls into *raptures*'! She then told the 200 boys and girls in attendance that they could go on dancing waltzes and valetas ... to records! The teenagers booed, and asked for their admission charge of 2s back. As ordered, The Phantoms packed up their equipment and left. They later received their full fee.

After a while Colin left the group, and the three remaining members continued as a trio. During this time they entered and won the prestigious Northern Song Contest at St George's Hall. Shortly afterwards Roy Waterworth replaced Colin on bass, and they continued with this line-up for two years, with the well-known Carl Gresham as their manager. With Carl's skills they became very popular, and a *Melody Maker* poll voted them the best band in Yorkshire. Their gimmick was to have their hair bleached (something almost unheard of in those days) and to wear matching suits with gold lamé glitter.

In 1964 the group took a step forward with a new manager, Farrel Kelly. Back came Colin Whiteley on bass and a new female singer to front them, Ann McCormack. They reformed as Branwell and the Brontebeats with Charlotte, a name synonymous with the local village of Haworth, its desolate moors and parsonage, although the choice of name did not go down well with rector of Haworth Church! The band wore traditional mid-Victorian outfits, and Ann wore floor-length dresses, including a bustle. TV appearances followed, and an old forty-two seater coach was converted into a travelling home for the group, with their name painted on each side. They began to be successful, but unfortunately they disbanded after only a few months.

In 1965 Peter Clegg and Ann McCormack decided to form a trio, and the new member to make up the trio was Radivoj (Danny) Danic, whom they had met while they were performing at the George Hotel in Low Moor. Danny was selling cockles and mussels to supplement his engineering job. When he told them he could sing and play the guitar he was in! The name of the trio was The Newarks.

One of their first bookings was at West Bowling Labour Club in Bradford. It was there that Tony Hartwell of Philips Records saw them, and after demos had been made and their name had been changed to the Three Good Reasons they were given a recording contract with Philips on the Mercury label. Their first single, 'Build Your Love', was unfortunately not a hit, but some success followed with a number one in Holland: this was a track from a Beatles album, 'Nowhere Man'. After their third single release, 'Moment of Truth', written by Marty Wilde, the Three Good Reasons parted, leaving their mark locally ... and in Holland.

Peter Clegg (b. 1947, Bradford) vocals and rhythm guitar
Living in Odsal, Peter attended Cooper Lane Infants School, Great Horton Middle School and Buttershaw Secondary Modern School. Leaving education aged fifteen, he joined his father's profession, becoming an apprentice weaving overlooker at Pepper Lees Mill in Wyke. He left the mill to be a professional musician, and later, when the Three Good Reasons disbanded, he became a painter and decorator. However, he soon returned to music, this time with a trio called Impakt, which gave him a season at Butlin's in 1968. In 1972 he joined a group called Crumbs of Comfort, later shortened to Comfort when they backed Rickie Valance and Heinz of 'Telstar' fame.

Peter later played with an assortment of bands, including the Dave Lee Sound – with whom he played bass guitar. Then he was with Hi-Fly, which went on the top of the bill at Batley Variety Club. Later, into the 1980s, Peter spent some time with a mobile disco as well as playing for occasional bands, the last being Everything in 2000. Peter is now retired, and still lives in the Bradford area with his family and grandchildren.

Brindley Jardine (b. 1947, Wilsden) drums
Son of a baker, Brindley was with The Phantoms from 1962 to 1964 and then Branwell and the Brontebeats with Charlotte. He later joined an orchestra and toured throughout the UK.

Chris Gibson (b. 1948, overseas) lead guitar
Chris was born abroad as his father was serving in the RAF. The family moved to Bradford weeks before he joined The Phantoms as lead guitarist in 1962. He stayed with the group until 1964, and remained with them when they re-formed as Branwell and the Brontebeats with Charlotte. After he left he became a session musician for Joe Meek, the record producer and songwriter.

Roy Waterworth (b. 1945, Bradford) bass guitar
Roy was with The Phantoms from 1962 to 1964, and later moved away from Bradford.

ROCK & TWIST

TO THE FABULOUS

PHANTOMS

on FRIDAY APRIL 5th 1963

7-30 to 11-45

at BINGLEY LITTLE THEATRE

Tickets 2/6 Light Refreshments

In 1965 Peter Clegg and Ann McCormack decided to form a trio with Radivoj (Danny) Danic, calling themselves the Three Good Reasons. Left to right: Peter Clegg, Ann McCormack, Radivoj Danic.

Colin Whiteley (b. 1948, Bradford) bass guitar
Colin played with The Phantoms, then left, but later rejoined Branwell and the Brontebeats and Charlotte until its break-up in 1965.

Ann Bailey aka Ann McCormack (b. 1950, Bradford) vocals
Ann lived on Buttershaw Drive, on the Buttershaw estate, and started in showbusiness at the age of eleven as a singer with a local band The Dyaks. Aged fifteen she became the lead singer with The Brontebeats, and then with Three Good Reasons. Later she formed the Bailey Moore Trio with her husband Jack and Duncan Moore, formerly of the Avondales. After many years she left the group to become a full-time mother, while her husband Jack went on to have great success with top country band Stroller, still with Duncan Moore. Ann's two sons are carrying on the tradition and playing in bands. Ann is now retired and still lives in the Bradford area.

Danic (Danny) Radivoj (b. 1944, Sabac, Yugoslavia) guitar
When Danny was eleven his family moved to England and settled in Brantwood Oval, in the Heaton district of Bradford. He began to play the guitar aged twelve and also became quite proficient on the banjo. It was after a chance meeting with Peter and Ann at the George Hotel in Low Moor that he joined them to make up the Three Good Reasons. After they broke up Danny continued to live and work in Bradford.

The Three Good Reasons went on to have a recording contract with Philips. Success followed with a number one hit – in Holland.

THE PRESIDENTS

rock 'n' roll

In 1957 Keighley produced one of its first rock 'n' roll groups. The Presidents were so called because three of its members played Hofner President guitars. The original line-up was Bruce Russell, bass guitar (although he was playing bass on a non-bass guitar, as bass guitars were not available at this time), Linda Nixon aka Linda Russell, lead singer, Colin Hodgson, vocals and rhythm guitar, Malcolm Nixon (Linda's brother), vocals and lead guitar, and Edward (Ted) Earle, drums.

The Presidents had started as a skiffle group called The Zephyrs, and for a short while mainly played at youth clubs in the Keighley area; however, they also did some club and dance hall work supporting the local dance bands at venues such as the Mechanics' Institute, Keighley. Later this position was reversed as rock 'n' roll became more popular, and groups replaced dance bands.

The Presidents' line-up changed as some members joined other groups, and in 1960 they consisted of Bruce Russell, Linda Russell, Colin Hodgson, Chris Kelly, drums, and Stuart Nixon (Linda's younger brother), lead guitar. A few months later they disbanded, as three members joined The Beatniks, to form the Beat Squad.

Bruce Russell (b 1939, Keighley) bass guitar

See Linda Russell and Bruce.

Linda Nixon aka Linda Russell (b. 1942, Keighley) vocals

See Linda Russell and Bruce.

Colin Hodgson (b 1940, Keighley) vocals and rhythm guitar

It's thumbs up from a young fan for the Zephyrs skiffle group playing at Cliffe Castle, 1958. Some weeks later they went all rock 'n' roll and became The Presidents. Left to right: Bruce Russell, Malcolm Nixon, Ted Earle (later the drummer), Colin Hodgson.

The Presidents entertain a youth club Christmas party in the early days, 1958. Left to right: Ted Earle, Linda Nixon, Malcolm Nixon, Bruce Russell.

The Presidents at Holden Hall ,Oakworth, 1959. Back row, left to right: Colin Hodgson, Stuart Nixon, Bruce Russell. Front row: Chris Kelly, Linda Nixon.

Colin was an accomplished ukulele musician, who went on to play guitar with several dance bands. His full-time career was that of a draughtsman.

Malcolm Nixon (1941–2004, Keighley) lead guitar
From 1958 to 1961 Malcolm played lead guitar with The Presidents. Later he formed a group with his first wife Kathleen as lead vocalist and his younger brother Stuart on second guitar. They were called the Gary Lee Three, named after Malcolm and Kathleen's two children). In 1964 Malcolm joined an early line-up of The Nomads, for whom he played on and off for three decades. He also played with other local groups, including jazz bands. Malcolm, a brilliant and well-respected lead guitarist, spent his last few years in Skipton, where he died in 2004.

Chris Kelly (b 1941, Keighley) drums and lead guitar
After The Presidents, Chris joined Rondo and Kelly's Heroes. In 1981 he joined The Nomads as lead guitarist.

Stuart Nixon (b. 1945, Keighley) lead guitarist, vocals and keyboard
Stuart was the younger brother of Malcolm and Linda. After The Presidents he joined Malcolm and his wife Kathleen as the Gary Lee Three, and later became musical director to his daughter Debbie with the Debbie Angel Show (now Angel and Korrel), an international success, especially on cruise liners.

Edward (Ted) Earle (b. 1940, Keighley) vocals and drums
Ted later played with the Beat Squad and The Keymen.

THE RATTLERS

rock 'n' roll

The Rattlers original members when they formed in 1964 were Spike O'Brien, piano, Keith Barrett, bass guitar, Harry Stott, drums, and a stand-in Manx guitarist. Their inaugural gig was six months at a huge 2,000-seater seven bar hotel complex called The Villiers in Douglas, Isle of Man. The season was a great success, bringing piano/guitar-based rock to an audience that had previously not heard it.

Back in the UK, in March 1965 the line-up changed, with Keith still on bass and also vocals, and Spike on piano; they were joined by Brendan Crowe, rhythm guitar, and John Fea, drums, Harry Stott having left. The Rattlers were once again booked for The Villiers, from April to September 1965. After numerous 'consultation visits' to Viv's Bar and a couple of rehearsals they set off to the Isle of Man. This six-month season was a unique experience, not least because the Manx opening hours were 10am until 6am the next morning. Opening hours on Sundays were more limited, but even so the group played twelve or thirteen lengthy sessions each week, honing both their playing and their social skills. Over this period they built up a huge fan base both locally and among visitors. It was a completely different scene from Bradford, walking home from the casino along the promenade at around 5.30 am on the Saturday morning, pretty much knackered after a long week's playing, with only the seagulls picking at last night's chip wrappers for company and the sun struggling to appear over the Liverpool horizon.

In September 1965, having signed up to return the following year, The Rattlers returned to Bradford for a brief rest, spending time with their families and settling back into Bradford life. Unfortunately immediate gigs were scarce, and following such an active season Spike and John's thoughts turned towards London to carry their careers forward. The Rattlers continued with two further seasons in the Isle of Man, augmented by new musicians, after which the group dispersed.

Brian (Spike) O Brien (1940–2000) piano

See profile.

The Rattlers attracted huge crowds to the Villiers Hotel, Isle of Man, in 1965. Here they relax with a couple of fans. Left to right: John Fea, Keith Barrett, Spike O'Brien, Brendan Crowe.

Keith Barrett (b. 1946, Bradford) bass guitar and vocals
Keith lived in Greengates. He was with several groups, including Jeff Green and the Bandits and was the only married member of The Rattlers: his wife was Janet and they had a baby son called Paul Leon. Keith was also an accomplished songwriter and vocalist. He was the only member of The Rattlers to attend all the Isle of Man seasons (1964–7).

Brendan Crowe (1944–85, Bradford) rhythm guitar
See Mick and the Tornadoes.

Harry Stott (b. 1944, Bradford) drums
Harry only played the first Isle of Man season with The Rattlers.

John Fea (b. 1945, Kent) drums and harmonica
John's family moved to Bradford in 1955, where he attended Belle Vue Grammar School and, for a short time, Bradford Art College – leaving to work for the Post Office. His forte was the drums and it was not long before he was playing in swing-jazz and rock 'n' roll groups, including for a short period The Tuxedos, Telecasters and The Jinx. In 1965 he joined The Rattlers for its successful season in the Isle of Man. In 1967 he returned there with the re-formed Rattlers for a six month season.

Fashion and music were rapidly changing, and it was the 'Flower Power' period of *Sergeant Pepper* and Scott Mackenzie. From 1968 until the 1970s and '80s John worked in a variety of bands on drums, including the re-formed

Overlanders (of 'Michelle' fame). John and Spike O'Brien, working in London, formed a great little harmony group called Pat's People, and some time later they re-formed The Rattlers in London, this time with original bassist Keith Barrett. It was during this period that John met and married Jill.

In the early '90s, while playing club gigs on drums he was privileged to play many sessions on blues harmonica with the likes of Cliff Bennett and the Rebel Rousers, Mike Berry and other bands involved in the Joe Meek Road Show. In the mid-1990s he was invited by The Dingos to replace their original drummer Smudge, which he continued to do until his lifelong buddy Spike's untimely death, just a few days into the new millennium.

John and Jill now live in Surrey. From time to time he enjoys playing in bars and clubs in Spain. He is an overlooked and very talented drummer and harmonica player, who deserves recognition for his contribution to our world of rock 'n' roll.

Richard Harding at Strawberry Studios, Stockport, 1964. The egg boxes used to deaden the sound didn't look great, but worked.

RICHARD HARDING

guitarist legend

Richard Harding is acknowledged to be one of the greatest virtuoso guitarists throughout the UK and beyond. He is admired by many world-renowned musicians, including Eric Clapton, Mark Knopfler, Paul McCartney and Tom Jones, and many local rock 'n' roll peers.

Richard Harding was born in Bramley in 1943, lived at 84 Hough Lane and was educated at Swinnow Primary School and Leeds Central High School. Richard's father, Arthur, although having a university degree in textiles, had also been a violinist in several West Riding orchestras. At home he had a recording studio in the attic, and as a skilled studio engineer with a home-made eight-track (mainly mono), he produced hundreds of demo tapes for a wide range of Yorkshire musicians. It was little wonder that Richard's knowledge of music electronics would be, as they say, a chip off the old block.

At a local youth club Richard knew a lad who had an electric guitar. Even though he couldn't play it he was in a group. Richard was very interested, especially in how the instrument was made, and set out to make his own guitar. In fact, he made three, and learnt to play them by listening to Bill Haley's 'Rock Around The Clock' over and over again.

It was not long before he became very proficient on the guitar, and it was in the last days of skiffle that he met local lad Mick Sagar and with three others formed The Tennesseans. They were soon playing at local venues, including the Students Club, the Gaumont and Majestic ballrooms and working men's clubs. Soon they were joined by Malcolm Clark and Ian Bannister, both from The Dingos, and The Cresters had arrived. Later, with an EMI contract, they recorded 'Deep Feeling', but this was not a success. Richard recorded a follow-up solo single, 'Temptation' and 'Jezebel', which was released in 1961. It was bad luck that the Everly Brothers released their version of 'Temptation' at the same time.

The group was now playing many venues around the UK, including a tour with Freddie Cannon, dates in the North of England and a full week at the notorious Glasgow Empire. Later in 1963, at the height of their popularity, they had a three day tour with The Beatles in Scotland.

Perhaps one of Richard's fondest memories is from 1965. It was during an one overnight stay in Manchester when they were playing at the Jungfrau Club, in a cellar in the city centre. While the group were sorting out their instruments Richard bumped into a tall fellow, then stepped back in amazement: it was Chet Atkins, Richard's hero! He was with Jim Reeves, and later they watched the group play, including a few instrumentals from Richard, and Chet told Richard how much he had enjoyed his playing. Richard will never forget it – partly because he caught chicken pox the following day!

Today Richard is still very much in demand, playing with the popular Dillinger and at the Bradford rock 'n' roll reunions. He is also very active in his recording studio in Bramley, producing radio commercials within the radio industry.

His lovely and talented wife Brenda was also quite a star in the Swinging Sixties, singing under the name of Brenda May. In 1967 she recorded 'I shouldn't care about you' on HMV, made many TV appearances and was on European cabaret tours. Today she is still well known and respected in the music business. As for Richard, no amount of text can do justice to the life of this extraordinarily talented guitarist. It has been a pleasure to know him for over fifty years.

ROBIN HOOD AND HIS MERRY MEN
rock 'n' roll

A name to conjure with was Robin Hood and His Merry Men, who were on the local scene for a short while in 1965–6. At one time they were all dressed in twelfth-century costumes, which was a sight to behold, but the loose garments interfered with their musical instruments and their movement on stage.

All local lads, the line up consisted of a keyboard player whose name is now forgotten, Mike Stephenson, rhythm guitar, Allen Marston, vocals, and Trevor MacParland, drums. The group had little success, although they had a certain following. There was talk of some members of the group moving to the south coast, but Mike Stephenson could see the writing on the wall and left the group to further another career. The keyboard player also moved on, leaving Allen Marston and Trevor MacParland to chase their dream. Moving to Southsea, they were joined by two local musicians and took the name Get Rich. Things were not going well, so they could not turn professional and took mediocre jobs to sustain a living. There were few bookings in Southsea, although the *Daily Mirror* published a large feature about the group in 1966. Allen was quoted as saying, 'We've got away from the working men's clubs of the North and that's the main thing. Audiences there only want to hear Beatles' music and the stuff they can sing along to. We couldn't play what we wanted or how we wanted and they kept telling us to turn the volume down. Here we can play the way we like.'

After a short while, however, Allen and Trevor returned home. Within days a new group was formed, with the input of rhythm guitarist Brian Wardley from the Five Leighs, and two of Bradford's top musicians, bass player Allan Davies from The Royalists and John Verity from The Chillas. With Allen taking lead vocals, the new name was Allen Pounds Get Rich. They took a short trip to London, but nothing much materialised although they released a record on Parlophone, 'Searching in the Wilderness'. They returned to Bradford, and by December 1966 the new group had folded. Perhaps if Robin Hood and his Merry Men had stayed in Yorkshire from the beginning they might have succeeded – we shall never know!

A modern Robin Hood and his Merry Men. Left to right: -?-, Mike Stephenson, Allen Marston, Trevor MacParland.

Allen Marston aka Allen Pound (b. 1946, Bradford) vocals
Allen lived in the Nab Wood area. For a while he worked as a representative for a loans company. He was with Robin Hood and His Merry Men from 1965 to 1966, and then Get Rich. In mid-1966 Allen reorganised the group, with new members and a new name, Allen Pounds Get Rich, but this was short lived. They released one single, 'Searching in the Wilderness', on Parlophone before they broke up in December 1966.

Trevor MacParland (b. 1948 Bradford) drums
Trevor was with Get Rich in 1966 and then Allen Pounds Get Rich. He joined Bonafide in 1967 and in the same year moved to another group, Success.

Mike Stephenson (b. 1938, Bradford) rhythm guitar
See Sansovenos.

Brian Wardley (b. 1946, Bradford) rhythm guitar
Brian joined Allen Pounds Get Rich from the Five Leighs.

John Verity (b. 1949, Bradford) lead guitar
See profile.

Allan Davies (b. 1945, Bradford) bass guitar
See The Royalists.

Originally know as the Rocking Spartans, the name was shortened to The Spartans, seen here at Ryshworth Working Men's Club, 1965. A Vox organ was part of this very popular group by now. Left to right: Ian Sanderson, Harry 'Henry' Horrocks, Tony Woodiwiss, Colin Wood.

THE ROCKING SPARTANS/SPARTANS

rock 'n' roll

The group was formed in Keighley in 1962, from members of the Crotona Youth Club that was then based in North Street, Keighley. Originally known as the Rocking Spartans, the founder members were Ian (Sandy) Sanderson, lead guitar and vocals, Roy Wood, drums, Tony Warmsley, bass guitar, and Jim Harrison, rhythm guitar. The group played in working men's clubs and local youth clubs, becoming The Spartans in 1964, with a final line-up of Ian Sanderson, Tony Woodwiss, bass guitar, Harry (Henry) Horrocks, Vox organ, and Colin Wood, drums. During the early rock 'n' roll years in Keighley, The Spartans and The Nomads were rivals, each with separate loyal fan bases.

In June 1964 they sent a demonstration disc to the television show *Ready Steady Go*, and also copies to DJ Jimmy Savile and Screaming Lord Sutch's pirate radio station. The song was 'All I Want', written by Tony Warmsley. As with so many groups at that time, which were pushing to be noticed, nothing happened.

Local bookings of note were the Crotona Club, Victoria Hall, Keighley, the Buffs Club, Oxenhope Social Club (known as the Idiot Hut), the American base at Menwith Hill, Harrogate, and the Imperial ballroom in Nelson. They had an offer to go on tour as a supporting group for Kathy Kirby, Freddie and the Dreamers and Heinz, but because they were only semi-professionals and had work commitments they could not accept it. The Spartans finally broke up in 1966.

Ian (Sandy) Sanderson (b. 1945, Keighley) lead guitar and vocals

Ian attended Keighley Grammar School. Leaving school at eighteen, he joined NSF (National Switch Factor) in 1962, and worked there until 1968, when he moved to Anderton Springs in Bingley. Ian started his musical career at the age of sixteen, when he watched local groups including The Presidents, Beat Squad and The Beatniks. In 1962, having taught himself to play the guitar, he helped to form the Rocking Spartans.

In 1966 Ian left to join The Nomads as lead guitar, remaining with them until 1975, at which point he played with a resident band at the Armitage Arms in Brighouse. As he was still working full time, as a sales engineer, he occasionally played with The Nomads, as every so often they re-formed, albeit with non-original musicians.

Later Ian went on to form his own company, Fish People, working from his premises in Keighley until he retired in 2010. Ian still plays with The Nomads and still lives in Keighley with his partner Kath.

Roy Wood (b 1943, Keighley) drums
Roy was a founder member of the Rocking Spartans, and left the group in 1964.

Tony Warmsley (b. 1947, Lancaster) bass guitar
A founder member of the Rocking Spartans, Tony left the group in 1964.

Jim Harrison (b. 1945, Keighley) rhythm guitar
A founder member of the Rocking Spartans, Jim left the group in 1964, and later joined Jovial Crew.

Tony Woodwiss (b. 1945, Keighley) bass guitar
Tony joined The Spartans in 1964 and left when they folded in 1966. He now lives in New Zealand.

Harry (Henry) Horrocks (b. 1945, Clitheroe) Vox organ/keyboard
Harry joined the Spartans from a Clitheroe group called Lee Barry and the MGs. He left in 1966.

Colin Wood (b. 1944, Keighley) drums
Colin left The Spartans in 1966, and worked for Austin Reed, the tailors, in Keighley

ROY AND THE FOUR ACES/BILLY ROYAL AND THE FOUR ACES

rock 'n' roll

Formed in 1962 as the Four Aces and subsequently reformed as Roy and the Four Aces, the group consisted of Alfred Nurse, drums, Peter Nurse, bass guitar, Michael Roberts, rhythm guitar and vocals, Stan Mawson, lead guitar, and Roy Copeland, vocals. All were resplendent in royal blue jackets and grey trousers. What was probably unique about the group was that a father and son were members: Alfred Nurse, who was manager as well as drummer, was in his fifties, and his son Peter was in his early twenties.

Many working men's clubs, dance halls and other venues were entertained by this up and coming popular group, who were transported to each venue in the usual Thames van. They played at the White Swan in Wibsey, Bankfoot and Dudley Hill working men's clubs and at Menston Working Men's Club, which gave them a regular booking simply because they were the only quiet group that did not disturb the neighbours. Other bookings followed, at the Slackside Working Men's Club, Tyersal Working Men's Club and Bradford's Transport Club, Sunbridge Road; they even ventured to a regular booking at the Crescent Club in York. They also played at local dance halls, including the Kings and Queens in Morley Street and the Majestic. The group's repertoire was an assortment of music that always proved very popular: Shadows and Merseybeats numbers, r&b, rock 'n' roll, ballads and even a skiffle spot.

Between 1963 and 1964 two young vocalists were introduced into the group, sisters Pat and Joan Gallagher. It was a good move as the girls added glamour as well as being extremely good vocalists, Pat with ballads and Joan with rock 'n' roll. At about the same time Roy Copeland, the vocalist, left to be replaced by Billy Bloomfield, and the group's new name was Billy Royal and the Four Aces. Mike Roberts also moved on in 1964, to be replaced for a short while by Paul Flintoff and then John Wilkinson as rhythm guitarists.

It was John Wilkinson who brought humour into the group, making it even more popular. They were now managed by the Gallagher sisters' father Leo. Although he had the group's interests at heart, and tried to keep them

Billy Royal and the Four Aces was originally Roy and the Four Aces. Left to right: Stan Mawson, Alfred Nurse, Paul Flintoff, Billy Bloomfield (Billy Royal), Peter Nurse.

The Four Aces. Left to right: Stan Mawson, Alfred Nurse, Paul Flintoff, Peter Nurse.

together, family commitments and career moves meant that in 1965 the lads and lasses moved on.

Stan Mawson (b. 1943, Bradford) lead guitarist
Stan attended schools in Pudsey, including the grammar school. He was first employed by Samuel Butler, Bridge Builders, and later Frank Wigglesworth in Shipley. However, his career took off with Clyde, Crane, Booth Limited of Rodley. He was still with them as proposals manager in 2008 when he retired.

Stan's musical ability came from his mother, who played the piano; not only did he learn her instrument, but he also taught himself to play the guitar. Like many young rock 'n' roll musicians of the time he built his own guitar, until with his mother's help he purchased an Antoria guitar.

After leaving the Four Aces Stan concentrated on his career. Now retired, he still plays his guitar from time to time and also plays the organ at a local church. He still lives in Clayton with his wife Pauline and family, two children and four grandchildren.

Peter Nurse (b. 1940, Bradford) bass guitar
Peter lived in Great Horton, where he attended Grange Infants School and Primary School, and later Grange Boys Grammar School. In 1958 he took up a radio and TV apprenticeship for Bolton Radio Services, moving later to the Bradford Central Workshops. When Peter left the Four Aces in 1965 it was to concentrate on his career. Over the next few years he was employed in many senior positions as a TV engineer with Baird Television, British Relay and DER (Domestic Electrical Rentals). In 1978, while with Bradford College as a senior lecturer in electronics, he was seconded to work in Oman, Saudi Arabia. Still with Bradford College, he retired in 2005.

Peter now spends most of his spare time with the vintage model aircraft clubs of Brighouse and Keighley and district. He lives in Allerton with his wife Mary, two sons and five grandchildren.

Alfred Nurse (1912–97, Bradford) drums and manager
Alfred was brought up in the Great Horton area. After schooling, he was employed by Bradford Transport Corporation as a tram and bus conductor; later he worked at Grattan Warehouse, until retiring in 1977. A self-taught musician, Alfred played drums, ukulele and guitar – and it was he who formed the Four Aces. It is a tribute to him that in his fifties he was a drummer in a teenage rock 'n' roll group. Albert passed away in 1997, aged eighty five.

Roy Copeland (b. 1944, Bradford) vocals
Roy was with the group from 1962 to 1964. He was employed as a manual worker for the local water board (before it became Yorkshire Water), and was based at Chellow Heights treatment plant in Sandy Lane, Bradford. Later he was a caretaker at a primary school in Addingham near Ilkley.

Billy Bloomfield (b. 1944, Bradford) vocals
Billy lived in Windhill and worked at Butterfields, engineers in Shipley. He took over from Roy Copeland on vocals in the Four Aces in 1964, and the

group's name then changed to Billy Royal and the Four Aces. Later he went to live in Bournemouth.

Mike Roberts (b. 1946, Bradford) rhythm guitar and vocals

Mike lived in the Thornton-Allerton area of Bradford, where he attended Fairweather Green Primary School and Belle Vue Boys Grammar School. His first job was as a trainee supervisor with a plastics company in Allerton, and it was during this time that he left the Four Aces to concentrate on his career. After working for a couple of dyeing and chemical companies for thirteen years, he moved into education for twenty-seven years, spending his last five years in educational research at Leeds University.

Mike, now retired, spends time with his main hobby of photography, which he took up when he was thirteen. The rest of his spare time is spent going to college and picking up qualifications related to his diverse career history. He now lives in the Riddlesden area of Keighley with his wife Maureen; they have a son called Simon, who works in Newcastle.

Paul Flintoff (b. 1946, Bradford) rhythm guitar

Paul came into the group for a short while in 1964, and was well known for playing his guitar in a Chuck Berry style.

John Wilkinson (b. 1941, Bradford) rhythm guitar

John was employed at Baird Television. He brought comedy and humour to the group when he took over from Paul Flintoff, adding a different and popular angle to the act until its demise in 1965.

Patricia Gallagher (1946–98, Bradford) vocals

Patricia lived in the Buttershaw area of Bradford. With her sister Joan she was with the group for eighteen months, her speciality being ballads.

Joan Gallagher (1949–2004) vocals

Joan lived in the Buttershaw area of Bradford. Like her sister Pat she was with the group for eighteen months, her speciality being rock 'n' roll. She later lived in Ilkley and became a representative for a cosmetic company.

THE ROYALISTS

rock 'n' roll

A mix and match group of local young talented lads got together in late 1963 to form a new group called The Royalists that would go on to be very popular at top venues and Butlin's holiday camps. The group consisted of Malcolm Murray, vocalist, Allan Davies, bass guitar and backing vocals, Roy Bould, piano and keyboard, and Vic Storey, drums and backing vocals.

After much practice, entrepreneur Tommy Crabtree, owner of the County Bars in Bradford, became mentor and promoter for the group for some time, until the lack of bookings prompted a move to the Flair Agency, which was run by two women. Again this was not very successful, so they decided to manage themselves. It proved to be a good move, as in February 1964 Owen Hammond, Butlin's agent, was in Bradford to hold auditions at the Engineers Club in Westgate. Many local groups attended, but the Royalists had that certain something that swung the balance, and they passed the audition. A contract was awarded for twenty weeks, from May until October 1964, at the Butlin's in Minehead, Somerset.

All went well at Butlin's, so much so that a recording contract loomed and a visit was planned to London in late 1964. Everything seemed to go well at the recording studio, but nothing came of it. It was suggested that if they could move to London then things could be different. They all agreed that this was a non-starter: as one group member said, 'If we get booked for the London Palladium then perhaps we would move!'

Returning from the London trip, it was back to playing at clubs and rock 'n' roll venues, and even a small Scottish tour. In March 1965 Butlin's was on offer again, with a week's pre-season booking at Bognor Regis. This was so successful that staff and campers sent a petition asking for them to be booked for the season. This wasn't to be, but The Royalists were booked for the season at Butlin's, Filey, for fourteen weeks from June to October. In 1966 they were again booked at Filey. Although as usual they were a big success, group members wanted to do other things and moved on. The Royalists were no more.

Malcolm (Mac) Murray (1939–2010, Bradford) vocals
Malcolm lived on the Canterbury estate and attended Wibsey Modern Secondary School. On leaving school he worked for a local cloth dye-house, then William Denby and Son, Hollins Hill, during which time he started singing part-time with Irene Ford as a double act in local clubs.

In 1963 Malcolm met Roy Bould and they teamed up to form The Royalists. When this group folded in 1966 he formed a duo with Roy Woodrow, until 1968 – when he got back with Roy Bould again. With the addition of John Hare they had a season at Butlin's as the Royal Trio. In 1970 Malcolm teamed up with Josh Grundy as the Eccentrik Duo.

In 1975 Malcolm went solo, performing at many venues in a professional and popular style until 2003, when he retired and went to live with his wife Kath in Spain. In 2010, Malcolm returned to the UK as he was ill, and lived in Bingley until October, when he passed away. He left behind a loving family.

Malcolm's singing exemplified the rock 'n' roll era, and he was a pivotal member of The Royalists and assorted duos and combos. He never seemed to change in looks, voice, charm or entertainment. Mac certainly deserves a place in Bradford's rock 'n' roll history.

Allan Davies (b. 1945, Bradford) bass guitar and vocals
Allan attended Carlton Grammar School. Leaving school aged sixteen, he was employed by Tanks and Drums in Bowling and later at St James's Market, Bradford. Allan sang and played the guitar from the age of fourteen, and with experience in skiffle helped form Clay Martin and the Trespassers.

After time in 1963 with the Great Pacifics, Allan formed The Royalists in 1964. After their demise in 1966 he joined Allen Pounds Get Rich and went to London as they had a recording contract with the agent Tito Burns. A demo disc was made but no recording contract was forthcoming, so Allan was soon back in Bradford. He joined the Blood Group from 1966 to 1968.

During the late 1960s and '70s Allan played with many groups. In the 1970s he spent time in Amsterdam and in London, where he played reggae soul with the group Indigo. For the next twenty-five years he was in great demand, and later he teamed up with ex-Royalist Roy Bould, entertaining at local venues.

Allan now spends most of his time at home in his music studio in Bradford composing folk, blues and country music, supported by his wife Josie.

Roy Bould (b. 1938, Eccleshill) piano
Roy attended Carlton Grammar School. In 1954 he joined the GPO in Bradford as a messenger boy, and in 1956 signed on in the Royal Signals before he was called up for his National Service. In 1959 he returned to the GPO.

Roy attended piano lessons from the age of four and was something of a child prodigy, receiving many music certificates. In 1963 he met Malcolm Murray and they played at clubs as a duo, Roy on keyboards and Malcolm on vocals. In 1963, with the addition of Allan Davies and Vic Storey The Royalists were formed. In 1966, when Allen went to join the Blood Group, Roy performed at Butlin's with Malcolm and John Hare as the Royal Trio. From

A Royalists publicity photograph taken at Butlins holiday camp. Left to right: Vic Storey, Roy Bould, Allan Davies, Malcolm Murray.

With all the paraphernalia of a 1960s rock group, The Royalists perform during one of their Butlins seasons. Left to right: Roy Bould, Malcolm Murray, Vic Storey, Allan Davies.

1970 to 1977 Roy played as resident musician at the Furnace Inn on Halifax Road.

In 1977 he joined Tetley's Breweries as manager of The Melbourne in Westgate. In 1980 he left Tetley's and was in residence for music nights in a range of pubs, including The Belldene, The Beehive in Westgate, The Beacon at Wibsey and for many years the Prince of Wales, Harrogate Road, until 1996.

After spending some time in Spain, playing at venues while on holiday, Roy ended his playing days as resident musician at the New Inn, Idle, in 2004. He now spends his time with his wife Dawn caravanning in England and Spain, but still lives in his home town of Bradford.

Victor (Vic) Storey (b. 1940, Bowling) drums

Leaving school aged sixteen, Vic worked for a sheet metal company, during which time he learnt to play the drums. In the late 1950s he worked as a stand-in drummer with many local groups, but with no regular position. In 1963 he answered an advert in the *Telegraph and Argus* for a drummer in the newly formed group The Royalists, and was accepted. He played with the group during its most successful years, 1963–5. With the break up of the group in 1966 Vic left the rock 'n' roll scene, and went on to have a successful business career. Now retired, he lives with his wife in the countryside of Haworth.

SAMMY KING

vocalist and songwriter

Although well known during the rock 'n' roll era and afterwards, perhaps what brought Sammy King to prominence was writing the popular song 'Penny Arcade', and having it recorded by Roy Orbison.

Alan Twohig, aka Sammy King, was born in Batley Carr in 1941 and attended St Joseph's RC Primary School in Batley and St Bede's Grammar School. A keen sportsman, he was captain of the school football team and was a talented player who wanted to become a professional footballer. However, all that was turned upside down when in 1954 he suffered a hip injury playing for St Bede's against Grange Boys Grammar School. The injury was so bad that he ended up in Pinderfields Hospital, Wakefield, for two years. The infection destroyed the cartilage in his hip, meaning he would never finish school – and his dream of becoming a professional footballer was over.

When Sammy eventually became mobile again he had no idea what to do for a living, so he went to art college because he was unfit to do any manual work. He had always been interested in music and could play the piano, so he joined the South Side Skiffle Group in Batley as a hobby. He was originally a drummer and then an acoustic guitarist before progressing to the electric guitar – which he picked up very quickly.

After the South Side Skiffle Group, Sammy joined a band called The Saints, then moved to The Dingos in Bradford for a few years. After the Dingos broke up he found himself without a group. One day he was in a bingo hall in Batley, sitting at the back with a bingo card that a mate (who ran the hall) had given him. A band called the Voltaires played during the interval, and when the singer walked out Sammy got up and sang a 'twist' song and then a ballad – because he knew the lads. He was so successful that he became their full-time singer, and the group was renamed Sammy King and the Voltaires.

The Voltaires went on to support many acts, including The Beatles (at the Queens Hall in Leeds, Sammy's only regret being that he never spoke to George Harrison). and the Rolling Stones. Sammy also appeared on stage with Shirley Bassey, Louis Armstrong, Dusty Springfield and Cilla Black. The pressure of performing with the group soon took its toll, and after taking a short break

The original South Side skiffle group. Sammy, far right, was quite a proficient drummer.

Later he would progress to the guitar to complement his vocal skills.

Sammy King with the Voltaires.

Sammy hit the road again as part of a duo. It was at this time that he went back to writing songs, but he didn't know what to do with them. A friend, Derek Smith, manager of the Batley Variety Club, told him that Roy Orbison was coming to perform at the club, and that Sammy should see if Roy thought his songs were any good.

After being given an introduction to Roy Orbison, Sammy approached him about his songs. After playing a few numbers on tape, Roy asked Sammy if he could take them, including 'Penny Arcade', back to his recording manager in Nashville, Tennessee. Sammy did not think he would like 'Penny Arcade', because he had written it with the Eurovision Song Contest in mind and it wasn't really Roy's style. He didn't hear anything for months, and then he received a tape through the post of Roy singing the song, and a note saying that it was going to be his next single. Roy Orbison insisted the song be featured on several of his albums, and it is still being played today forty years on.

Sammy King, friend of the stars, who in early life had many trials and tribulations, is at the top of his profession and has spent his life giving pleasure to others. He is still playing and writing music and is always on call, especially at the Bradford rock 'n' roll reunions. He lives in Heckmondwyke with his wife Linda, and has recently published his bestselling autobiography entitled *Penny Arcade* (Bank House Books, 2009).

The bass player at far left is Chris Charlesworth, playing with the Craven group the Rocking Pandas. Chris had previously played with Sandra and the Montanas until their name change to the Mark Russell Four.

SANDRA AND THE MONTANAS/THE MARK RUSSELL FOUR

rock 'n' roll

In 1964 a group of young lads and a beautiful vocalist called Sandra from the Craven area entered the rock 'n' roll scene. The group was the idea of Jeff Birtley, formerly of The Flamingos and The Dalesmen. Their manager was Jeff's mother, Margaret, who was very competent. The group line-up was Jeff Birtley, lead guitar and vocals, Chris Charlesworth, rhythm guitar, Dave Beresford, bass guitar, Malcolm Whittaker, drums, and Sandra Winterburn, lead vocals.

Soon they were accomplished enough to take bookings (arranged with zest by their manager). Most of the venues were working men's clubs in Yorkshire, although they had a regular weekly booking at St Thomas's Hall in Sutton. As this was local they soon had quite a fan club. They played many times on the same bill as another popular local group The Nomads, whom The Montanas looked up to. The group went from strength to strength, even if it was a fairly low key success.

However, all was not well. One day Margaret had a telephone call from Roy Allen, the manager of a Birmingham rock 'n' roll group called The Montanas. They had recently sealed a contract with Pye Records, and in no uncertain terms the manager had threatened the Bradford Montanas to change their name or else! Having no barristers or queen's counsel in the family, they had to comply – and the group became the Mark Russell Four. Mark Russell was the name of Jeff Birtley's son, who had just been born!

Sandra had already left The Montanas, as had rhythm guitarist Chris Charlesworth, bass player Dave Beresford and drummer Malcolm Whittaker. The new members were Alan Senior, bass guitar, Joe Haigh, drums, Norman Crabtree, lead guitar, and the only original member Jeff Birtley, still on vocals but now playing rhythm guitar. Joe and Norman joined from The Nomads.

The Mark Russell Four continued to be in demand as a very professional group from 1966 well into the 1970s, keeping up with changing fashion and music.

Jeff Birtley (b. 1946, Keighley) lead guitar and vocals
See The Flamingos.

Sandra Winterburn (b. 1946, Steeton) vocals
Sandra later married the bass guitarist Dave Beresford.

Chris Charlesworth (b. 1947, Bingley) rhythm guitar, violin, bass guitar
In 1950 Chris's family moved to Skipton, and he later attended St Peter's School, York. At the age of ten Chris first came under the spell of rock 'n' roll when he heard Little Richard singing 'Tutti Frutti', and seeing The Beatles in 1963 at the Gaumont in Bradford inspired him to buy a guitar. A year later he was the rhythm guitarist with Sandra and the Montanas. Later he was with Skipton group the Rocking Pandas (Mark II) for a short time; this was a short-lived second line-up that followed the original Rocking Pandas, who had existed for two years.

After training as a journalist, Chris joined the Bradford *Telegraph and Argus* – and wrote their first pop column in 1968. Two years later he became a full-time music writer on the staff of *Melody Maker*, first as their news editor and in 1973 as their US editor, based in New York. In seven years he interviewed and/or wrote just about every rock icon of the era, and his sole regret is never seeing Elvis.

After a spell working for a management company in New York and at RCA in London, Chris began writing books, including biographies of The Who, David Bowie, Deep Purple, Slade and Cat Stevens. In 1983 he became the editor of Omnibus Press, whose editorial fortunes he has guided ever since – having commissioned and edited over 500 rock and pop books, probably more than anyone else in the world. Outside Omnibus, Chris's long association with The Who resulted in his compiling and co-producing their *30 Years of Maximum R&B* box set, released in 1995.

Though now mostly occupied with book ideas, and editing the work of other writers, his occasional musings have appeared in *Record Collector*, national papers and on RBP.

Fifty years on the lad from Bingley lives in a village near Guildford, Surrey, with his wife Lisa, son Sam and daughter Olivia.

Dave Beresford (b- 1947, Sutton) bass guitarist
Dave later married vocalist Sandra Winterburn.

Malcolm Whittaker(1946, Crosshills) drums
Malcolm was also a very talented trumpet-cornet player, later playing with local dance and brass bands.

Alan Senior (b. 1945, Bradford) bass guitar
Alan lived in Bingley. After his time with the Mark Russell Four, he went on to play with Jackfield Farm in 1970. In 1977 he was with the Band Size 2, in 1983 Size 2 by 2 and into the 1990s with Size 5.

Joe Haigh (b. 1944, Oxenhope) drums
See The Nomads.

Norman Crabtree (b. 1944, Keighley) lead guitar
See The Nomads.

Sandra's fabulous voice could have made her the next Connie Francis.

SANDRA (SANDIE) ANSTEY

pop singer

Sandra (Sandie) Pauline Anstey was born in Bradford in 1937 and lived in the Little Horton area, where she attended Grange Girls Grammar School. She first started singing at Dudley Hill Cricket Club in her early teens, about the same time as her younger cousin Pauline Matthews (Kiki Dee). During 1955–6 she was employed by Hayden Robinson (of Dunedin Players Band fame) in Kirkgate Market. He was one of the first to promote the sale of sheet music in a manner that was popular in the USA: Sandra sang pop songs to the customers from the sheet music, especially rock 'n' roll numbers.

Sandra, with a voice not unlike Connie Francis, became so popular that she began to accept bookings from local clubs and even small parts in local pantomimes. In 1957 after an article in the *New Musical Express* she was offered an audition for EMI in London. She had a new publicity photograph taken, and prepared for the event, but she was ill and unable to attend. Later, other commitments meant that she refused a second offer.

Sandie passed auditions for the popular TV programme *Top Town*, and was later very popular at the Fiesta Club in Sheffield. However, because of family commitments she decided to forego her musical career and move into the world of fashion, to spend a lifetime as a model, fashion designer and fashion house proprietor. Now she is retired, and still lives in the Bradford area.

Sandie really was a fashion-plate model, with a perfect figure, blonde hair, a lovely smile, and highly trained in modelling and singing. If she had had that lucky break and the EMI audition, there is no doubt that she would have been top of the bill with no trouble at all. Unlike her cousin, Sandie missed out on what might have been a glamorous musical career.

It was while working at Burtons Tailors in the mid-1950s that John Hockney and I used to pop into Kirkgate Market, not only to hear her but just to see her. She was beautiful. Both of us really fancied her, but she was way out of our league – although sometimes she gave us a smile. Once she even said hello to me when she passed by in Godwin Street. I was so chuffed that I didn't look where I was going, and fell over a small child. The child's mother started shouting and bawling at me and I went crimson. I only hoped that the beautiful singer had not seen or heard the fracas. Oh to be seventeen again!

A classic dress of the 1950s worn by Sandie Anstey outside her Bradford home.

SANDRA DAY
pop singer

Sandra Ainsworth aka Sandra Day was born in Batley in 1942 and attended Foxcroft Girls School at Mount Pleasant, Batley. Leaving school aged fifteen, she became a window dresser for Woolworth's in Commercial Street, Batley. Her talent as a rock 'n' roll vocalist was discovered by Mel Clarke, and for two years she performed at many top venues with Sandra Day and the Mel Clarke Four.

In 1959 Sandra and her widowed mum went to live in Canada, during which time she sang on the Canadian radio show CHUM. They returned in 1960 because her mum missed her family and could not settle. Back in Batley, Sandra returned to Woolworth's but working on the counter. In her absence the store had been modernised leaving only two small shop windows, and therefore no place for a window dresser! She was soon back with the Mel Clarke Four.

Sandra was as popular as ever, and soon an opportunity arose to become part of a new trio called The Vocalairs with her brother Ken and her future husband John Wagstaff. Highly talented, they soon became much sought after, especially on the new nightclub circuit. The Vocalairs had tremendous success in the late 1960s and into the '70s. They played a season in Malta, many times at the Batley Variety Club, and at the famous Astor Club in London, which was owned by the infamous Kray twins: there were plenty of their associates in the audience each night. In 1971 they appeared on *Opportunity Knocks* and came second. After a few years at the top the Trio parted. Sandra went on to marry John, who in 1982 established Flair Records. Flair was responsible for the popular group Black Lace and their big hit of 1984 'Agadoo'. Sandra now works with her husband, who later became the manager of Smokie; he still is to this day.

In 1991 Sandra was included in a compilation recording of Bradford groups of the 1960s, when she gave a fantastic rendition of Connie Francis's hit 'Stupid Cupid'. Now retired, Sandra lives in the Brighouse area with her husband and family. From time to time she sings with the Mel Clarke Four at functions. In 2010 she was on top form singing at the Bradford rock 'n' roll reunion at the Hilton Hotel. Sandra is a lovely lady with a wonderful voice.

The lovely Sandra Day, who captivated audiences throughout Bradford and beyond.

THE SANSOVENOS

rock 'n' roll

In 1959 a group of enthusiastic young men got together to form The Sansovenos. Perhaps you are thinking that whoever chose what is surely a unique name for a rock 'n' roll group had an interest in the arts, as Jacopo Sansovenos was a sixteenth-century Italian sculptor. However, the truth is that one of the group's members picked the name from a newspaper: Sansoveno was a racehorse.

The line-up was Mike Stephenson, rhythm guitar, Mick Kershaw, vocals, Dave Pickup, lead guitar, Barry Lane, bass guitar, and the drummer, remembered only as Dave. For a while they did well, with bookings that included the Students Club, and the Gaumont and Majestic ballrooms.

In 1960 the group changed its name from The Sansovenos to Mick and the Tornadoes, with a new line-up.

Mike Stephenson (b. 1938, Bradford) rhythm guitar

Mike was educated at St Mary's RC School. Aged eleven he learnt how to read music and took up the accordion, becoming quite proficient. Leaving school in 1953, he was employed at Listers Mill in the weaving department. In 1956, with National Service looming he signed on for three years in the RAF. It was during this time he taught himself to play the guitar, and when home on leave he played at local clubs.

In 1959, when he was demobbed from the RAF, Mike joined The Sansovenos, and carried on when the group's name was changed to Mick and the Tornadoes. He left in 1962 and played for a short while with Vince Wayne and the Falcons, leaving them the next year to join Terry Sexton and the Telecasters. With all these groups he acted as manager and was responsible for all bookings, which was no mean feat.

Leaving The Telecasters in 1964, Mike was with another short lived group, Robin Hood and his Merry Men, from 1965 to 1966. He turned down many offers to turn professional, with bookings in Germany and the continent, as he had begun to think of life outside music and thought it was time to settle down in a secure career. Mike had had a few mediocre jobs since leaving the RAF, back at Listers Mill, then Grattan Warehouse, and a short time with the *Telegraph and Argus*, but from 1970 to 1989, when he was offered early retirement, he found his niche with a well-known insurance company.

Mike still lives for his music, and plays the keyboard for his wife Doreen and family and friends in the Bradford area.

Mick Kershaw aka Mick Novak (b. 1942, Bradford) vocals and rhythm guitar

After leaving school Mick was employed at Grattan Warehouse, Ingleby Road. He joined The Sansovenos, his first group, in 1959. In 1960, after the group changed its name, he led the group on vocals – under his new stage name. Mick was especially popular with female fans: his good looks compared with any of the famous male pin-ups of the time. He continued with Mick and the Tornadoes until the group folded in 1963, then went on to play with the Del Rio Four. He was with them when they changed their name to The Chapters, a name that came from singer Kenny Lynch. Mick was also part of the group when they recorded 'Can't Stop Thinking About Her' on Pye; this did reasonably well.

When The Chapters folded Mick was off the road for a while. In 1967 he formed The Guests with some other good musicians. He had become professional by now, and had become quite an accomplished rhythm guitarist as well as a vocalist. In the early 1970s The Guests succeeded in obtaining a recording contract with RCA, and their first recording was 'Baby You've Got to Stay', co-written by Mick and another group member. The record was not a success, and soon afterwards the group disbanded.

Mick was offered a job at the Mecca Locarno on Manningham Lane, singing and playing rhythm guitar with the Terry Blakely Quartet, which was in residence at the ballroom. Twelve months later he was back with The Guests, who had re-formed with a different name: Punch. The band went on to have tremendous success in the 1970s, playing at many of the top clubs in the UK. Such was their popularity that a TV documentary was made about them and their life on the road; they also appeared on the BBC's *Look North*. Things could not have been better, and success seemed to be just around the corner when they released a record and an appearance on *Opportunity Knocks* was booked. However, the record flopped and they came nowhere on *Opportunity Knocks*. Mick was disappointed, as he had thought his time had come

Bouncing back, in the late 1970s Mick was compèring shows at the popular Talk of Yorkshire in Bradford, and in the 1980s he was in a new group called Phase Four, which mostly played at hotel functions but was also booked on cruise ships, going as far as the Caribbean. They also found time for a season at Pontin's. When he left Phase Four Mick joined other bands, including a trio called Festival with whom he played for fifteen seasons at Haven Holidays Group camps. In 1999, because of family commitments, he called it a day on their last engagement in the Isle of Wight.

Back home and settled after all the trials and tribulations of being on the road, Mick continued to play as a semi-professional. In 2000 he joined a band called Kraka, but in 2004 and now in his sixties he decided to call it a day and to settle down in something different. Mick now lives in Wakefield, and spends his spare time looking after the maintenance at Fieldhead Hospital.

Mick was an extremely talented guitarist and rock 'n' roll vocalist, one of the best.

Dave Pickup (b. 1940, Bradford) lead guitar
Dave lived in the Great Horton Road area. He left the Sansovenos when the group changed its name to Mick and the Tornadoes. During this time Dave was employed by Brown, Muffs.

Barry Lane (1940, Bradford) bass guitar
When Dave left The Sansovenos he joined other local groups for a while. He was employed by Brown, Muffs.

Dave ? (b. 1941) drums
Dave lived in Bradford, and was with the Sansovenos for only a short time.

The newly formed Sansavinos, all smartly dressed, look to the future, 1959. Left to right: Mike Stephenson, Mick Kershaw, Dave ?, Dave Pickup, Barry Lane.

The Seeds of Tyme, on stage at the Cameo Club as Tony and the Fadeaways, a name that lasted only a few weeks. Left to right: Bruce Wilson, David ?, Tony Butterworth, Keith Alred and Paul Coleman.

Time out for discussions: the Seeds of Tyme at East Bowling Unity Club, 1965. Left to right: Paul Coleman, Keith Alred, Bruce Wilson, Tony Butterworth.

THE SEEDS OF TYME

rock 'n' roll

In 1964, towards the twilight days of rock 'n' roll, a new group came along that introduced itself as Tony and the Fadeaways. Within three months, after much discussion, the group's name did fade-away, and the Seeds of Tyme sprang to life. The two lads who formed the group were colleagues working for the Midland Bank in Market Street – Keith Alred, lead guitar and vocals, and Paul Coleman, rhythm guitarist and backing vocals. Soon they were joined by drummer Tony Butterworth, who was not only a talented drummer but also a good rock 'n' roll vocalist, quite an addition to any group. The bass player was Bruce Wilson, affectionately known as Stan by the other group members. Rehearsals were held in a hall at the Synagogue Spring Gardens and the Belle Vue Hotel on Manningham Lane. Their repertoire was largely rock of the 1950s and '60s, with pop chart music added, and a few country and old time numbers for the club circuit. Favourites were Buddy Holly, Little Richard, Eddie Cochran, Bo Diddly, The Shadows, The Kinks, The Animals, The Searchers and Chuck Berry.

By 1965 the Seeds of Tyme were well established, with a manager, and agents Harry Morris and Mark Jordan were finding them more than enough bookings. Such was their demand that double bookings had to be resolved on occasion! It was a busy time, and the list of venues played 1965 and 1966 ran into hundreds, on the working men's club circuit and also at clubs and dance halls, including (in Bradford) the Mecca Locarno, Lyceum Rainbow, Connaught Rooms, Fountains Hall, Excel Bowling Alley 2, the Top Twenty, Shipley Bowling Alley and almost every Bradford C&IU affiliated working men's club, as well as social and sports clubs, including North Bierley, Birkenshaw, Hepworth and Grandage Social Club, Homewood Social Club, with the comedian Ken Platt, Lidget Green Social Club, Windhill Cricket Club, and many more – spreading out into the old West Riding of Yorkshire.

The group's transport was provided by a milk van driver called Ludwig and his co-pilot wife April. The cost to the group was always 10s irrespective of mileage: 100 miles or 1 mile was the same! Ludwig had to get up for milk deliveries at 3.30 am after driving the group home, sometimes only finishing in the early hours of the morning, and he only broke down once in two years – quite a record.

In 1967, as suddenly as the Seeds of Tyme had sprung up, the lads split up to go their own ways because of work commitments. Another Tyme, another place, who knows? This was another group of talented lads who loved their music but did not quite make it. As founder member Keith Alred said, 'It was the buzz every night we played of being up on stage enjoying ourselves, and hopefully everyone listening was enjoying it too.' There was sadness when they took their last bow and the applause died down, when they knew that they had achieved as much as they had hoped for, and more than they had expected.

Keith Alred (b. 1945, Wakefield) lead guitar and vocals

Keith's family moved to Bradford when he was a year old, and he attended Bolton Lane Infants and Swaine House School. Passing his scholarship, he went on to Belle Vue Grammar School at the same time as Mike Priestley of the *Telegraph and Argus*, actors George Layton and Edward Peel, and TV film producer Barry Hanson. Keith played senior football for the school alongside George Layton and David Roper, who later played for Bradford City. Keith was spotted by a Bradford City scout while playing in goal in the Sunday Amateur League for Lane Close Mills and was given a City trial. He was certainly a spectacular goalkeeper, and earned many accolades in the local press for his acrobatics between the posts. The City trial was not a success, however, as Keith was a tad short, at 5ft 5in.

Leaving school, Keith joined the Midland Bank in Bradford as a junior teller. It was while working there that he and his pal Paul were asked to put something together for the bank's Christmas party – but they were not allowed to play or sing, just mime, while holding and gesturing with their guitars. This must be a unique beginning for two budding rock 'n' roll stars.

After his time with Seeds of Tyme Keith continued in the banking profession for a short time before moving to Viking Lamps in Baildon, as wages manager. In 1978–9 he sang and played rhythm guitar for the Skipton group Blue Touch, and spent an enjoyable couple of years treading the boards again. In the 1980s he started to work for Oil-Gear Towler Brothers in Rodley, where he stayed for some years.

Keith is now retired and lives with his wife Jean in Eccleshill. He relaxes by playing pool at the 147 Cabaret Club in Thornbury and stamp collecting, and hopes to find time to renovate his Burns guitar.

Paul Coleman (b. 1944, Bradford) rhythm guitar

Paul worked at the Midland Bank in Bradford, later progressing to management within the industry.

Tony Butterworth (b. 1945, Bradford) drums and vocals

Tony was a very talented drummer who had learned his profession from his father: his parents were resident drummer and pianist at the Sun Inn in Cottingley for many years. While he was playing with the Seeds of Tyme Tony was working as a coppersmith at Rycroft's in Bradford.

Bruce (Stan) Wilson (1945–84, Bradford) violin and bass guitar
Bruce lived in the Girlington area. He also worked as a coppersmith at Rycroft's during his years with the Seeds of Tyme. Sadly he passed away in 1984, but is well remembered by his friends.

The original Senators, 1961. Left to right: Des O'Hara, Brian Dobson, Bob Eals. Centre: Geoff Chew. Front: Pete Holland.

THE SENATORS/THE LADYKILLERS

rhythm group

This band was formed by Geoff Chew in 1961 when playing a melody of his chord to his cousin Peter Holland, who happened to know the first two lines of 'Be Bop a Lula' in something like the same key. This intolerable din was hailed as a great success, so The Senators were born. Geoff was on lead guitar and Peter on vocals, and they added Ben Eales, rhythm guitar, Des O' Hara, bass guitar, and Brian Dobson, drums. After a short time they were joined by female vocalist Doreen Pritchard, with the stage name Bobby's Girl. An audition was given to John Riggott, who really couldn't play anything but had a car! A bass guitar was obtained on the promise of payment to follow, but unfortunately it didn't, and the owner of the guitar, a Mr Soulsby, forcibly repossessed the instrument. John Riggott was demoted to transport manager.

For the next few years the group had varied success in quite an assortment of venues, some of which were established in the mid-1960s and today are just memories, such as the Dungeon, Coffin and the Witchbarn clubs. Other venues included Bradford Bowl and Bradford ice rink, the Queens Hall and the Market Tavern, a favourite for this type of group, which also played r&b. They also had many bookings at the Majestic dance hall (just before bingo took over!) and at private parties. They ventured to the Leeds area as well, and were quite popular at the Las Vegas in Dewsbury.

During these successful years Peter Holland left, and his place was taken by Johnny Philips. Then Ben Eales left, his place being taken on rhythm guitar by John Horsfall, as did Brian Dobson, being replaced on drums by Mike Larvin. Towards the end Martin Taylor, a rhythm guitarist, and Barry (Clem) Clements, lead vocals, were also members, albeit for a short time.

In early 1965 The Senators changed their name to The Ladykillers for a short time, and then the group dissolved. Geoff Chew and Mike Larvin merged with The Tarantulas in the same year to form a new group called Moldy Warp.

Geoff Chew (b. 1945, Otley) lead guitar, bass guitar and drums

Geoff lived in Otley. He attended Ilkley Grammar School, Harrogate Art College and Becketts Park Training College, before becoming a teacher. Geoff was only sixteen when he formed The Senators. Already a gifted guitarist, he later became a bass guitarist and drummer. Following his time with The Senators and The Ladykillers, he joined The Tarantulas and Moldy Warp. In the meantime Geoff became a teacher at Seacroft Middle School. As Head of Art and Music he introduced pop music into the curriculum.

Later Geoff was a member of Hi-Fly, Broughton Blues Band and Brass Tacks. In 1991 Moldy Warp re-emerged after a long hibernation, sporting a nucleus of original members that included Geoff.

Geoff is a well-respected music teacher, and for over twenty years his rock music school has taught lead and bass guitar and drums to over 500 pupils aged between seven and seventy. He hopes to pass on his fifty years of experience, giving his pupils the opportunity to have as much fun and enjoyment as he has had from performing music. It is fair to say that his musical ability and knowledge run from A to Z.

Geoff lives in Burley in Wharfedale in retirement with his wife Linda.

Peter Holland (b. 1940, Bradford) lead vocals
Peter lived in Heaton. Peter was one of The Senators' original members and a good rock 'n' roll vocalist. When the musical style changed to Beatles numbers and r&b n he left the group. Peter still lives in the Bradford area.

Ben Eales (b. 1943, Bramhope) rhythm guitar
Ben attended Leeds Grammar School. Another original member of The Senators, he left in the early 1960s to emigrate to Kingston, Jamaica.

Brian Dobson (b 1943, Burley in Wharfedale) drums
A keen sportsman, Brian left The Senators as his sports commitments increased. He played first team rugby for Otley and in the summer played cricket for a local team. Brian still lives in Burley.

Des O' Hara (b. 1946, Menston) bass guitar
Des was a very active member of The Senators. He later went on to form The Kingpins and was also part of The Ladykillers and Moldy Warp. Throughout his musical career he played with numerous bands, and he is still very active on the Yorkshire music scene. Des enjoyed a varied career, ranging from sheet metal work to computer operator at Leeds University. A very talented bass player, he is still highly regarded by his peers.

Doreen Pritchard aka Bobby's Girl (b. 1946, Otley) lead vocals
Doreen joined The Senators in its early days as lead female vocalist, and also played the electric-piano. She still lives in Otley.

Johnny Philips (b. 1942) lead vocals
Johnny joined The Senators in its early days. He studied at Harrogate Art College with fellow musician Geoff Chew. Later he played electric guitar with The Ladykillers, and then became a DJ, most notable for his appearances at the popular Town and Country Club in Leeds. Johnny is also well remembered for his beard and stetson hat.

The Senators' new line-up, c. 1964. Back row, left to right: Mick Larvin, Johnny Philips, Doreen Pritchard, John Horsfall. Front row: Des O'Hara, Geoff Chew, Martin Taylor.

John Horsfall (b. 1943, Guiseley) rhythm guitar
John lived in Guiseley. A valuable member of The Senators, he stayed with them when they became The Ladykillers. He eventually left and emigrated to Australia, where he joined the police force.

Mick Larvin (1945–2010, Leeds) drums
Mick joined The Senators when Brian Dobson left, and stayed with the group when it became The Ladykillers. He helped to form Moldy Warp with Geoff Chew, and later played at Brian London's nightclub in Blackpool, going on to play on cruise ships; he finally became entertainments manager for P&O Cruises. Unfortunately Mick passed away in Blackpool in 2010. He was a very fine musician, and is greatly missed.

Martin Taylor (b 1943, Leeds) rhythm guitar
Martin lived in Leeds. He played in the latter days of The Senators and the early days of The Ladykillers.

Barry (Clem) Clements (b 1946, Doncaster) lead vocals
Barry was only with The Senators for a short time. He later became an actor and can be seen in numerous films.

THE SIDEWINDERS

skiffle group

In 1957 a group of Bradford students led by Dave Simpson got together to establish a skiffle group. The Sidewinders was one of those groups that from the start seemed to fit well with this popular music, and such was their popularity that they became the resident group at the Bradford Topic Folk and Skiffle Club. In 1958 they entered a skiffle group competition at the Gaumont Cinema, the prize being an appearance on the live touring show of the TV series *The Six-Five Special*, featuring among many others Don Lang and his Frantic Five, on the following Saturday night. The winning group would also appear on the show again at a later date. The competition was hosted by Jim Dale, and The Sidewinders went on to win the final. They were shocked to discover that the other stars would not perform with them unless they joined the Musicians Union – and the cost of this was £30 per group member – at that time around six to eight weeks' pay for most people, and The Sidewinders were students. At that time Musicians Union policy was to enrol amateurs where they were in direct competition with professional musicians, ensuring they could demand the minimum union rate. Why the many Bradford amateur groups taking part were not made aware of this clause before the show was an indictment of some showbusiness at this time. However, The Sidewinders each paid their £30, and were perhaps in debt to their families for many months.

Not long afterwards the group dissolved to concentrate on their careers, and so disappeared into life outside skiffle. They left their mark on the early days of skiffle in Bradford, and who knows what would have happened if they had progressed to rock 'n' roll?

Spike O'Brien, without doubt the jewel in Bradford's rock 'n' roll crown. His death was a sad loss to his many friends and fellow artistes.

SPIKE O'BRIEN

rock 'n' roll pianist

Brian Holt aka Spike O'Brien was born in Bradford in 1940 and attended Hanson High School. He learned to play the piano from the age of four his father was a classical pianist. Leaving school in 1956, he was employed in the offices of Listers Mill as an office boy, because his mother wanted him to have a steady job!

Music and playing the piano were Spike's main interest, and most of his thoughts were on rock 'n' roll. This resulted in the office manager telling him he could either have a good career in office work or go about like a pop star, and asking him to make a decision. Spike made his decision – and gave in his notice.

For a while he drifted from job to job, at one time driving a small truck for the BDA (Bradford Dyers Association). He was playing the piano at many venues in the Bradford area, and it was about this time that he acquired his stage name. At one venue some girls asked him what his name was: having heard him being called both Brian and Spike, they wanted to know which it was – Spike or Brian. Hence the name Spike O' Brien was born.

In 1959 Spike joined The Dingos. At this time they were probably the most prominent and professional local rock 'n' roll group. However, after a short period of time he left and joined another local group, The Tuxedos; then in 1963 he decided to get together some other local artists to form a new group, The Rattlers.

After three successful seasons with The Rattlers at Douglas, Isle of Man, Spike joined Don Partridge's backing group, The Wildfowl. Don was a 'one man band!' In 1973 Spike recorded 'Poor Little Fred', a skit on the popular 'Big Bad John', and he had moderate success. Later in the 1980s and '90s he was still touring the Bradford circuit with local groups, especially The Dingos, and was as popular as he had ever been. His later highlight was playing at the rock 'n' roll reunion dances at the Pile Bar and the Bradford Midland Hotel.

Spike was a piano genius, embodying pure rock 'n' roll in its most reckless and high-spirited form, with such piano-pounding rockers from the late 1950s as 'Whole Lot of Shaking Going On' and 'Great Balls of Fire'. Spike's larger than life personality and energetic performance had the crowd shaking, shouting, rocking and rolling! When he passed away in 2000 the rock 'n' roll world lost a truly great artist and friend of many fellow musicians, who held him in high esteem. Spike is sadly missed, and fully deserves a place of honour in the Who's Who of Bradford rock 'n' roll.

The last time I spoke to Spike was on the phone a few days before he passed away: he was waiting for a lung transplant. During our conversation I asked if there was anything I can get him. With that wonderful sense of humour, back came his reply: 'Yes, Dal, a new pair of f—ing lungs'!

THE STROLLERS/BRIAN T. STROLLERS

rock 'n' roll

The Strollers were latecomers who 'strolled' onto the rock 'n' roll scene in 1962. The founders were brothers Tony and John Rourke and Clive Royston, who met at St Walburga's Youth Club. Clive's father Clifford not only offered to manage their affairs but also sold his car and replaced it with a van, so he could transport the group and their equipment. Two new members joined them, and the line-up became Adrian Gunn, vocals, Tony Rourke, lead guitar, John Rourke, bass guitar, Clive Royston, rhythm guitarist, and Charlie Whelan, drums. With good management and a professional approach the group soon became very popular. However, after just a few months Adrian moved on, to be replaced in May 1962 by Colin Rawlinson, a very competent vocalist. Soon the group had top bookings at the Mecca and Majestic ballrooms as well as Cleckheaton and Dewsbury town halls and an assortment of the better working men's clubs in Yorkshire.

In mid-1963 Colin Rawlinson left to further his career in textiles, as did Charlie Whelan. A new vocalist called Brian Tordoff and the experienced rock 'n' roll drummer Phil Mitchell soon filled their places.

In 1963 news filtered through that there was a group in the south of England also called The Strollers – so they added Brian T. to their name. This well-liked group, with Brian Tordoff in top billing, always took to the stage immaculately dressed, which gave a good first impression – and when they got down to play it was obvious they were not short of talent. They were now playing at many venues in Yorkshire and beyond, including the Empire in York, Palins in Halifax, the Empress in Mexborough, the Majestic in Leeds, the Lyceum Rainbow Club in Bradford, the Royal Hotel in Harrogate and Blackpool South Pier. It was at this latter that Brian T. and the Strollers reached the semi-finals of the Lancashire division of the National Beat Contest. They never knew why they were grouped with top Liverpool and Manchester groups! They also played as a supporting group to The Applejacks, with another Bradford group, the Del-Fi's, in Harrogate, and later they backed Mike Preston on tour.

The original Strollers, 1962. Left to right: Charles Whelan, Adrian Gunn, Clive Royston, John Rourke, Tony Rourke.

The Strollers with a new line-up, 1962. Left to right: Tony Rourke, John Rourke, Clive Royston, Colin Rawlinson, Phil Mitchell.

The Brian T. Strollers, 1963. Back row, left to right: Phil Mitchell, Brian Tordoff ('Brian T'), Clive Royston. Front row: John Rourke, Tony Rourke.

Unlike so many groups of the mid-1960s the Brian T. Strollers concentrated solely on dance hall engagements and rarely played to pub and club audiences. They preferred gentler pop music to the more raucous r&b that was beginning to become popular. It was during 1964 that Sharon Vaughan, late of The Caravelles, joined the group for a short while. Given the right sort of breaks they might have reached stardom, but in November 1964 they lost momentum when Brian Tordoff left to continue as a solo artist. Popular Colin Rawlinson returned on vocals in December until March 1965. The following year the group, now with Paul Minchella on drums, went on tour with Ricky Valance. In 1966 the inevitable happened: the group disbanded.

In 1993 the group re-formed, with original members Clive Royston, Tony and John Rourke, Paul Minchella and Brian Tordoff. The group is still playing, with a slightly different line-up and alas without Clive Royston, who passed away in 2007.

Adrian Gunn (1943–19??, Bradford) vocals
Adrian was an excellent rock 'n' roll vocalist and founder member of The Strollers, but he soon left the group.

Clive Royston (1944–2007, Shipley) rhythm guitar
Clive lived at Gaisby Mount in Shipley. After attending school he studied textiles at Bingley Technical College, and in 1962 he helped to form The Strollers, continuing with the group until it folded in 1966. After a spell as a clerk with the North Eastern Gas Board, he later worked in textiles, forming his own company and becoming a well-respected businessman. When the group was reformed in 1993 Clive was in his element. Sadly he suddenly passed away in 2007.

Tony Rourke (b. 1944, Bradford) lead guitar
Tony lived in Baildon. He was educated at St Bede's Grammar School and was a founder member of The Strollers; it was claimed that he was the serious one. When the group folded in 1966 Tony worked in Germany for some years, and in 1993 he joined the re-formed Strollers for a short while.

John Rourke (b. 1940, Bradford) bass guitar
Brother of Tony, John lived in Baildon and was educated at St Bede's Grammar School. John studied accountancy on leaving school and was later employed as an accountant at AIS (Allied Industrial Services). Like his brother he was a founder member of The Strollers and joined them again in 1993. He is still with them today.

Charlie Whelan (b. 1941, Bradford) drums
A founder member of The Strollers, Charlie left within a year. In the 1980s he went on to play in working men's clubs.

Colin Rawlinson (b. 1940, Bradford) vocals
Colin lived in Quarry Street in Heaton, attending Cooper Lane Infants School, Grange Primary School and Grange Boys Grammar School. His first job on leaving school in 1955 was as a textile pattern room assistant for Pitchon and

The glamorous Sharon Vaughan joins The Strollers, 1964. Here she shares a duet with Brian T.

Co. of Bradford. In 1956 he attended Bradford Institute of Technology and Bradford Technical College to learn all aspects of the textile industry. At the same time he, like many other young lads, became interested in the new rock 'n' roll music. He began by purchasing an acoustic guitar and had a few lessons from his uncle, who had a Les Paul Gibson. Colin's first public appearance was singing a few songs with his own accompaniment at an international youth gathering at Bradford Cathedral annexe. He sang Frankie Vaughan's hit number 'The Garden of Eden', which was not considered appropriate. He thought, however, that being a vocalist was much better than playing the guitar.

In the late 1950s, with college and his career, rock 'n' roll took the back seat, but in 1962 Colin found himself back in the music world. In the adjoining office to him at the Courtaulds Group in Girlington was Clifford Royston. He told Colin that his son Clive played rhythm guitar with a recently formed group called The Strollers, and that their vocalist Adrian Gunn was leaving. They were going to hold auditions for a replacement. Colin went along to St Walburga's to meet the other members and sang a couple of Chuck Berry songs, after which he was asked if he would like to join them.

From May 1962 Colin was an asset to The Strollers, and his diary shows many bookings – in most cases twenty a month. However, in April 1963 he decided to leave, and his place was taken by Brian Tordoff. In November 1964 Colin was asked if he would return, and he accepted. Many bookings followed until March 1965, when owing to pressure of work and a lack of interest, he resigned. Married to Hazel in 1967, his career was now his priority, and after a series of job changes because of redundancies and closures in the rapidly shrinking textile industry, he found solace with the family owned A. Riddell as production assistant, where he spent many happy years.

The final 1964 line-up. Standing at the back are Brian T. and Tony Rourke. In front, kneeling, are John Rourke, Paul Minchella and Clive Royston.

Ten years later Colin is still working in textiles. He has many happy memories and still plays the guitar and sings the songs of his youth. In 2001 he sadly lost his wife.

Phil Mitchell (b. 1942 Bradford) drums
Phil lived in Cullingworth. He took over as The Strollers' drummer in 1962 when Charlie Whelan left. A joiner by trade, he was with the group until 1964.

Paul Minchella (b. 1947, Bradford) drums
Paul was of Italian descent. He attended St Mary's RC School in Bradford, and left aged fifteen to make a career in the printing industry. It was as a teenager that he took lessons as a drummer, and he was soon established locally, joining The Strollers in 1965. As well as The Strollers, he also played with Sammy King and the Voltaires and the Sammy King Five. Later he went on tour, backing Wee Willie Harris.

Paul still works for the Post Office and lives in Wyke with his wife Christine and family. When not supporting the Bradford Bulls he plays drums with the re-formed Strollers.

Brian Tordoff aka Brian T. (b. 1946, Redcar) vocals
When Brian's family moved to Bradford he attended Queensbury Secondary Modern School. Leaving aged fifteen, he became an apprentice motor mechanic. In 1962, shortly after winning a talent contest at the seaside, he

joined The Strollers as a vocalist, and the group's name changed to Brian T. Strollers.

Leaving the group in November 1964, Brian continued for the next twenty-five years as a solo artist. He played the guitar and sang, most of the time as a semi-professional: he was still working full-time for the Electricity Board in Halifax. He still went under the title of Brian T., and became very popular in the pubs and clubs of the north of England as well as Scotland. Brian worked with many top-line artists, including comedians Charlie Williams and Bernard Manning; he also had bookings with The Casuals, the popular Bachelors and Ronnie Hilton, but his highlight was working with Billy Fury at the Bierley Labour Club in Bradford.

Brian is still playing in the twenty-first century with some of the original members of The Strollers, and still loves the sound of rock 'n' roll music. He is unassuming, modest, well respected, and a credit to his musical profession. Moving towards retirement, he now lives with his wife Ann in Denholme.

Sharon Holt aka Sharon Vaughan (b. 1942, Bradford) vocals
See The Caravelles.

The Stormsville Five, 1962. Left to right: Mike Brodie, John Truelove, Paul Long, Eric Brodie, Harry Parking.

Open for Engagements

THE STORMSVILLE FIVE
RHYTHM COMBO

NANI TAL,
WESTFIELD DRIVE,
GUISELEY.
Tele. Rawdon 3618

THE STORMSVILLE FIVE

rock 'n' roll

In 1957–8 a group of young lads from the Shipley area got together to form what would be for the next few years the Stormsville Five. Practice time was spent at one of the lad's houses, which was normal for many groups in the early days. They all worshipped Buddy Holly and his music, and it was during one of their practice sessions on 3 February 1959 that they heard the news on the radio of Buddy's death. Originally the group played rock 'n' roll instrumentals, and they built up quite a repertoire, including the popular numbers 'Fickle Chicken', 'The Swag', 'Rumble' and many others.

The line-up was Eric Brodie, lead guitar, Mike Brodie, rhythm guitar, Brian (Baz) Bastow, bass guitar, and John (Fido) Fielding, drums. It was Baz who came up with the name the Stormville Five, at about the same time that a vocalist called Harry Parkin joined the group. In the early days each member wore a lurid purple brushed mohair sweater. What class! One of their first bookings was a function at the local drill hall in Baildon. With a shortage of amplifiers, the lead and rhythm guitarist played through one 10 watt amplifier, and the bass guitarist and vocalist played through another. It worked, although whether the crowd could distinguish any sounds is another thing. Well, needs must!

With early success, and full amplification, they began to play at the many venues in and around Bradford including the Gaumont and Majestic ballrooms, the Students Club, the Mecca, local firms' dances at the popular Kings and Queens and many local pubs and clubs. During these many months of playing there were only two changes to the group's line-up: John (Fido) Fielding left and was replaced by Paul Long on drums, and John Truelove took over from bass player Brian (Baz) Bastow.

For the next five years the five lads had much success. Almost every week the *Telegraph and Argus* included an advert that said where the Stormville Five were appearing. The end came in 1965 when, with changes in style and music, and careers pending, the band members went their own way – leaving fond memories for themselves and for local rock 'n' roll teenagers.

Brian (Baz) Bastow (b. 1941, Birmingham) bass guitar
Brian's father was a proper Yorkshireman, whose war work took him to the Midlands. In 1944 Brian's mother passed away, so Brian and his father moved back to Yorkshire and took up residence in East Morton near Bingley. Brian later attended Bingley Grammar School. It was during the years 1957–8 that he began his rock 'n' roll career as a founder member of the Stormsville Five. Later in 1960 Brian joined Lee Chevin and the Ravers. It wasn't until many years later that he found out he wasn't the player they wanted, but he was the only one able to take over the hire purchase on the previous bass player's Fender Precision.

Brian was with The Ravers (Riders) during their most successful years and played bass on the record 'Darling Jean'/'Memories of You' in 1963, co-writing 'Darling Jean' with Dave Pannett. After The Ravers folded in 1965 he stood in for various rock, blues and jazz bands until the mid-1970s, when he formed (in the Skipton area) a folk/rock band called Jig Saw and later a country-rock band called Custer's Last Band. In 1996 Brian moved to America and now plays in a Christian rock band, also playing out as a cover band, anything with great harmonies. Brian is currently working on new CDs.

Eric Brodie (b. 1942, Shipley) lead guitar
Cousin of Mike Brodie, Eric attended Bradford Boys Grammar School. He was noted as being a very proficient guitarist, who could emulate Scotty Moore's guitar playing on the early Presley Sun recordings.

Mike Brodie (b. 1943, Shipley) rhythm guitar
Mike was the cousin of Eric Brodie.

John (Fido) Fielding (b. 1942, Shipley) drums
An original member of the Stormsville Five, John left in the 1960s.

Harry Parkin (b. 1941, Bradford) vocals
Harry was a very accomplished rock 'n' roll singer, especially in the early style of Elvis Presley.

John Truelove (b. 1943, Bradford) bass guitar
John joined The Stormville Five in 1960 when Brian (Baz) Bairstow joined Lee Chevin and the Ravers.

Paul Long (b. 1943, Bradford) drums
Paul joined the Stormsville Five when John (Fido) Fielding left in the early 1960s.

THE TARANTULAS

rock 'n' roll

The story of The Tarantulas is a tangled web, but when it is unravelled it is an absorbing story! Based in Ilkley, they came together in the summer of 1963 as Shadows soundalikes. They were Pete Dickinson, lead guitar, Stan Dobson and Tony Idle, rhythm guitars, Clive Steele, bass guitar, and Andrew Horton, drums. Feeling the need to broaden their repertoire, they approached singer Brian Bailey, a perennial winner at the Wharfedale Music Festival. Brian took up the challenge, and coarsened his voice to perform rock 'n' roll!

The group's debut was a private party at the Bluebird Café in Ilkley on the evening of 22 November 1963, which unfortunately coincided with the assassination of John F. Kennedy. The news of which somewhat detracted from the group's performance. From then on they became a regular act at the Blue Genes Club in Ilkley, where Gene Hartley championed their cause and spread the word, leading to bookings at the Stoney Lea Hotel in Ilkley as featured act. They also supported other groups, such as the Four Pennies, Rev. Black and the Rocking Vicars, and The Wheels from Belfast. The Tarantulas also played at the Leeds and Bradford Mecca ballrooms, and also the Coffin Club, Top Twenty Club, the Dungeon and the popular Majestic ballroom, all in Bradford. Big Daddy's Club in Halifax was a particular favourite.

Brimming with confidence, The Tarantulas entered the Battle of the Bands contest at Keighley Victoria Hall, where they emerged winners, in the process beating The Grumbleweeds, who had yet to adopt their comedy persona. Within weeks, in April 1964, The Tarantulas entered a larger contest: Beat Unlimited the Yorkshire Sound, organised jointly by Star Cinemas and Coca-Cola. They reached the finals in Brighouse, their opposition comprising The Zendas from Morley, Clive and the Crestas from Sherburn-in-Elmet, the Fabulous Phantoms from Bradford, The Ravens from Huddersfield, The Gleneagles from Leeds, The Astrals from Leeds, and Danny and the Talismen. Winning the contest, they received a cash prize and a TV appearance, a test recording for Fontana Records and promotion by Star Cinemas. The members of the group are still waiting to enjoy the latter three accolades, but the cash prize came in handy! From then on widespread venues included Cleveleys,

The Ilkley-based Tarantulas, who had a very successful two years on the road from 1963 until 1965. Back row, left to right: Peter (Stan) Dobson, Brian Bailey, Andrew Horton, Clive Steele. Front row: Tony Idle, Pete Dickinson.

Blackpool, Bradford and Leeds universities, and the Cavern Club in Liverpool, where they shared the bill with the Clayton Squares and The Hideaways.

In 1965 Pete Dickinson left the group, followed by Tony Idle. George Speller joined them on keyboards. Later The Tarantulas amalgamated with two members of The Ladykillers to form, with a change in fashion and music, Moldy Warp .

Pete Dickinson (b. 1945, Ilkley) lead guitar

Pete attended Ilkley Secondary School and Keighley Technical College before taking up an apprenticeship with the Yorkshire Electricity Board. He eventually became a respected project engineer with a large company, his job taking him all over the world. In 2000 he underwent a successful quadruple heart bypass operation. Now retired, he enjoys music and walking in the Dales.

Peter Stanley (Stan) Dobson (b. 1945, Ilkley) rhythm guitar

Stan attended Ilkley Secondary School and Harrogate Art College. He then went into retail, before eventually becoming a hospital theatre porter. It was

Stan who helped to organise the merging of The Ladykillers and The Tarantulas into Moldy Warp. Now retired, his interests are music and walking in the Dales.

Tony Idle (b. 1944, Ilkley) rhythm guitar
Tony attended Ilkley Secondary School and Harrogate Art College. After leaving The Tarantulas Tony moved to London to become a partner in a very successful graphic design agency. They created the memorable metal Martian creatures in the Smash potato ads!

Clive Steele (b. 1945, Ilkley) bass guitar
Clive attended Ilkley Grammar School and a teachers training college, which naturally led to a career in education. After The Tarantulas he was part of Moldy Warp for a short time. Music is still an important part of his life.

Andrew Horton (b 1945, Ilkley) drums
Andrew attended Ilkley Secondary School and Keighley Technical College before becoming an electrician with the Yorkshire Electricity Board. Now retired, his abiding interests are electronics and music.

George Speller (b. 1945, Ingrow, Keighley) keyboards
A member of The Tarantulas from 1965, he was with Moldy Warp for a short while. When he left he took up a post within the BBC, and handled the controls on many programmes – including early Terry Wogan radio epics.

The original Telecasters, 1962. Terry Sexton is on vocals. Back row, left to right: Terry Sexton, Ray Smith, Mike Stephenson, Dave Wiggins. Front: Brian Fillingham.

A gyrating Terry Sexton leads the Telecasters into a dynamic pose.

THE TELECASTERS/TERRY SEXTON AND THE TELECASTERS/TERRY SEXTON AND THE SHAKES

rock 'n' roll

Formed in the early 1960s, The Telecasters were probably one of the most professional local groups, taking top billing with Mike Sagar, The Cresters and The Dingos. The Telecasters consisted of Raymond Smith, bass guitar, Brian Fillingham, drums, Dave Wiggins, lead guitar, and Mike Stephenson, rhythm guitar (he also acted as their manager). In 1962 the group was joined by Terry Sexton, vocals, and their name was changed to Terry Sexton and the Telecasters. It was a sound move, as Terry brought several things to the group: his good looks, a reliable Commer van, which could be used for engagements, and best of all his girlfriend. Barbara Pell could sing, and, known as Diana Stevens, was soon part of the group.

The Telecasters now became one of the best-dressed groups in the region, Terry being resplendent in a silver lamé suit made of gold coloured teddy bear fur. He also had a bronze satin suit, and the other group members mirrored his fashion by wearing lime green and turquoise outfits. Later, more sophisticated classical grey mohair suits were worn.

Soon Terry and the group became so popular that many local dancehalls and other venues competed for their talent. Diana, with her talent and beauty, was a very popular group member and was an audience favourite. She had originally trained as a classical soprano, although she adapted well to rock 'n' roll: her renditions, with Terry, of the duets 'Hey Paula' and 'Deep Purple' were always requested. The musical ability of the group was of the same high standard, and their rendition of The Animals' hit 'The House of the Rising Sun' was always a favourite.

It was during this period that The Telecasters loaned Gerry and the Pacemakers their musical instruments and equipment for their show at the Majestic ballroom, when the van carrying the Pacemakers' equipment broke down in Manchester. The Telecasters saved the day, preventing what could have been a riot.

Terry Sexton, one of Bradford's top rock 'n' roll artistes.

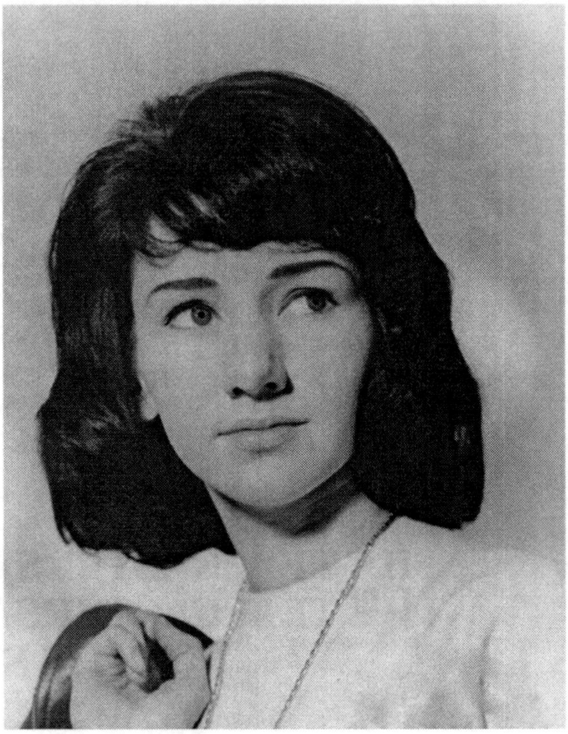

Diana Stevens (Barbara Pell) would go on to be a professional singer at many of the Locarno venues.

Diana Stevens adds glamour to the line-up, 1962. The group's name later changed to Terry Sexton and the Shakes, and Terry Sexton and the Shakes with Diana Stevens in 1964. Back row, left to right: Ray Smith, Brian Fillingham, Mick Stephenson. Front row: Terry Sexton, Dave Wiggins, Diana Stevens (Barbara Pell).

The Shakes at one of their many appearances at the Majestic. Left to right: Terry Sexton, Brian Fillingham, Mike Stephenson, Dave Wiggins, Diana Stevens, Ray Smith.

A young Dave Wiggins practises in his home with pictures of his heroes on the wall, including Elvis and Eddie Cochran.

In 1964 a change of name took place, to Terry Sexton and the Shakes. They still had the same line-up, except that rhythm guitarist Mike Stephenson had moved on to join Vince Wayne and the Falcons. It was during this time that Diana was taken onto the payroll, although she was not paid as much as the male members. Everything was going well, with many bookings; they also shared a billing with The Hollies. It seemed that the world was their oyster.

In late 1964 The Shakes passed auditions for Butlin's and Continental Tours, but they could not persuade one or other of their band members to go (a usual occurrence at this time). They continued into 1965, until their last booking at the Thornton Working Men's Club. A short while later they became part of Pete Nelson and the Telecasters, for a short time with a new female vocalist, Ann Broadbent. The group finally folded in the mid-1960s.

Terry Sexton (b. 1944, Bradford) vocals

Terry lived at Rand Street, before moving to Oulton Terrace with his mother to live with his grandparents. He attended Princeville Infants School, Grange Primary School and Princeville Secondary Modern School. Aged thirteen, he contracted tuberculosis and spent six months in Middleton Sanatorium in Ilkley: it was said that he had probably been infected by swimming in the Apperley Bridge Canal. Back at school he excelled in many subjects – because he had had one-to-one tuition at the sanatorium.

Leaving school aged fifteen, Terry became an apprentice electrician for Collinson Brothers in Bradford. Out of his savings he bought himself a Lambretta, but then he fell in love with a 1953 Jaguar with 10,000 miles on the clock, and just one owner! It was £279 – so he sold his Lambretta for £65, borrowed the rest, and purchased the car. Passing his test, he used it to travel to and from work, until he was told in no uncertain terms that if he came to work in 'that Jaguar' again he would be sacked, because it was a bad image for the company. Terry came to work in his Jag, was sacked, and joined Inman Joyce and Company.

While this was all taking place Terry had entered the world of rock 'n' roll. Aged sixteen, thinking he could sing, he entered a talent competition while on holiday at Butlin's in Filey. His rendering of Cliff Richard's 'Please Don't Tease' failed, as did a similar rendition the same week at the camp in the Pig and Whistle Bar. Back home, after much practice, he auditioned for Mike Stevenson, a member of the popular Tornados group, and for a short while was with Mick and the Tornados until joining The Telecasters and so began his career as a top rock 'n' roll artist.

In 1965 Terry Sexton played his last engagement, at Thornton Working Men's Club. A year later Terry married Carol, and within two years was the proud father of two boys, Darren and Conrad.

Still in the electrical business, which he had pursued since he was fifteen, and after many managerial positions, including seventeen years with Sharpe and Law shopfitters in Carlisle Road, in 1985 he formed his own company, becoming one of the region's most successful businessmen. Terry retired in 2000, and spends a considerable amount of time in Majorca with his wife.

Raymond (Ray) Smith (b. 1938, Bradford) bass guitar
See Vince Wayne and the Falcons.

Brian Fillingham (1938–2008, Bradford) drums

Brian lived in Raleigh Street and attended Paley Road School. Leaving school at fifteen, he became an apprentice wool sorter at a local mill. From an early age he practised drumming: he would set up his drums almost anywhere and in some cases all day. Music was his life, and by the age of seventeen he was an accomplished drummer. Just as he was beginning to be noticed for his talent, in 1956 he was called up for National Service in the RAF.

In his spare time in the forces Brian played his drums with other musical National Service lads. Although he liked rock 'n' roll music he also had an affiliation with jazz. On returning home in 1958 he worked in the Low Moor Head Office of the BDA (Bradford Dyers Association). Back on the music scene he was soon in demand, and in the early 1960s he became the drummer for The Telecasters and its other incarnations, until the group folded in 1965.

In 1967, now married to Pat, Brian moved to South Wales and for ten years ran a café. During this time he played in jazz bands, and was soon playing at top venues – and many times on Radio Wales. Now semi-professional, he was also a music tutor in education for the schools programmes in Wales.

When Brian became ill, a musical benefit was organised for him. It was thought that about 100 would attend, but in fact the total was well over 300 – indicating just how popular and respected he was. Sadly he could not attend the benefit, and a short while later, in 2008, he passed away. Brian was another Bradford lad who left his mark in the world of music.

David (Dave) Wiggins (1947–2008, Bradford) lead guitar

Dave attended Grange Boys Grammar School. His grandfather had been an orchestral clarinet player, and Dave had an interest in the same instrument. Aged nine, he won a musical scholarship, but his parents thought him too young to accept it. In his early teens Dave's taste was jazz, but seemingly overnight he realised he preferred rock 'n' roll. Soon he was a self-taught lead guitarist.

While still at school Dave and Ray Smith formed an instrumental group called The Sapphires, but after a short while he was firmly established as lead guitarist with the Telecasters. Having left school at sixteen, he became an apprentice sampler at a local woollen mill. Dave played with The Telecasters, then The Shakes, until the group was dissolved in 1965. Aged eighteen, he stood in with local groups until in June 1966 there was a knock at the door of his parents' house in Lidget Green. The door was opened to reveal Johnny Kidd and his bass player Nick Simper who, having heard of Dave's talents, were asking for his help. Johnny, who was on the verge of a comeback, asked him to join his group, but Dave, now in a 'proper job' and engaged to be married to Pamela, declined. Sadly, four months later Johnny Kidd died in a motor accident in Bury, returning from a cancelled booking. Nick Simper was badly injured.

Dave was working for Bird's Eye, the frozen food manufacturers, but was made redundant in the late 1980s. Thanks to his redundancy payment and his

The likeable and popular Brian Fillingham was an integral part of the group throughout its existence.

love of guitars, he opened a guitar shop in Lidget Green called Guitarcade. The business did well for a few years, but eventually he called it a day and joined an engineering company in Halifax. In 2008 Dave passed away, a few weeks before he was due to retire.

Dave Wiggins was a young, vibrant and well-liked Bradford musician in the 1960s – not only an accomplished lead guitarist but with the good looks of Buddy Holly and Hank Marvin. Who knows what may have happened if he had taken up Johnny Kidd's offer?

Mike Stephenson (b. 1938, Bradford) rhythm guitar

See The Sansovenos.

Barbara Pell aka Diana Stevens (b. 1946, Brighouse)

Barbara attended Longroyde Junior School and Brighouse Girls Grammar School. Leaving school in 1961, she became a photographic artist. In 1962 she joined The Telecasters and worked in the fashion world for Noel Fashions in Bradford, later joining the Provident Clothing Company, also in Bradford.

In 1967 Barbara turned professional singer with Tiffany's in York with the Alan Paul Set, then transferred to the Locarno in Burnley with the new stage-name of Pandora. For a few years from 1967 she appeared at Leicester Palais with the Ivor Kenny Sound and the Midlands Dance Orchestra, then moved to Tiffany's in Derby with the Ivor Kenny Sound. In the late 1970s and early '80s she was with the Mike Miller Band at the Nottingham Palais, then the Nottingham Commodore with the Gary Stuart Band. Barbara then went freelance for a few years. In 1986 to date she has been a children's entertainer.

Barbara has made many TV appearances, including *Name that Tune*, *Catchphrase* and *To Buy or Not to Buy*. She now lives in the lovely countryside of Upper Saxondale in Nottinghamshire with her husband Roger. In 1967, when Barbara auditioned at Leicester Palais, Ivor Kenny (who played the keyboards) asked the ballroom manager Roger Lakin to give his opinion of the various vocalists. Roger chose Barbara, and in July 1968 they were married. The rest, as they say, is history and as Barbara says, she has enjoyed many years of not doing a proper job!

Peter Nelson (b. 1941, Bradford) vocals

Peter headed the reformed Telecasters for a few months during 1965–6.

Ann Broadbent (b. 1940, Bradford) vocals

For a short time Ann was part of the re-formed Telecasters, one of the few female rock 'n' roll vocalists of the time in Bradford. She went on to be quite a popular solo artist.

Doreen, Marian and Nora, the lovely Three Ds, who made a bid for fame betweeen 1959 and 1960.

THE THREE Ds

pop trio

The three young ladies, Doreen, Marian and Nora, who were billed as the Three Ds, were employed at English Electric in Bradford, and had formed a close friendship. The girls attended many dance venues playing rock 'n' roll, like the Queens in Idle, the Majestic, and many more. When they realised that they had the same goal to be in the music business, singing and even recording records, they decided in about 1958 that they would create their own trio. Thus the Three Ds was born. It was Garth Cawood of The Dingos who pushed them into making this decision, hoping that they would sing with his group. As the trio's members lived in different parts of Bradford, they practised in the English Electric social room until they had learnt their repertoire. At this point they were formally asked to join The Dingos.

The girls invested in their own dresses, to be made by a local dressmaker – indicating their commitment. They always went to enormous trouble to look the part. They were probably Bradford's only close harmonising girl group in 1959 and 1960. Only in show-business for a short time, they became very popular, appearing with The Dingos at local pubs, clubs and dance halls like the Gaumont and Majestic.

With a similar style to Connie Francis, Helen Shapiro, The Poni-tails and the Vernon Girls, singing the pop songs of the time as a trio or backing The Dingos, it looked as if a full-time career might be on the cards. Making a demo-tape was considered from time to time and the Three Ds even wrote their own rock 'n' roll number called 'I Got a Boy and His Name is Jack'. Contact was made with Carol Levis (of Carol Levis Discoveries), but to no avail. All this happened with their own managerial skills – and mostly using buses to attend bookings! Intermittently Helen McCaffery of Tomboys fame sang with them, with the stage name Dee Laurence.

Things did not work out for the Three Ds, as Marian and Nora acquired boyfriends and they reluctantly broke up the trio: the usual case of what might have been! However, these three girls tried for stardom, and have their well-deserved place in the rock 'n' roll Who's Who of Bradford.

Doreen Burns (b. 1938, Bradford) vocals
Doreen attended Lilycroft Infants School and Bowling Back Lane Junior School. In 1949 she was one of Sir Francis Laidler's world-famous Sunbeams. Doreen left Tyersal Secondary Modern School in 1953 for shop work in the centre of Bradford, and in 1956 she joined English Electric as a fettler. It was there that in 1958 she formed the Three Ds with her fellow employees Marian and Norma. Doreen later married and raised a family, and worked for Kay's Catalogue until retiring in 2002. She still lives in Bradford.

Marian (b. 1940, Bradford) vocals
From 1956 she was employed at English Electric. She was a member of the Three Ds from 1958.

Nora (b. 1940, Bradford) vocals
From 1956 she was employed at English Electric. She was a member of the Three Ds from 1958.

THE TOMBOYS WITH HELEN

rock 'n' roll

Most Bradford rock 'n' roll groups were made up of teenagers, but the popular Tomboys was made up of mature men, some in their thirties and married with families. In 1956 the group was formed as a duo, with Tommy Butler and Dennis McCaffery both singing and playing the guitar. They proved very popular, playing at many local pubs, most notably The Sedgefield, Horse and Jockey, Oddfellows and Listers Arms. Around the late 1950s they were joined by David (Emil) Hardacre, lead guitarist, Terry Lee, drums, and Harry Foster, vocals. It was at about the same time that Dennis's daughter Helen became part of the group; and they were named the Tomboys with Helen. For the next few years they were in great demand, joining the club circuit and playing throughout Yorkshire. What made them almost unique was that all the group members, including the drummer, could sing and harmonise. They were very talented, and soon built up an army of fans.

It was Helen's voice that tipped the scales; that and her charisma on stage. The group had a couple of stand-in singers (Margaret Hennessey and Margaret Brewin) for the rare occasions when she was unavailable. After a few years at the top, in 1964, Dennis and daughter Helen emigrated to Toronto, Canada, and the group broke up. When old rock 'n' rollers reminisce about this era in Bradford, the Tomboys with Helen is one of the groups that are at the forefront of memories.

Tommy Butler (b. 1930, Bradford) rhythm guitar and vocals

Tommy attended Ryan Street School and All Saints School. At the age of fourteen he left to join his father, also named Thomas, in the family coal merchant business, eventually taking over the reins from him.

In 1956 Tommy formed a duo with Dennis McCaffery, The Tomboys – which later developed into the Tomboys with Helen. In 1964, when Dennis and Helen emigrated to Toronto, he declined the invitation to join them because of family reasons and business commitments.

Tommy resumed playing, and took up residency at the Listers Arms in Manchester Road, with Dougie Lamb on bass and Terry Lee on drums, and

From the mid-1950s unil the mid-'60s the Tom Boys with Helen were considered to be one of Bradford's finest groups. Back row, left to right: Dennis McCafferey, Helen McCaffery (Ellen), David 'Emil' Hardaker, Harry Foster. Front row: Tommy Butler, Terry Lee.

Helen sometimes sang as Dee Lawrence with the Three Ds, backing The Dingos.

Tommy Butler sang and played the guitar well into his sixties.

calling themselves The Waysiders. The Listers was renowned for its open mic sessions and the opportunity it gave young musicians to cut their teeth. The trio continued here for a couple of decades, and is still frequently mentioned and fondly remembered.

Tommy went on to join The Bees on keyboard, a group made up of his sons: Tom junior, rhythm guitar and vocals, Neil, bass and vocals, Jim, lead guitar, and Russ, drums. Surely father and four sons in one group could be a unique occurrence!

After The Bees disbanded there were various re-formations under different names, the most notable being the Berlin Wall, formed in 1989. Tommy was back on guitar and vocals, Peter Davison, his son in law, on guitar and vocals, Dave Hughes on bass, and Jim and Russ as before. Tom junior and Neil went on to achieve success with other bands, while Jim and Russ eventually welcomed the younger end of the family, with brothers Daz on bass and Scott on rhythm guitar and vocals.

In the late 1980s Tommy started a Sunday residency at the Gatehouse Club in Clayton with Mel Clarke, Drew Charles, Dougie Lamb and Alan Walker. He went on to perform under the name of Tommy and the Boys at the City Hotel, Beck Hill Club and Hoffman's in Little Germany. Among the many who accompanied him at this time were Mel Clarke, Allan Davis, John Jake Pullan, Josh Grundy, Jim Butler, Mick Waite, Dougie Lamb and Eric Holt.

In the mid-1990s Tommy was forced to give up playing because of illness; otherwise, no dooubt, he would still be playing on his Fender Stratocaster today. He is enjoying his retirement, with his many grandchildren and great-grandchildren, and lives in Wibsey.

Dennis McCaffery (1924–90s, Bradford) bass guitar

Dennis was educated at St Bede's Grammar School. In 1956 he formed a duo with Tommy Butler, and in 1958 formed the Tomboys with Helen. When Dennis emigrated to Canada with Helen they formed a group called The Bradfords, enjoying some success with their recordings. Dennis later moved to Washington State, and passed away in the 1990s.

Ellen McCaffery aka Helen (b. 1946, Bradford) vocals

Ellen attended St Joseph's RC School in Packington Street. While still at school she was regarded as a good singer and an accomplished accordionist. Leaving education at fifteen, it was not long before she was appointed as vocalist for The Tomboys, which became the Tomboys with Helen. In the beginning the press assumed her real name was Helen when in fact it was actually Ellen; from then on she used the name Helen as her stage name.

Aged sixteen, Helen left home to get married in Gretna Green, making headlines in the *News of the World*. However, the marriage did not last, and she was soon back home with her father and the group.

Helen sang with The Dingos for a short while, with the stage name Dee Lawrence, and also supported the Three Ds – but she spent most of her time with the Tomboys with Helen until 1964, when she emigrated to Canada with her father.

It appears that Helen moved around for some years, living in Minnesota, America, and Vancouver, Canada, where she ran an English fish and chip café and bar. A remarkable woman, Helen had a wealth of talent, and is always remembered when local rock 'n' roll is discussed.

David (Emil) Hardacre (b. 1937, Bradford) bass and lead guitar
See Mike Sagar and the Cresters.

Terry Lee (b. 1938, Shipley) drums
Born in Shipley, Terry and his family moved to Laburnham Place in Manningham, where he attended Green Lane Infants School, Green Lane Primary School and Drummond Road Secondary School. He left school at fifteen to work in Drummonds Mill and then at Foster Square railway station, before settling with the General Cleaning Company.

As a teenager Terry enjoyed the usual activities, particularly football, and even played a season with Bradford Park Avenue as a goalkeeper – but he never pursued it as a career. In 1957 he was called up for his National Service, and after two years with the Royal Signals he was demobbed in 1959. Back in Civvy Street he started to take an interest in the local rock 'n' roll groups. On a visit to North Bierley Labour Club Terry saw The Dingos, led by Garth Cawood. He became friendly with the band, and followed them for quite a while as he had his own transport. Some time later Garth asked Terry if he would like to transport the band to their venues, so he started to run The Dingos around, later enlisting the help of a lad called Stuart Ellis, who later became one of The Dingos' bass players. Terry had now become a roadie, and transported the band for over a year. In that time he had become friendly with The Tomboys.

The City Hotel in Bradford had a resident duo, Jack Kershaw, piano, and Les Warburton, drums, with whom Terry also became friends. Becoming interested in the drums, he picked up hints and tips from Les, who after a while asked him if he would stand in for him for a week while he was on holiday. Shortly afterwards, Dennis and Tommy of The Tomboys, obviously impressed by Terry's drumming, asked if he would like to join their group. Terry thought that if they saw talent in him then he had to give it a go. He informed Garth and The Dingos of his intention, and so began a drumming career that was some of the most enjoyable years of his life.

Terry stayed with The Tomboys for about five years, until just after he married Maureen. On leaving the band he did various session work, including playing with Raymond Ramon, the Earl Darren Sound and Colin Dean. For many years he played with Tommy Butler and Dougie Lamb as the trio The Waysiders at the Listers Arms. He later applied for a position at the Idle Working Men's Club, where he stayed for twenty-two years.

A self-taught percussionist, Terry had a wonderful semi-professional career spanning thirty-five years, during which time he met some lovely, interesting and friendly people. He realised what a wonderful era he was living in and thoroughly enjoyed the nightlife of Bradford and surrounding areas in the 1950s and '60s, whether he was playing or socialising. Terry Lee, a credit to his musical profession, lives in the Idle area with Maureen.

Harry Foster (b. 1925, Bradford) vocals
See profile.

TONI STAR AND THE METEORS

rock 'n' roll

Originally known as The Meteors, this group was formed in the early 1960s: Malcolm Bradshaw, bass guitar, brother Dennis, lead guitar, and Robin Hemingway, drums. After a while they were joined by a vocalist, who went under the name of Tony Star. They were soon making a name for themselves, but then Tony decided to go solo. This was a problem, as advance bookings showed the group's name to be Tony Star and the Meteors. They need not have worried, as a young singer named Jennifer Cook-Speight eagerly joined them. She was given the name Toni Star, so the group's name could remain unchanged. Like most groups of the time they were immaculate in their appearance, with royal blue satin trousers and tops, with the letter M embroidered at the front: these were known to them as their spacesuits – and they were made Malcolm and Dennis's mother. Their father provided the transport to and from venues (who said all mums and dads were squares?).

The group were regulars at the Majestic ballroom and other dance halls including the Kings and Queen's and the newly opened Mecca Locarno on Manningham Lane. They were also very popular at cinemas, playing on stage during the interval, which was all the rage for a short time, and they appeared at many of the local working men's clubs. It seemed that they had everything – but everything suddenly changed when Jenny left in mid-1964. For a short while the group continued as The Meteors, and another female singer joined them, but it was too late. They had begun to fizzle out, and in late 1964 they disbanded.

Dennis Bradshaw (b. 1948, Bradford) lead guitar

Dennis lived in Buttershaw and was a very proficient guitarist, a key member of the Meteors until they folded in 1964.

Malcolm Bradshaw (b. 1946, Bradford) bass guitar

Malcolm lived at Buttershaw with his brother Dennis and family. A member of The Meteors until they folded in 1964, he joined the Caravelles in 1965, following Len Fox as bass player. A versatile musician and vocalist, he formed a duo with Vicky Lee, the Two Ms, when the Caravelles disbanded. Having mastered the keyboard, they had much success until 1968, when they parted company. Malcolm was a carpet fitter, but later had a career in security.

Robin Hemingway (b. 1946, Bradford) drums

Robin lived at Buttershaw. He was a very competent drummer with The Meteors, and joined the Caravelles when they disbanded, replacing Dave Marshall in 1965. During his musical career he was employed in food retail at the Cooperative Society in Fair Road, Wibsey, later going into management.

Tony Star (b. 1941, Bradford) vocals

When Tony left The Meteors for a solo career, his place was taken by Jennifer Cook (later Speight), who adapted his name to Toni.

Jennifer Cook (later Speight) aka Toni Star (b. 1944, Bradford) vocals

Jennifer attended Thornbury Infant School and Junior Schools, and was a pupil at Lapage Street Secondary School. Leaving aged fifteen, she started work at the well-known fashion house Novello's on the corner of Westgate and Kirkgate, where she trained as a sales assistant in the gown department. She was really enthusiastic and enjoyed her work in this famous establishment; but her ambition was to become a rock 'n' roll singer.

Answering an advert in the local paper, she auditioned with the Phil Cleary Orchestra at the Midland Hotel, Leeds. Being young and naïve she thought it was a rock band as the advert had said 'Girl singer wanted', so she had a shock! Jennifer's audition went well, but she was told that she would have to look older as they played at many dance halls – and she was only seventeen.

Jenny really wanted to be with a rock 'n' roll group, and her chance came in 1962 when, now aged eighteen, she was asked if she would like to join Tony Star and the Meteors. Changing the group's name to Toni Star and the Meteors was an easy matter. Jenny soon made an impact, as there were few rock 'n' roll groups with a female vocalist. With her good looks, fine singing voice and excellent backing from The Meteors, Toni was much in demand.

In 1964, after nearly two successful years with the Meteors, Jenny decided to call it a day and left the Meteors. Marrying in 1968, she moved to Blackpool, where she still lives – near her son Mark and two grandchildren. Now retired, her hobbies are walking on the seafront, shopping and horseracing. Toni Star, one of yesterday's stars!

THE TRADESMEN

rock 'n' roll

The Tradesmen were in existence for only three years, from 1963 until 1966. Starting the group showed what can be done with talent and determination, even when you have no funds to speak of. Although they did not make it to the top, they fully deserve a place in the annals of Bradford's rock 'n' roll. It all came about when Mike Betts, who had been taking guitar lessons for two years, got together some friends. The line-up was John (Andy) Anderson, lead guitar and vocals, Mike Betts, rhythm guitar and vocals, Mick Higgins, bass guitar, and Robert Castle, drums. John and Mick had no guitar-playing experience and had to be taught the rudiments, while the drummer had to teach himself. They all knew there was much to do, and they set about purchasing guitars, drums, amplifiers and a PA system. This was quite a challenge, as they were all apprentices with an average of £8 to £10 per week in wages. Budding drummer Robert bought a cheap drum-set and started taking lessons on Saturday mornings. Mike Betts had his own guitar, while Mick and Andy purchased secondhand guitars. Not being able to afford a bass guitar, they took the strings off one of them, purchased four bass strings and converted it. With all the equipment complete, Mike set about teaching the other two guitarists basic chords and scales, and even purchased sheet music from Fred Power's bookshop in Kirkgate Market.

All that was now required was a place to practise, and they were soon meeting at Mike's house (when his mum had gone out). The next item they needed was a cheap amplifier with a couple of speakers, which was not the ideal output for three guitarists – but they had to make do. Practising at Mike's home was a problem with amplification, and his mum did not always go out! A new venue was required, and as two of the lads were in the Boys Brigade at Idle Baptist Church, Mr Carter, who was the deacon, let them practise in the Sunday School, which had a stage, on Saturday afternoons at no cost.

Progress was slow, but each week they improved. Soon they could play some rock 'n' roll music, including Beatles, Rolling Stones, Hollies, Searchers and Shadows instrumentals. It wasn't enthusiasm that was letting them down but their equipment, so they took the major decision to pool their money and

Practice time on stage at the Idle Baptist Sunday school, 1963. Left to right: Mick Higgins, Robert Castle, John Anderson, Mick Betts.

Mick Higgins and John Anderson show off their new equipment.

Mike Betts at home, together with his new Italian guitar with aluminium scratch-plate.

Drummer Robert Castle practising the drum solo from 'Wipeout'.

take the giant step of purchasing two amplifiers from Harmony House, one to be used by the bass guitarist and the other by both lead and rhythm guitarist. To complement these there were two Goodman's speakers. Having to put down a deposit and buy them on hire purchase was a massive undertaking. On the day that they finally received all this new equipment they took it straight down to the Sunday School. They were now a new group with a completely different sound; it had been worth the many months of practice. Now they were getting somewhere.

After purchasing another amplifier, so each guitarist had his own amplifier, it was time to meet the public and show off their rock 'n' roll repertoire. The Tradesmen had arrived, and played their first booking at a youth club church dance at St Luke's down Barkerend Road in early 1963. It was a thrill for all the lads when they were well received by a young audience, and they had their first payment of £20! It had been a long struggle.

After their first booking there was nothing else immediately in the pipeline, so the lads went on practising regularly. Eventually they were asked to play at their youth club at Idle Baptist Church – for nothing, as they used the Sunday School for practice. They agreed that it would be a good venue, especially as the audience would contain many of their friends. They must have gone down well, as two twenty-first birthday celebration bookings quickly followed, one of which in particular, at Idle Working Men's Club, went very well. When not practising or playing The Tradesmen went around pubs and clubs listening to other local groups. They agreed that every other group was better than they were, and they accepted that they had a long way to go.

One venue they visited was Greengates Social Club, affectionately known as the Red Den. After mentioning to the concert secretary that they had a group, they were given their first top booking – for the following Saturday night. They drummed up as much support as they could among friends and family, and they turned up on the night to help fill the Red Den. The concert secretary's introductions were always of the same standard and generally in a broad Yorkshire accent: 'I would like you to give a big hand to our special group of the night as they are all local lads living in Idle – so let's hear it for The Tradesmen.' At first they were very nervous, but after a few rocking numbers and generous applause they soon acquired confidence, and it was a very successful evening. They felt they were on their way, especially as the concert secretary gave them another booking and advised them to contact other concert club secretaries. They took his advice, and soon had many bookings, playing mostly on Saturday evenings and at lunchtimes. Sometimesthese were quite far afield – but a friend, John King, borrowed his brother's Austin A55 van and later a more up-market Bedford Workabus with seats in the back, sliding doors and a column gear-change.

The Tradesmen were beginning to be noticed. This gave them the impetus invest in new outfits, and a friend offered to make these at a reduced price, payable monthly as the money came in from their bookings. The new attire consisted of black dinner suits, white shirts, black ties and black shoes and socks, which made them look professional. They also felt it was time to upgrade their instruments, so Robert the drummer went back to Harmony House in Bradford and traded in his old kit for the upmarket Rodgers drumkit and new

Zym cymbals (also top of the range). The three guitarists travelled to Kitchens of Leeds, looking for a good part exchange on their guitars. Mick Higgins purchased a Fender Solid bass, John Anderson had a Gibson Semi-Acoustic and Mike Betts a Gretsch Chet Atkins Tennessean semi-acoustic with a Bigsby Tremolo arm. The cost of Mike's guitar alone was approximately £178, a fantastic sum of money in 1965, although free hard guitar cases, extra strings and plectrums were given to each member.

With new suits and expensive instruments The Tradesmen filled their repertoire with the popular numbers of The Beatles, Rolling Stones, Billy J. Kramer, The Shadows, Bob Dylan, Donovan, The Hollies, The Searchers, Joe Brown and many others. Now firmly established on the working men's club circuit, they were a very popular local group, and earned enough money to pay for their suits and instruments, with a little left over. Among the many popular clubs they performed at were the Idle Working Men's Club, Laisterdyke Social Club, Dudley Hill Social Club, the City Band Club, East Ward Labour Club, the Woodend Club in Windhill and the Railway Club. They had many bookings at their first club venue, the Red Den, and were the first choice for many twenty-first birthday parties, which were very lucrative. Perhaps one of the strangest venues was Bolton Villas Cricket Club in Wrose, where they were engaged to play on 5 November, at the bonfire night event. The group was on the outside edge of the cricket pitch, with various long extension leads from the clubhouse to supply their power.

At about this time the Top Twenty Club opened in Idle, in The Tradesmen's back yard. It was promoted by Frank Thorpe of Thorpe's Ice-Cream fame, and it proved to be very popular – especially with Garth Cawood at the helm. As they were a local group, Frank let The Tradesmen practise at the club, and gave them the odd booking to supplement their many other venues.

In 1966 the mother of one of the group wrote to Hughie Green, suggesting that The Tradesmen should appear on *Opportunity Knocks*. The group forgot all about it and continued to play, but girlfriends were now on the scene and other priorities took over. Suddenly, after years of trials and tribulations, they realised deep down that they would never make it big time: they really just weren't good enough. In mid-1966 they closed the book on The Tradesmen and sold all their equipment back to the shops. Then three months later a letter arrived for Mike Betts, asking if The Tradesmen could attend an audition at The Gaumont in Bradford for *Opportunity Knocks*. But it was too late: The Tradesmen were no longer available.

Like so many other groups of that time, a book could be published about The Tradesmen alone. Much of what happened to them happened in some way to other local groups. Few members of the public who saw them perform would have had any idea of the effort it took to put them on the stage, smartly dressed, performing well, and all smiling and hoping.

Mike Betts (b. 1944, Swinton) rhythm guitar and vocals.

When he was six months old Mike's parents moved to Bradford, living at Stanley Street in Idle. Mike attended Thorpe Infants School and Greengates Junior School. Later, when the family moved to Moorfield Place, he then attended Thorpe Secondary Modern School, and also joined the Boys Brigade at Idle Baptist Church. Leaving school at fifteen he became an apprentice plumber and heating engineer with local firm Alfred Keighley Ltd, the offices being in the old fire station in Idle. He worked on the new housing estates that were springing up.

In 1961, increasingly interested in music in general, and rock 'n' roll in particular, Mike decided to learn to play the guitar, and bought an old acoustic model from a secondhand shop for 30s; but how to learn? Someone pointed him to Errick's photography shop in Keighley. A brilliant musician called Ray Smith worked there, and in his spare time he gave guitar lessons for 10s. Mike began to learn from him, and was soon influenced by the sounds of Django Reinhardt and Chet Atkins. He soon upgraded to a solid electric guitar, which did not work. Ray advised him to buy an Italian guitar, which was very thin and not solid. For two years Mike continued with his lessons, and was so successful that Ray asked him to join him on stage at The Alma in Windhill, playing rhythm guitar, and later at the Kings Head in Bingley. Mike was elated and said he would think about it, but eventually said no – because his mates wanted someone like him to teach them the basics and help them to form a group.

It would be many months before they performed in public, but perhaps this was the best decision Mike had ever made. From 1963, for three years, The Tradesmen was a formidable group. When they folded in 1966 he sold his beloved Gretch guitar back to the shop he had purchased it from. The same year he married Joyce.

Mike carried on with his former work, and later formed his own plumbing business. After a few years he became a manager at Christian charities in Leeds before finally retiring. He and his wife Joyce had three children, Jonathan, James and Catherine, and still live in the Thackley area. Although he never joined another group, Mike still enjoys playing the guitar as well as his other hobbies of photography, railway modelling, listening to classical music and walking in the Dales.

John (Andy) Anderson (b. 1944, Bradford) lead guitar

John lived on Leyton Drive in Idle, and attended Thorpe Infants School and Greengates School. After education he joined Rundels of Idle as an apprentice architectural metalworker, and it was here that he met Mick Higgins. In about 1961 he and Mick began to attend Idle Baptist Church Youth Club, where they met up with the other lads who would go on to form The Tradesmen. John fancied being a lead guitarist, so Mike Betts taught him, starting with a few chords and chromatic scales. After much practice he soon became quite proficient, and an integral part of The Tradesmen. He was with the group until they disbanded in 1966.

John never joined another group, and in 1968 he went to live in Australia, at Townsville in Queensland. Soon he was working in the building industry. He was married to Genette and they had two boys, but unfortunately the marriage ended, and John now lives in Melbourne. He has returned to the UK a few times, but he likes it over there and is content to be an Aussie!

Robert Castle (b. 1941, Bradford) drums

Robert lived in the Idle area, where he attended Thorpe Infants School, Swaine House Junior School and Thorpe Secondary Modern School. Leaving school aged fifteen, his first job was working on a local farm. However, this was not to his liking, and his father managed to get him an apprenticeship as a motor mechanic, for National Carriers on Canal Road, Bradford.

Robert had joined the 3rd Company Boys Brigade based at Idle Baptist Church, and when he and a few friends decided to have a go at forming a pop group he decided that he would be the drummer. He started drumming lessons at Woods Music Shop then on North Parade. Having saved up enough money, he purchased a cheap drum kit from Mr Bryant of Harmony House in Great Horton Road. It would be many months before he and the other members had enough experience to fulfil their ambition

Later, when The Tradesmen had some success, Robert bought an expensive Rodgers drum kit. He was with the group until it disbanded in 1966. Shortly afterwards he and lead guitarist John Anderson went on holiday to the Channel Islands – and it was there Robert met his future wife Gillian, on holiday there from Middlesex. When they married they moved to Pinner, Middlesex, as a trained mechanic Robert worked on the new Deltic diesel locomotives.

Later Robert and Gillian decided to move back to Bradford, and bought a bungalow in the Thackley area. He became a postman in Idle, but badly injured his back and was pensioned off by the Post Office. Sadly Gillian passed away in 2009. Robert now lives in a nursing home in Bradford. He still looks back to the really good times and many laughs he had with the group, and says that he is so glad that he was part of that scene.

Mick Higgins (b. 1946, Bradford) bass guitar

Mick lived on Highfield Road in Idle, where his father was an wholesale egg merchant; he kept hens in fields on Idle Moor. Mick attended Thackley Primary School, Esholt Village Junior School and Belle Vue Boys Grammar School. When he left education he started work at Rundels of Idle as an apprentice architectural metalworker, where he served his full apprenticeship. It was here that he met John Anderson – and in about 1961 he formed a friendship with other lads who wanted to form a group. He was invited to play bass guitar, so he purchased a secondhand guitar and Mike Betts taught him a few chords. With much practice and determination Mick soon became a good bass guitarist, and when The Tradesmen finally started in 1963 it was he and lead guitarist John Anderson who painted their logo on the drum. Later, while playing at the Railway Club in Wakefield Road, he met his future wife Patricia, whom he married in 1968.

After completing his apprenticeship Mick left Rundels to join Leggots of Bradford, in the same industry. Later a move to Cullingworth Fabrications brought him much success: the company really looked after its staff, with bonuses and family trips. However, the job involved lots of travelling, so in 1983 he left to start his own business. After some time he secured a very lucrative contract with a German company, supplying balustrades and handrails to Marks and Spencers. Mick is still self-employed, and as involved as ever with his architectural metalwork – but he is hoping to retire soon. Mick and Patricia went on to have two children, Angela and Paul. Sadly Patricia passed away in 1998.

Today Mick spends his spare time growing fruit and veg on his allotment, and enjoys visiting air shows. He puts his fifty years of specialist skills to good use by restoring old cars, and has just completed a 1963 Humber Super Snipe. Mick never joined another group after The Tradesmen, but he left his mark like those other lads from Idle, the village where he still lives.

THE TUXEDOS

rock 'n' roll

The Tuxedos were formed on the back of the skiffle craze and originated from Highfield Secondary School and the East Bierley/Birkenshaw areas. At the Christmas 1957 school concert Martin Cook, trumpet, Ian (Jungle) Smith, guitar, George Minchull, guitar, and others did a Presley song, and continued to practise after the event.

Much teenage activity in those days centred around youth clubs, and Martin, Ian and George gravitated to Holme Lane Methodist Club, close to Highfield School. There were many who fancied their chances in the cut and thrust of those early rock group days, but eventually this thinned out to Dave Mortimer, drums, Martin Cook, Ian Smith and George Minchull, all on guitars, and various singers, including John Dowson. Calling themselves the Skiff-Rocks, the name of a chord book used by Ian and George, they went on to play at various youth clubs.

Ian and George used to meet up every Saturday morning at Morley's Corner in Bradford. In those days sheet music for the Top Ten was available at Hayden Robinson's music stall in Kirkgate Market, where you could browse through the sheets and memorise the chords for your practice sessions. They also wandered over to Moore's music shop in North Parade, and sometimes if things were quiet they could play various guitars. The most coveted were the solid rock guitars, which produced the bright treble sound of lead guitars. It was during one of these visits that they first saw a solid guitar that was black and white, called Tuxedo. From that day their group became known as The Tuxedos.

The group now had a new name and a revised line-up: John Dowson, vocals, Martin Cook and Ian Smith, rhythm guitars, George Minchull, lead guitar, Dave Sunderland, bass guitar, and Dave Mortimer, drums. The year 1960 was the start of a very successful period, when they played regularly at the Majestic and Gaumont in Bradford and at Yorkshire's many dance and town hall events. A manager was now required to organise their activities, and their roadie Trevor Lever, whose job had been to make sure they arrived at venues on time, took over this role. He obtained and confirmed many bookings, and

The Tuxedos have a jam session at their club in the Unity Hall. Left to right: George Minchull, John Dowson, Trevor Lever (manager), Irvin Smith, Spike O'Brien, Ian Smith.

also controlled the finances. In those halcyon days a night's earnings could be all of £10 minus 10 per cent agent's fee.

In 1961 Martin Cook, the rhythm guitarist, left the group to go to college in Hull, and a year later Dave Sunderland, bass guitarist, and Dave Mortimer, drummer, also left, which caused a major headache. Relief came unexpectedly when The Dingos broke up, and the very talented Spike O'Brien and Irvin (Smudge) Smith, drums, became available. Ian Smith transferred very successfully to bass guitar, allowing Spike's superb piano skills full rein. His solos included B. Bumble and the Stingers' 'Nut Rocker', which was an arrangement of Tchaikovsky's 'March of the Wooden Soldiers': Smudge was on drums and George on lead guitar. John Dowson's vocals led from the front in powerful interpretations of 'Shaking All Over' and the contrasting 'Spanish Harlem'. The group was now in great demand, even playing on the same bill as Sounds Incorporated and Johnny Kidd.

In 1963 Spike and Smudge left, as did bass guitarist Ian. John and George did a few bookings with a reduced band, with stand-in bass guitarists and drummers, but after a relatively short time they called it a day.

John Dowson on vocals, with the voice, looks and charisma of any of the top popstars of the day.

John Dowson (1942–2010, Birkenshaw) vocals

John lived on a farm in Station Lane, Birkenshaw. Educated at Whitcliffe Mount Grammar School, he started work as a laboratory assistant in 1959 at Firths Carpets, Brighouse, transferring to a new laboratory at their sister company Firth Furnishings, Heckmondwyke, in 1961. John stayed at Firths (now called Rieter) all his working life, during which time he became their technical guru. The business supplied many of the world's car manufacturers. He retired in 2003 to spend more time with his wife Jill, and they enjoyed their passion for gardening, French wines, genealogy and travelling. They had two sons, one of whom works in Switzerland. Sadly John passed away in September 2010.

George Minchull (b. 1943, Bradford) lead guitar

George lived in the Abb Scot Lane area of Low Moor. Educated at Highfield Secondary School, he began work as an apprentice TV engineer, later moving into electronics, then computers. He became manager of National Repair Centre for the UK division of Bell Atlantic. He later became a Fellow of the Institute of Engineering Technology and is an Incorporated Engineer. George officially retired in 2003, but continues to work with his wife Hilary in their own catering business (the Quality Wedding Company), which specialises in weddings in the UK in the summer and in India in the winter. George has married twice and has four children, Tim and Donna from his first marriage and Claire and Christian from his present marriage of thirty-nine years to Hilary.

A founder member of The Tuxedos, George stayed with the group until it disbanded. Afterwards he played with The Telecasters for a short while. His hobbies now are playing the guitar, playing squash and building electronic gadgets. He now lives in Huddersfield with his wife

Ian (Jungle) Smith (b. 1943, Bradford) rhythm guitar

Ian lived in East Bierley and worked as a wool sorter in Bradford. After leaving The Tuxedos he joined a group called the James Boys.

Martin Cook (b. 1943, Bradford) rhythm guitar

Martin lived at Dudley Hill. His parents had a large furnishing supply business in Greengates.

Dave Sunderland (b. 1944, Bradford) bass guitar

Dave lived opposite the Ring of Bells in Idle, where his parents had a very successful fish and chip shop. Dave worked for Charles Sydney in Bradford and later as service manger at Tordoff's Porsche garage in Yeadon.

Dave Mortimer (b. 1943, Bradford) drums

Dave lived in Shirley Road off Tong Street.

Brian Holt aka Spike O'Brien (1940–2000 Bradford) piano

See profile.

Irvin (Smudge) Smith (b. 1942, Bradford) drums

See The Dingos.

Trevor Lever (b. 1942, Brighouse) manager and roadie
Trevor lived in Brighouse. Educated at Rastrick Grammar School, he started work at Firth Carpets in the laboratory where his life-long friendship with John Dowson began. Trevor bought an ex-army pick-up in 1959 and became a roadie with The Tuxedos, soon taking on the management of the group.

In 1982 Trevor started Avocet Dye and Chemical Company Ltd, manufacturing products for the textile industry. This family company is now exporting over 70 per cent of its production from its factory in Brighouse. His wife Doreen is financial director, their son Michael is managing director and daughter Janette is production director. Outside the business Trevor is a cyclist and walker. With Doreen he has walked and trekked in many parts of the world, including ascending Kilimanjaro in 2006.

Vince Wayne and the Falcons practise at the Boy and Barrel pub on Westgate. Left to right: Dave Barraclough, Vince Wayne, Dave Marshall, Alan Thornton.

Vince Wayne and the Falcons: a publicity pose at the Boy and Barrel pub. Left to right: Dave Barraclough, Dave Marshall, Alan Thornton. Front: Vince Wayne.

VINCE WAYNE AND THE FALCONS

rock 'n' roll

A local group that lots of people remember is Vince Wayne and the Falcons, which had quite a following in the early 1960s. It all started in 1959 when Vince and his best pal Alan Thornton, who both played the guitar, went around the pubs and clubs as a duo, with Vince also on vocals. However, after a short while they decided to form a full rock 'n' roll group, and started to look for new members.

It was in the youth club close to Moore's music shop that Vince met a young Dave Marshall, who wanted to join a group as a drummer. Dave had his own drum kit, was keen and talented, so he was welcome. Next came Dave Barraclough, a good rhythm guitarist, followed by the competent Ray Smith on bass guitar. With Alan on lead and Vince on vocals, Vince Wayne and the Falcons was complete – with fame and stardom just around the corner!

They rehearsed at the Boy and Barrel pub in Westgate, and were the resident group on Fridays and Saturday for many months for the grand sum of £3 per performance. They found it was rather cramped. and soon moved to the Oddfellows Arms at the bottom of Manchester Road. Here they could also rehearse, and for the next two years were booked playing alternate Saturday lunchtimes with the Tomboys with Helen. They were paid £4 and also received a few free drinks.

In between these regular bookings they played at many other venues, including the Majestic and Gaumont ballrooms, the Students Club and the Textile Hall in Westgate, and many local pubs and clubs in Bradford, Halifax, Huddersfield and Leeds. They were also regularly on stage at the Gaumont Theatre's Saturday morning teenage show, at which local groups performed between 10am and 12 noon.

During this time Dave Barraclough left to join The Caravelles, and his place was taken by the very experienced and talented guitarist Mike Stephenson. At the same time Dave Marshall moved on, also joining The Caravelles. A new drummer was soon found to fill the spot, the very experienced Dave Archer, late of The Ravers.

Garth Cawood was now being noted as a very proficient theatrical booking agent and with his contacts he obtained many bookings for the group. Things began to change, though, and when Alan left with his family for Canada it was the beginning of the end. New members came and went, and it was not long before the group was no more.

Selwyn Kershaw aka Vince Wayne (b. 1939, Bradford) vocals and guitar

Vince lived in Thornton before moving to Queensbury, where he attended Foxhill School. Later, when living in Buttershaw, he went to Wibsey School at the same time as those other rock 'n' rollers Garth Cawood and Malcolm Murray of The Royalists. His best mate was Alan Thornton, his right-hand man during The Falcons years. Vince's first job was as a warp twister at A. and S. Henry's Mill in Great Horton, but this was not to his liking and he became a waiter at the Midland Hotel. After time performing as a duo with Alan, and an exciting few years singing with Vince Wayne and the Falcons, he returned after The Falcons folded as part of the Vince Wayne Combo, performing with an assortment of talented musicians. Later, in 1967, he was with a trio called 2 Plus 1, which had a season at Butlin's, Skegness.

For the next few years Vince kept his hand in playing the guitar and singing at venues throughout the North of England. Having worked in the hotel business for many years, including the prestigious Clifton Arms and the Palm Court Hotel in Blackpool, he decided to start a scrap metal business in Withernsea. In 1992 he formed another group, the Moody Guys, who were quite successful for a couple of years.

In 1995 Vince had to retire from his business because of ill health, and he now lives in the Knottingley area, West Yorkshire. In his spare time he dabbles in property and plays his guitar. As he says, the 1950s and '60s music will forever be in his heart! Vince is now writing songs, and is hoping to have that big hit! Vince was, and still is, quite a character, a very good vocalist and a favourite of the teenagers, and he is well remembered by his peers of the 1950s and '60s.

Alan Thornton (b. 1941, Bradford) lead guitar

In 1959 Alan and his best friend Vince Wayne started to go round the pubs as a guitar and vocals duo. This led to Vince Wayne and the Falcons. When the group broke up Alan emigrated to Canada with his family.

Dave Barraclough (b. 1942, Bradford) rhythm and lead guitar

Dave lived on Beckside Road. After leaving school he spent his early years as a cloth examiner. After several years with Vince Wayne and the Falcons he left to join The Caravelles. Dave was the only group member to continue with them until they dissolved in 1966. Later he went to live in Sunderland.

Ray Smith (b. 1938, Bradford) bass guitar

Ray attended St Cuthbert's RC School, and St Bede's Grammar School. Leaving school at sixteen, his first job was with William Rigg and Son, textile pattern makers. This was followed by training as an apprentice jockey with Captain C

A publicity pose at the Boy and Barrel pub. L-R: Dave Barraclough, Dave Marshall and Alan Thornton. Front centre: Vince Wayne.

Boyd Rochford's stables in Newmarket (at the time he was the Queen Mother's and Queen's trainer). After an assortment of jobs Ray signed on in the RAF for five years, but after twelve months he was pensioned out having smashed his leg in a motor-cycle accident.

Still in his late teens Ray started playing the guitar, a Rosetti Lucky Seven that he bought on hire purchase. When going around the youth clubs he met another pair of would-be stars, Dave Wiggins and Arthur (whose surname is forgotten), who were playing as The Sapphires. It was suggested that he join them as bass guitarist, which he did, but the group fizzled out after a short time. Many other offers came his way, most notably Vince Wayne and the Falcons, which he joined in 1960.

During the following months, as bass players were in demand, Ray was inundated with offers, and during his time with The Falcons he did session work with The Toledos, backed Vince Eager in Barnoldswick and also backed local pop singer Johnny Apollo (Vince Beresford).

In 1961, still with The Falcons and after much reorganisation and new members, Ray finally joined up with Terry Sexton under his new band name Terry Sexton and the Telecasters. Back with his old mate Dave Wiggins, Ray settled in with one of Yorkshire's most popular groups for a few years, until they folded in 1965.

Ray went on to play for other groups, but finally decided to sell his pale blue precision bass guitar and buy a saxophone. He was so keen that he took lessons from Ronnie Varo at Moore's music shop in Westgate. In between lessons he went onto the local moors to practice! Soon he had learned enough to get by, and joined a nine-piece local band called Lykes of Witch, playing soul music and practising in a shed in a field in Thornton.

In 1966, now married, Ray had to stop playing the sax after having some teeth removed. He purchased another bass guitar, and over the next few years played with many groups. In 1975 he joined a group called Night Traffic, with a stunning singer called Beverley Day. Ray was now playing all over the country, and more or less making a living out of it. A season in Jersey was followed by a German tour; then he returned to Jersey. Later the group played at Batley Variety Club, Morecambe Bowl and, in 1977, worked with Wee Willie Harris for twelve months.

After ten years with Night Traffic it was back to a proper job! Now in his late thirties, Ray worked as a sales representative, which stopped most of his music touring; he was with the same company until retirement. A few years before he retired Ray took to flying, and he had a private pilot's licence for eighteen years, until deafness became a hindrance. Ray has many other hobbies, including photography, kite making and flying, computer work, and supporting Bradford City since 1969. He still lives in Elland with his wife Sheila.

Dave Marshall (b. 1944, Plymouth) drums.
Dave later lived in Baildon, where he attended Ferniehurst Primary School. He moved to Lidget Green in 1954 and attended Lidget Green Junior School and Clayton Secondary Modern School. Leaving aged fifteen, he was apprenticed at Fields Printers and Son, Lidget Green. Another of Bradford's many self-taught drummers, between 1960 and 1966 he went on to be a stalwart member of The Caravelles following his time with The Falcons.

When he left The Caravelles, Dave formed a group with other ex-Caravelles, the Hornets and Carolanne, after which he concentrated on his career in printing. He married Tina in 1965, and had two children, Amanda and Timothy. He was with W.N. Sharpe and Company (Greeting Cards) on Bingley Road for twenty-five years, but was made redundant. After time with Fine Arts in Low Moor and later UK Cards Ltd in Keighley, from which he was made redundant in 2004, Dave retired at sixty. A keen gardener, he and his wife live in the Queensbury area.

Mike Stephenson (b. 1938, Bradford) rhythm guitar
See The Sansovenos.

Dave Archer (b. 1943, Bradford) drums
See Lee Chevin and the Ravers.

Kenny Gough (b. 1941, Bradford)
See Mike Sagar and the Cresters.

THE WINGBEATS
rock 'n' roll

A set of local young lads and lass got together in 1962 to form The Wingbeats, and aimed for the top. The group consisted of Margaret Brewing, vocals (she sang in the style of Helen Shapiro), Terry Noble, lead guitar, Colin (surname unknown), rhythm guitar, Keith Knowles, bass guitar, and Ken Hickey, vocals and drums. Sadly, the group only lasted a few months, although they secured a weekly booking, every Friday night at Sutton Community Centre Tyersal, for which they each received 10s. Ken Hickey's drum kit was taken to this venue each week in a bubble car!

Margaret Brewing (b. 1947, Bradford) vocals
Margaret lived in Lupton Street off Manningham Lane and attended Midland Road Infants School and Frizinghall Secondary Modern School. Margaret was vocalist with The Wingbeats for the short time that the group was together. Later, from time to name, she stood in for Helen of The Tomboys, if Helen wasn't available.

Terry Noble (b. 1946, Bradford) lead guitar
Terry attended Bradford Art College.

Colin ? (b. 1947, Bradford) rhythm guitar

Keith Knowles (b. 1947, Bradford) bass guitar

Kenneth (Ken) Hickey (b. 1947, Bradford) drums and vocals
See profile.

The New Victoria (Gaumont), 1931–2000?

The way we were, 1960. The smart and wonderful staff of the Gaumont, from an age gone by. Phil Cox was the manager, wearing glasses. On his left is assistant manager Norman Ridler. At the back on the left, with gloves and epaulettes, is Commissionaire George – well loved by the many Saturday Morning Club youngsters in the 1940s and '50s.

Epilogue
NOSTALGIA

We know in our heart of hearts that the 'Good Old Days' were not always so great. However, despite that, the widespread perception that many of them were is all part of the phenomenon known as nostalgia, in which we gloss over the difficulties and tribulations of decades gone by with our rose-tinted spectacles firmly in place. It is a wistful desire to return to a former time in our life, to our home, family and friends, a sentimental yearning for the happiness of a former place or time. It is also a desire not to see tangible links with that former place and time needlessly destroyed. Anyone who remembers the Bradford of yesteryear with nostalgia will probably still refer to the radio as wireless, to the City Hall as the Town Hall, and will still mourn the passing of trolleybuses (or 'trackless'). During 1954 to 1966, the years of rock 'n' roll, we still had some wonderful buildings in Bradford, most notable being the Swan Arcade and Kirkgate Market. These, with many others, were swept away – a wanton act of destruction led by outsiders with no thought for Bradford's heritage and no compassion for those who cared so much about it.

At the moment Bradford is going through a similar process, with more iconic buildings set to be demolished to make way for the next 'Legoland' replacement. One such is the Odeon (New Vic), known to thousands of Bradfordians over the years from the Saturday Morning Clubs of the 1940s and '50s to the pop shows of the 1950s and '60s. Nothing is sacrosanct in Bradford.

While many of us are in favour of progress if it leads to genuine improvements, it is so sad that Bradford, home of our forebears, has in the last forty years lost its way through ill-advised schemes. The replacements for Bradford's iconic buildings are hotels, apartments, glass buildings and wine bars. All the while the city centre stagnates, with shops boarded up and only a few businesses left, surrounded by charity and pound shops. I, like many of Bradford's older generation (which includes many original rock 'n' rollers), may not be available for comment in twenty or thirty years when a new generation of consultants descends on Bradford to provide schemes to replace those of the twenty-first century. We need to make our voices heard now if there is to be anything left of the city that meant so much to us.

ABOUT THE AUTHOR

Soldier, Author and Explorer of Kwa Zululand

Derek Lister was born on 2 May 1938 at Walden Drive, Heaton, Bradford, and attended St Patrick's RC school in Westgate. Leaving school aged fifteen, he worked at the famous Bradford store Brown Muffs and later Burtons the tailors in Westgate. Called up at eighteen for National Service, he signed on and saw active service in Aden and Cyprus. Derek returned to 'Civvy Street', working for a while at Grattan's Warehouse, then Stenhouse Insurance Brokers in Wells Street, Bradford. During this time he had rock 'n' roll groups called Dal Stevens and the Blue Jays and Dal Stevens and the Four Dukes. For five years from 1960 he also worked as a semi-professional DJ for Top Rank at The Gaumont and Majestic ballrooms in Bradford (see his *Bradford's Rock and Roll: The Golden Years 1959–1965,* Bradford Libraries, 1991).

In 1965 Derek embarked on a career in selling, and sold insurance, advertising for the well-known *Bradford Pictorial* Magazine, trolls and prams. In 1966 he married Diana and had two children, Alexander and Angelique. In 1969 he joined Concord Lighting, working as a representative in Yorkshire and the North-East. After being made redundant in 1980 he joined the leisure industry, selling and later marketing equipment to sports and leisure centres. Sadly in 1998 his lovely wife Diana passed away.

Derek retired in 2003. During his last two years of employment and into retirement he wrote the popular book *Bradford's Own*, published by Sutton Publishing in 2004. In 2008 his third book was published by Bank House Books, *Bradford Born and Bred*, an epic of 137,000 words and over 150 photographs, which chronicles his life from 1938 until he was called up for National Service in 1956. His family tree goes back to the monarchs of the Mercian kingdom, with Hereward the Wake (1032–73) among his ancestors.

Derek's hobbies include writing non-fiction, especially local history, training at the gym, metal detecting and collecting medals. He is a member of the Orders, Medals Research Society and an authority on British campaign medals. He visits South Africa annually, primarily Kwa Zululand, where he lives with the Zulu people and explores the areas involved in the Zulu Wars of 1877–9. He is an authority on the defence of Rorke's Drift and the Battle of

Isandhlwana. Among the highlights of these trips was contracting tic fever and a confrontation with one of the world's deadliest snakes, the black mamba. In 2006 he broke his wrist while crossing the Buffalo River in flood and in 2009 climbed the heights of Isandhlwana for the fifth time. Incidentally he is also banned from two fish shops in the Bradford area (don't ask!).

INDEX

Group names are in italics.

Lightning Source UK Ltd.
Milton Keynes UK
UKOW010743170612

194575UK00001B/2/P

9 781904 408994